How the World Changed Social Media

WHY WE POST

PUBLISHED AND FORTHCOMING TITLES:

Social Media in
Southeast Turkey
Elisabetta Costa

Social Media in
South Italy
Razvan Nicolescu

Social Media in
Northern Chile
Nell Haynes

Social Media
in Trinidad
Jolynna Sinanan

Social Media in
Rural China
Tom McDonald

Social Media in
Emergent Brazil
Juliano Spyer

Social Media in an
English Village
Daniel Miller

Social Media in
South India
Shriram Venkatraman

Visualising Facebook
Daniel Miller
and Jolynna Sinanan

Social Media in
Industrial China
Xinyuan Wang

How the World
Changed Social Media
Daniel Miller et al.

Find out more: www.ucl.ac.uk/ucl-press

Why We Post

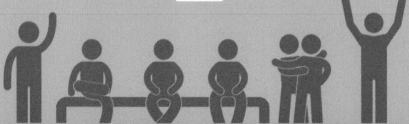

How the World Changed Social Media

Daniel Miller

Elisabetta Costa

Nell Haynes

Tom McDonald

Razvan Nicolescu

Jolynna Sinanan

Juliano Spyer

Shriram Venkatraman

Xinyuan Wang

⌃UCLPRESS

First published in 2016 by
UCL Press
University College London
Gower Street
London WC1E 6BT

Available to download free: www.ucl.ac.uk/ucl-press

A CIP catalogue record for this book is available
from The British Library.

ISBN: 978-1-910634-47-9 (Hbk.)
ISBN: 978-1-910634-48-6 (Pbk.)
ISBN: 978-1-910634-49-3 (PDF)
ISBN: 978-1-910634-51-6 (epub)
ISBN: 978-1-910634-52-3 (mobi)
DOI: 10.14324/111.9781910634493

Introduction to the series Why We Post

This book is one of a series of 11 titles. Nine are monographs devoted to specific field sites in Brazil, Chile, China, England, India, Italy, Trinidad and Turkey. These will be published during the course of 2016–17. The series also includes this volume, our comparative book about all of our findings, and a final book which contrasts the visuals that people post on Facebook in the English field site with those on our Trinidadian field site.

When we tell people that we have written nine monographs about social media around the world, all using the same chapter headings (apart from Chapter 5), they are concerned about potential repetition. However, if you decide to read several of these books (and we very much hope you do), you will see that this device has been helpful in showing the precise opposite. Each book is as individual and distinct as if it were on an entirely different topic.

This is perhaps our single most important finding. Most studies of the internet and social media are based on research methods that assume we can generalise across different groups. We look at tweets in one place and write about 'Twitter'. We conduct tests about social media and friendship in one population, and then write on this topic as if friendship means the same thing for all populations. By presenting nine books with the same chapter headings, you can judge for yourselves what kinds of generalisations are, or are not, possible.

Our intention is not to evaluate social media, either positively or negatively. Instead the purpose is educational, providing detailed evidence of what social media has become in each place and the local consequences, including local evaluations.

Each book is based on 15 months of research during which time most of the anthropologists lived, worked and interacted with people in the local language. Yet they differ from the dominant tradition of writing social science books. Firstly they do not engage with the academic literatures on social media. It would be highly repetitive to have the same discussions in all nine books. Instead discussions of these literatures are to be found here in this single, overall comparative volume. Secondly the monographs are not comparative, which again is the primary function of this volume. Thirdly, given the immense interest in social media from the general public, we have tried to write in an accessible and open style. This means the monographs have adopted a mode more common in historical writing of keeping all citations and the discussion of all wider academic issues to endnotes.

We hope you enjoy the results and that you will also read some of the monographs – in addition to this summary and comparative volume.

Acknowledgements

The individual authors provide acknowledgements for the people who assisted them in their research in their own respective volumes. With regard to this volume we would acknowledge that our primary funding is from the European Research Council grant SOCNET ERC-2011-AdG-295486. The participation of Nell Haynes is funded by the Interdisciplinary Center for Intercultural and Indigenous Studies in Santiago, Chile – ICIIS, CONICYT – FONDAP15110006. The participation of Xinyuan Wang is funded by the Wenner Gren Foundation.

For comments on individual chapters of this book and other assistance we would like to thank Justin Bourke, Isabel Colucci, Elijah Edelman, Augusto Fagundes, Marina Franchi, Nick Gadsby, Rebecca Stone Gordon, Thomas Haynes, Laura Haapio-Kirk, Sonia Livingstone, Omar Melo, Carolina Miranda, Jonathan Corpus Ong, Joowon Park, John Postill, Pascale Seale, Emanuel Spyer and Matthew Thomann.

This book is a collective creation, but Xinyuan Wang deserves a special mention for creating all the infographs.

Contents

Summary of contents

Chapter 1 What is social media?

Social media should not be seen primarily as the platforms upon which people post, but rather as the contents that are posted on these platforms.

These contents vary considerably from region to region, which is why a comparative study is necessary. The way in which we describe social media in one place should not be understood as a general description of social media: it is rather a regional case.

Social media is today a place within which we socialise, not just a means of communication.

Prior to social media there were mainly either private conversational media or public broadcasting media.

We propose a theory of scalable sociality to show how social media has colonised the space of group sociality between the private and the public. In so doing it has created scales, including the size of the group and the degree of privacy.

We employ a theory of polymedia that recognises our inability to understand any one platform or media in isolation. They must be seen as relative to each other, since today people use the range of available possibilities to select specific platforms or media for particular genres of interaction.

We reject a notion of the virtual that separates online spaces as a different world. We view social media as integral to everyday life in the same way that we now understand the place of the telephone conversation as part of offline life and not as a separate sphere.

We propose a theory of attainment to oppose the idea that with new digital technologies we have either lost some essential element of being human or become post-human. We have simply attained a new set of capacities that, like the skills involved in driving a car, are quickly accepted as ordinarily human.

Chapter 2 Academic studies of social media

We accept that our definition and approach is merely one of many, and that every discipline contributes its own perspective on the nature of social media.

Social media platforms such as Orkut and MySpace are frequently being replaced, while others, for instance Facebook, are constantly changing. As a result our definitions and approaches also need to be dynamic.

Platforms and their properties are less important as the cause of their contents (i.e. the reason *why* people post particular kinds of content on that platform) than we assume. Genres of content, such as schoolchildren's banter, happily migrate to entirely different platforms with quite different properties.

We reject the idea that the development of the internet represents a single trajectory. Some of the most important features of social media seem to be the exact opposite of prior uses of the internet. For example, the internet's problem of anonymity has become for social media a problem of the loss of privacy.

Chapter 3 Our method and approach

Our anthropological scholarship is established by our commitment of 15 months of ethnographic research in each of our nine communities, and by our willingness to give up initial interests and instead focus on what we discovered to be most important to each of these communities. We required 15 months in order to engage with the full variety of people present in each site – older and younger, less or better educated, different economic levels, etc. – and to gain the level of trust required to participate in more private domains such as WhatsApp.

Ethnography reflects the reality that no one lives in just one context. Everything we do and encounter is related as part of our lives, so our approach to people's experience needs to be holistic.

The primary method of anthropology is empathy: the attempt to understand social media from the perspective of its users.

Unlike much traditional anthropology this project was always collaborative and comparative, from conception to execution to dissemination.

Chapter 4 Our survey results

We present the results of a questionnaire administered to 1199 inform-ants across our nine sites. It explored 26 topics, ranging from whether – and with whom – they share passwords and the different categories of followers to whether users respond to advertising or whether social media increases their political activity.

In general we show that results need to be treated with consider-able caution, since often the most plausible explanation for the survey responses is that people interpreted the questions in different and cul-turally specific ways.

The results of such comparative quantitative surveys can thus be properly interpreted only with the additional background knowledge of qualitative ethnographic work.

Chapter 5 Education and young people

There is considerable public anxiety that social media distracts from edu-cation and reduces the social skills of young people – despite an exem-plary body of prior research that rejects any such simple conclusions.

In several of our field sites we show that low-income families often see social media activity as a useful skill, enhancing literacy and pro-viding a route to alternative, informal channels of education. By con-trast higher-income families see it more as a threat to formal education. However, we have also researched in field sites where the opposite would be true.

The topic illustrates the dangers of generalising about China, given that the two Chinese sites discussed in this chapter demonstrate both the highest and the lowest levels of devotion to formal education.

The best way to appreciate the impact of social media is to focus on specific sets of relationships: those between schoolchildren, between teachers and schoolchildren and between both of these groups and par-ents. We examine each in turn.

Chapter 6 Work and commerce

In this case the primary anxieties focused upon in popular journalism include surveillance by companies, new forms of commodification and social media as a distraction.

Although social media platforms are themselves owned by private companies, social media does not necessarily favour the interests of commerce. For example, following precedents such as email, they are powerful tools by which the public has radically repudiated attempts by commerce to separate the world of work from that of the family. In the case of south India, social media helps to keep jobs within the family.

In most of our field sites people were far more concerned about surveillance by other people they knew than by companies.

However, in our southeast Turkish site there is concern over surveillance by the state, while in our English site the rise of targeted advertising reveals a level of company knowledge that rebounds in negative attitudes to social media companies.

Social media in most of our sites was more important in fostering small-scale enterprises that leverage people's personal connections (such as local bars in Trinidad or sales of second-hand clothing in Chile), rather than in representing large-scale commerce.

This topic exposes clear differences in the way different societies see money as integral to, or opposed to, personal relations. This is reflected in the contrast between a site such as Amazon, which tends to be impersonal, and the Chinese equivalent Taobao, which fosters personal communication within commerce.

Chapter 7 Online and offline relationships

In this case the primary anxiety is whether shallow, inauthentic online relationships are displacing deeper offline relationships. In most cases our evidence is that online interactions are in fact another aspect of the same offline relationships. Rather than representing an *increase* in mediation, social media is helpful in revealing the mediated nature of prior communication and sociality, including face to face communication.

In our industrial China site we feel that the migration from offline to online may have done more to bring people closer to the modern life to which they aspire than the move from villages to the factory system. In some societies, such as Trinidad, the enhanced visibility of people through social media leads users to see this representation as potentially more truthful than offline observations of those around them.

In some societies, such as in our Brazilian and Trinidadian sites, social media fosters a tendency to befriend the friends of one's friends or relatives. In others, for instance our rural Chinese site, social media fosters entirely new relationships, including the befriending of strangers.

The use of social media may complement rather than reflect other forms of socialisation. For example, in our south Italy site people felt they already had sufficient social engagement, and therefore made less use of social media.

Chapter 8 Gender

Our field site in southeast Turkey is one of several suggesting that public-facing social media, such as Facebook, may enhance the appearance of conservatism or become an ultra-conservative place. Changes in offline life are not represented on this public space owing to the surveillance of relatives. Conservative representations of gender are also fostered in south India, rural China and our Chilean sites.

At the same time private-facing social media, such as WhatsApp, has had a liberalising effect on the lives of young women in the same Muslim southeast Turkish site; it has created unprecedented possibilities for cross-gender contact and the fulfilment of romantic aspirations.

In our south Italian site women repudiate their pre-marital forms of posting in order to appear as wives and mothers. In Trinidad, however, women strive to show how they have retained their ability to look sexy despite marriage and motherhood.

Social media enhances our ability to see how gender differences and stereotypes are visualised and portrayed – often through consistent associations such as beer (male) and wine (female) in our English site or manual labour for men and care work for women in our Chilean site.

In our Brazilian site there is some evidence for the enhancement of gender equality, and in several sites there is increasing visibility of non-normative sexuality online.

Chapter 9 Inequality

Our comparative evidence shows how important it may be to recognise that while social media and smartphones can create a greater degree of equality in capacity for communication and socialising within highly unequal societies, this may at the same time have no impact whatsoever on offline inequality.

The way in which people's aspirations are portrayed online is highly variable. Chinese factory workers portray a fantasy of their future lives, but evangelical Brazilians focus on the evidence for their advances in respectability.

People use social media equally to disparage pretentious claims to wealth and education through the use of humour and irony, but also to display such claims to wealth and education.

In our Chilean site social media is used to suppress differences in income, alongside other claims to distinct identity such as indigeneity and ethnicity, in order to express communal solidarity in opposition to the metropolitan regions that residents feel exploit them economically and are superficial.

In south India we can see how social media has added a new dimension of social difference – the relative cosmopolitanism revealed in postings – to many traditional forms of inequality such as caste and class.

Chapter 10 Politics

Most prior studies of social media exaggerate its impact upon politics by focusing upon easily observable political usage, such as debates or activism visible on Twitter. By contrast our study simply observes the degree to which political posting appears within the content of people's everyday use of social media.

Our site in the Kurdish region of Turkey shows why politics may appear less on social media in places where this is dangerous and fraught. Most posting here, as in south India, is cautious and conservative. A primary concern is with the potential impact of their postings on their social relationships.

In many sites, for example those in England and Trinidad, politics is mainly exploited by social media for purposes of entertainment.

While there is limited use of social media to comment on local political issues, social media is used to create local solidarity through negative posting on national issues, such as corruption in Italy or China.

In China censorship rarely descends to these kinds of communities, and it is the social media company that controls the dissemination of news. In southeast Turkey, however, there is a personal risk if people post anti-government sentiments.

Chapter 11 Visual images

A major effect of social media is that human communication has become more visual at the expense of oral and textual modes.

Memes are particularly significant as a kind of moral police of the internet. By using them people are able to express their values and disparage those of others in less direct and more acceptable ways than before.

Generalisations about new visual forms such as the selfie are often inaccurate. There are many varieties of the selfie which are often used to express group sentiment rather than individual narcissism.

The increase in visibility is often associated with increasing social conformity, and in some cases such as southeast Turkey safe topics such as food are preferred to photographs of people that could give rise to gossip. By contrast enhanced gossip and 'stalking' is regarded in Trinidad as a welcome pleasure fostered by social media. The case of Trinidad alerts us to cultural differences in the way in which people associate visual materials with truth.

The ability to communicate in primarily visual forms is especially important for people who struggle with literacy. Examples of the latter include older, low-income Brazilians; the youngest users, who choose platforms such as Instagram and Snapchat; and groups with precarious social relations, for instance Chinese factory workers.

Chapter 12 Individualism

There is an anxiety that social media, along with almost every other technological innovation, will foster individualism at the expense of social life. Our evidence, however, is that while earlier forms of the internet favoured ego-based networking, social media represents a partial return to prior group socialisation, such as the family, in many sites. This may include 'Confucian' traditions of family respect in rural China, but also encompasses caste in India or the tribe for the Kurdish community in Turkey.

In more traditional contexts, however, there are also enhanced opportunities for individualised networking – as is often the case, our evidence shows that social media can enhance two opposing trends simultaneously. Scalable sociality can foster both traditional groups and, in the case of WhatsApp, small-scale, often transient groups.

Social media is not simply a form of friending. As in our 'Goldilocks Strategy' found in England, it is often used to keep other people at just the right distance. In other sites scalable sociality is employed to differentiate platforms as more private or more public sites for socialising.

The public debate over privacy and social media is revealed as quite parochial. While seen as a new threat to privacy in many countries, in others, such as south India and especially China, social media may provide the first opportunity for some people to experience a genuinely private space.

Even where social media is used to express individuality, the enhanced visibility tends to make this increasingly conformist to accepted cultural styles of individualism.

Chapter 13 Does social media make people happier?

The study of social media can help us to critique any simple or over-generalised concepts of what it means to be happy or to claim to be happy.

Even when taken in terms of local conceptions of happiness, in most cases we see little evidence to support journalistic contentions that social media has made people generally less happy or content. Yet there are locally expressed fears that, along with gaming, social media emphasises more transient pleasures, or that, alongside choosing clothes, social media creates additional stress over public appearance.

Social media has increased the pressure at least to appear happy online. Yet it may also be the place where people can visually articulate their aspirations for a happy life, as in the case of an emergent class in our Brazilian site or a new domestic respectability in Chile.

By contrast in other sites social media may express adherence to and contentment with traditional values. These may include those of the family in rural China, ideals of beauty in Italy, of community in Trinidad, of Islam in southeast Turkey or of close kinship in south India.

Chapter 14 The future

This chapter starts with an acknowledgement of the inseparability of social media from the new ubiquity of smartphones as part of everyday life. This trend is likely to continue, especially with respect to the lowest income populations and to the older populations who were previously less present on social media.

It is possible that, following the continual invention of new platforms that take up niches between the private and the public, we will come to accept media in general as constituting a scale of sociality, without the need to designate a separated group of platforms as 'social media'. In any case these platforms may be dissipated within a broader spectrum of phone apps.

In general our work has suggested that the more conservative the society, the greater the impact of social media – even though the effect may be to reinforce conformity and conservatism as well as to create unprecedented opportunities for freedom.

As with most digital technologies, social media usually enhances opposite trends simultaneously. Examples of this are an increase in decommodification and commodification, political freedoms and political oppression, localism and globalism.

Again alongside other digital technologies, social media can in itself be used to represent the future, though this role will decline over time.

Conclusion

In the future, just as much as today, we will need comparative qualitative anthropological fieldwork that can empathetically engage with social media from the perspective of its users in order to keep answering the question of what social media is – because the world will continue to change it.

List of figures

List of tables

List of contributors

Elisabetta Costa is Postdoctoral Research Fellow at the British Institute at Ankara (BIAA). She is an anthropologist specialising in the study of digital media, social media, journalism, politics and gender in Turkey and the Middle East.

Nell Haynes is Postdoctoral Fellow at Pontificia Universidad Católica de Chile in Santiago. She received her PhD in Anthropology from the American University in 2013. Her research addresses themes of performance, authenticity, globalization, and gendered and ethnic identification in Bolivia and Chile.

Tom McDonald is Assistant Professor in the Department of Sociology, The University of Hong Kong. He received his PhD in Anthropology from UCL in 2013, and has published numerous academic articles on internet use and consumption practices in China.

Daniel Miller is Professor of Anthropology at UCL, author/editor of 37 books including *Tales from Facebook, Digital Anthropology* (Ed. with H. Horst), *The Internet: an Ethnographic Approach* (with D. Slater), *Webcam* (with J. Sinanan), *The Comfort of Things, A Theory of Shopping,* and *Stuff*.

Razvan Nicolescu is Research Associate at UCL, where he obtained his PhD in 2013. Trained in both telecommunication and anthropology, he has conducted ethnographic research in Romania and Italy. His research interests focus on visibility and digital anthropology; political economy, governance, and informality; feelings, subjectivity, and normativity.

Jolynna Sinanan is Vice Chancellor's Postdoctoral Research Fellow at the Royal Melbourne Institute of Technology (RMIT). From 2011-2014, she was a Research Fellow in Anthropology at UCL. She is co-author (with D. Miller) of *Webcam*. Her areas of research are digital ethnography, new media, migration and gender in Trinidad, Australia and Singapore.

Juliano Spyer is pursuing his PhD at the Department of Anthropology, UCL. He obtained his MSc from UCL's Digital Anthropology Programme. He wrote the first book about social media in Brazil: *Conectado* (Zahar, 2007) and was digital adviser for the presidential candidate Marina Silva in 2010. He is originally trained as an oral history researcher.

Shriram Venkatraman is a PhD candidate at the Department of Anthropology, UCL. He is also a trained professional statistician and prior to his doctoral studies at UCL, held leadership positions at Walmart, USA. His research interests include technologies in work places, organisational culture and entrepreneurship.

Xinyuan Wang is a PhD candidate at the Department of Anthropology, UCL. She obtained her MSc from the UCL's Digital Anthropology Programme. She is an artist in Chinese traditional painting and calligraphy. She translated (Horst and Miller Eds.) *Digital Anthropology* into Chinese and contributed a piece on Digital Anthropology in China.

1
What is social media?[1]

Many previous studies of social media emphasise specific platforms, including books and papers devoted to just one particular platform such as Facebook or Twitter.[2] It is clearly important to understand Twitter, for example, as a platform: the company that owns it, the way it works and the very idea of social media based on messages that must remain below 140 characters. From an anthropological perspective, however, if we ask what Twitter actually *is* it makes more sense to think of the millions of tweets, the core genres, the regional differences and its social and emotional consequences for users. It is the *content* rather than the platform that is most significant when it comes to why social media matters.

As will be described in our individual ethnographies of social media around the world, genres of content happily migrate between quite different platforms, being seen one year on Orkut and the next on Facebook, one year on BBM and the next on Twitter. Platforms such as Facebook have themselves often changed functionality, developing and introducing new features. This research project is not therefore a study of platforms: it is a study of what people post and communicate through platforms, of why we post and the consequences of those postings. We have found this content to be very different across the nine field sites in which we worked. Content manifests and transforms local relationships and issues. Our study has thus turned out to be as much about how the world changed social media as about how social media changed the world.

Clearly this is not entirely a one-way process. These technologies have changed us. They have given us potential for communication and interaction that we did not previously possess. We need first clearly to establish what those potentials are and then to examine what the world subsequently did with those possibilities. It is easier to understand what social media is if we go back to a time before it existed. So wind back though Snapchat and Tinder, past Facebook and QQ, through MySpace and Friendster to life before all that.

Prior to all these technologies, there were two main ways in which people communicated using media. The first was public broadcast media such as television, radio and newspapers. With such media anyone at all, providing that they can gain access to it, can be the audience. The broadcaster has no direct control over who makes up their audiences, though they may try and persuade people to join them. Also available for quite some time were media that facilitated private communication between two people as one-to-one conversations, for example a telephone conversation. This is also called 'dyadic' communication. People could meet in groups face to face, but it was uncommon to create group-based interactions within media such as the telephone.

With the development of the internet, this polarisation between public and private media started to change. An email could be sent to a group. There were bulletin boards, specialised forums, chat rooms and blogging, which appealed to wider audiences, as well as other group media such as CB radio. Nevertheless most everyday communication through media remained dominated by the two prior forms, public broadcasting and the private dyadic. The initial development of social networking sites was, in effect, a scaling-down of public broadcasting to become individuals posting to groups. Usually these groups included not more than a few hundred people. In addition the people who formed those groups would interact among themselves, for example commenting upon the comments of others.

At the same time the development of text messaging and internet services such as MSM and AOL took place. These developed further with the rise of the smartphone, in particular BlackBerry Messenger (BBM), the proprietary messaging platform for Blackberry phones; its global impact has generally been considerably underestimated and it was the precursor to WhatsApp. Such services took private messaging and moved it upwards in scale by including various group functions. This trend has been consolidated over the last three years with the remarkably rapid rise of platforms such as WhatsApp and WeChat. These tend to be used to form smaller, more private groups than QQ or Facebook, often around 20 people or less. They may not be centred upon any one individual. Generally all members can post equally; these are groups rather than the networks of any one person. They are particularly important since for young people such text-based communication has largely replaced voice-based use of the phone.[3]

Clearly to define what social media is based only on those that presently exist is limiting. For our definition and approach to be sustainable we also have to bear in mind the new social media platforms that are constantly being developed, and the likelihood that some will become very successful in the future. It helps that we are starting to see a pattern in the way new forms of social media emerge. Some of these platforms have scaled down from public broadcasting, while others have scaled up from private communication. With the addition of new platforms in the future, we are likely to end up with a result that in effect creates some scales between the private and the public, along which we can locate these platforms.

We can envisage two key scales. The first is the scale from the most private to the most public. The second is the scale from the smallest group to the largest groups. At one end of both of these scales we still see private dyadic conversation and at the other end we still see fully public broadcasting. What is it that is being scaled? The core to the study of social science is the way in which people associate with each other to form social relations and societies. This is called sociality. The best way to define what is popularly called social media but also includes prior media is thus to describe the new situation as increasingly 'scalable sociality'.[4]

One of the clearest examples of how social media has created online scalable sociality emerged from the research on schoolchildren in the English village field site. Based on a survey of 2496 students, Miller

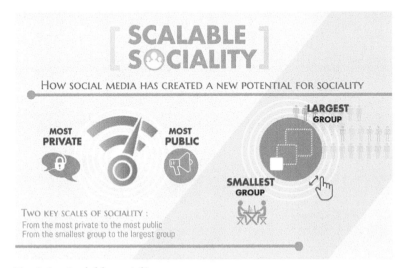

Fig. 1.1   Scalable sociality

found that most of them were using five or six different social media from a young age (Fig. 1.2).

In an earlier work, along with Madianou, Miller had developed an approach called 'polymedia',[5] which recognises that none of these platforms can be properly understood if considered in isolation because the meaning and use of each one is relative to the others. Previously people might have assumed that cost or access explained why users chose one media or platform rather than another. Today, however, people seem increasingly free to choose between these platforms, and so may be judged on their choices. For example, children living abroad who want to tell their parents gently about something that will not please them, such as a new tattoo or a need for more money, might for that reason avoid a medium that includes a visual element or one that allows a person to respond immediately – perhaps, in such a case, in anger.

With polymedia people can also map different kinds of sociality onto the diversity of their social media platforms. In the case of these

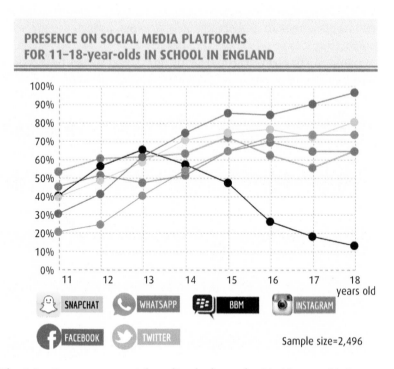

Fig. 1.2 Presence on social media platforms for 11–18-year-olds in schools in England

school pupils we can start with the continuity of dyadic communication, as they message or phone to chat in private to someone like their *Bestie* or *BFF* (Best Friend Forever). Next comes Snapchat which, because it often includes items such as a particularly ugly photograph of one's own face, relies on trust. Indeed it may be used to establish and maintain trust within a small group. The next size up consists of groups created in WhatsApp. Typically in a school class there will be one WhatsApp group that includes all the boys where they could talk about girls (or vice versa). There may be another that includes all the class. Reaching a still larger group are Tweets that reach all those who follow an individual on Twitter. This is the main site for school banter, and may include pupils from other classes in the year. Beyond the class is Facebook, mainly used by these school pupils as their link to family, neighbours and others beyond the school. Finally we have Instagram, where each pupil's social circle is often comprised of the same school pupils. However, it is also the only site where they actually welcome strangers – because the contact shows that someone who the children do not know has appreciated the aesthetic qualities of the image they have posted on Instagram (Fig. 1.3).

The use of social media by English schoolchildren demonstrates scalable sociality in that each of these platforms corresponds to a position of greater or lesser privacy and smaller or larger groups. There are no rules behind this. Groups and platforms may overlap, but mostly we find platforms become associated with specific genres of communication

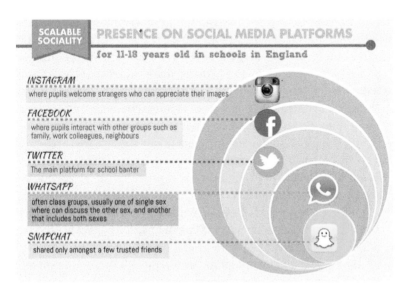

Fig. 1.3   The scales of social media use by English school pupils

which people see as appropriate for the group engaged with that particular platform.

In the schoolchildren's case the differences between platforms were used to illustrate this principle. However, scalable sociality can exist just as well within a single platform. A person may post a comment or image on their social media which will make sense only to the people to whom they are close, who understand what it refers to. Other people may be on the same site, but they will not get the significance – and are thereby excluded despite being present on this same platform.[6]

We have started with this example of scalable sociality in order to address the question of defining social media. While definitions may be useful, however, they are not the primary aim of this project. Through our ten key questions, each of which forms a chapter of this book, we investigate the very wide range of contexts within which social media now plays an important role: from the increasing importance of visual communication as opposed to textual communication to the impact of social media on education and whether equality online impacts upon inequality offline.

Platforms remain central to our analysis since these are the primary units through which we think about and use social media. Yet we should be careful in presuming that there are properties of the platforms that are responsible for, or in some sense cause, the associations that we observe with platforms. These same schoolchildren provide evidence for why we should not infer cause simply from association. Firstly the way they use Twitter, primarily for banter between themselves, contrasts sharply with the adult use of Twitter as mainly a source of information. Is the 'true' Twitter the one used for information or the one used for banter? Furthermore this school banter used to be on BBM; it then migrated to Facebook and is now almost entirely on Twitter. This suggests that a genre of interaction may remain quite stable despite migrating between supposedly very different platforms. Such an example, if sustained by others in our studies, would suggest that the platform is surprisingly irrelevant to finding explanations for why and how people use social media. It provides the place, but not the cause nor the explanation.

When all nine field sites are considered, it becomes apparent that in each region every new social media platform quickly becomes standardised around quite specific groups of users and implicitly understood appropriate and inappropriate usage, though these will continue to change. Again differentiation of groups may occur within the same platform or by exploiting a contrast between platforms. For example in

2014–15 there was a trend in several of our field sites to differentiate the more public-facing platforms such as Facebook or QQ from the more private-facing platforms such as WhatsApp/WeChat.

How new forms of social media map onto prior social groups, or indeed create new groups, varies considerably from one field site to another. In our south Indian field site, for example, the groups that associated around social media are mainly traditional social units such as the family or the caste. By contrast in our industrial Chinese site the floating population of migrant workers have largely lost their traditional forms of sociality, and in effect create social groups adapted to a new life spent mainly moving from city to city. Their more constant social life is actually on social media rather than offline. In some cases the more private platforms have radically changed people's lives, as in our site in southeast Turkey on which young women and men can more easily chat with each other. Meanwhile in our Chilean field site most people use public posting to patrol their own local community, whose values they regard as contrasting with the more metropolitan values of the capital city. More details for of all these claims will be found within this book.

Two other points should be already clear. When the study of the internet began people commonly talked about two worlds: the virtual and the real. By now it is very evident that there is no such distinction – the online is just as real as the offline. Social media has already become such an integral part of everyday life that it makes no sense to see it as separate. In the same way no one today would regard a telephone conversation as taking place in a separate world from 'real life'. It has also become apparent that research on social media is no longer the particular purview of either media or of communication. Our research provides considerable evidence that social media should be regarded rather as a place where many of us spend part of our lives. As a result the study of social media is as much one of sociality as of communication. Much of this book is not about media, nor about scalable sociality. It is about social media as another place in which people live, alongside their office life, home life and community life.

If we have defined here the term social media, what about 'the world'? Clearly we cannot study the world or the 'global' as a whole. But we can hope to study sufficient numbers of locations to be able to make statements about diversity and generality around the world. The contents of this book are based on the research of nine anthropologists, each of whom spent 15 months looking at the use and consequence of social media in one particular location. The unique character of this book is that it is almost entirely comparative. A brief account of the nine field sites may be found in an appendix.[7]

Finally we would couch these questions in terms of an approach developed by Miller and Sinanan called a 'theory of attainment'[8]. As we shall see in respect to the ten popular questions/topics considered in this volume, new technologies are often accompanied by a kind of moral panic, frequently fostered by journalism. These suggest that as a result of this new technology we have lost some essential element of our authentic humanity. For example, such panics incorporate the idea that face to face communication is richer or less mediated than communication employing digital technology, or that we are losing cognitive abilities such as long-term attention spans. These responses to technology have been common ever since Plato argued that the invention of writing would damage our capacity for memory. At the same time others have a utopian view that new technologies make us in some manner post-human.

Our theory of attainment argues that these technologies make no difference whatsoever to our essential humanity. The sociologist Goffman[9] showed convincingly how all communication and sociality takes place within cultural genres, including face to face. There is no such thing as unmediated, pre- or non-cultural sociality or communication. Instead we should recognise that whatever we do with new technologies must be latent in our humanity, i.e. something that as human beings we have always had the potential to do and to be. Such a capacity is now attained as a result of the new technology. This theory does not claim to adjudicate on whether any new capacity to send memes or selfies through social media, for example, is either good or bad. It just acknowledges that this has now become simply part of what human beings can do, as has driving a car.

2
Academic studies of social media

Definitions of social media

In the introduction to this volume we have defined social media as the colonisation of the space between traditional broadcast and private dyadic communication, providing people with a scale of group size and degrees of privacy that we have termed scalable sociality. However, we would not wish our definition to be seen as too tight or absolute. There were many prior examples of group communication online, such as bulletin boards and chat rooms. It would also be pedantic to insist that WhatsApp is a form of social media when used for a group, but not when used between just two people. Our definition is not absolute, nor does it contain firm boundaries; rather it is a heuristic device which helps to clarify the parameters of our study. Our discussion includes sites such as Tinder where the communication is dyadic but accessed by a group, as well as gaming consoles that today can function as social media platforms. It is also possible for some blogs and YouTube to be considered, but they rarely appear here – partly because most on YouTube is posted as a form of public broadcasting, though by individuals as much as by companies. It is not as though we even chose the name 'social media'. When we started our research we thought we were studying 'social networking sites'. We have simply followed the colloquial term used by the general public. So this is not a scientific label, but a popular term always subject to the vagaries of public semantics, and we can only be responsible for the way we use the term within this volume.

Furthermore ours would not be the generally accepted definition. The clear pioneer in the study of social media has been danah boyd,[1] and the most influential paper[2] to date was the 2007 publication *Social Network Sites: Definition, History, and Scholarship* by boyd and Nicole Ellison.[3] This provides not only a history but also a summary of academic work prior to 2007. As boyd points out,[4] the initial social networking sites in the US were places where people could actively network to find 'friends of friends' or, as in sites such as Friends Reunited, to reconnect with friends.[5] After a while these sites were transformed, largely by their users, into places of more constant interaction; this occurred more between established friends, so the sites became less concerned with expansive networking. In a way, therefore, social networking sites did become social media, if the labels are taken literally.

boyd was also a pioneer in trying to define and characterise social media. She described these as 'networked publics' and suggested that they possessed four main affordances which were persistence, visibility, spreadability and searchability.[6] The terms were certainly helpful for the time in which these ideas were being developed, on the basis of the huge success of Friendster and then MySpace, followed by Facebook, and these concepts remain helpful in understanding such platforms. A recent book on Twitter expands the discussion to the various kinds of public that are networked, and the ways in which users have developed and directed these.[7]

Over the last few years, however, and during the period of our study, the main growth has been in platforms – not only WhatsApp and WeChat,[8] but also Instagram and Snapchat. These platforms do not particularly align with the affordances of earlier ones. They are not especially searchable, persistent or even spreadable, but they do consolidate a trend towards scalable sociality. It is perhaps not surprising that as anthropologists we would favour a definition that focuses upon the topic of sociality, because that is what we study. Other disciplines will see things differently. For example, a recent book on social media from a scholar within communication studies develops an approach based on concepts of connectivity, including sections on YouTube, Wikipedia and Flickr alongside Twitter and Facebook.[9] Different definitions are likely to suit the perspectives of different disciplines.

There is a natural temptation to see things historically, assuming that technology 'evolves' in neat and discrete stages. In this view social media appears to be merely the latest popular use of the internet, especially when in some countries many people believe that Facebook and the internet are synonymous. There is now an established field of Internet Studies, which obviously would tend to assimilate the study of social media into the field.[10] However, the debates concerning the internet that took place prior to social media[11] were often the very opposite in their orientation to more recent debates over social media. When the internet first developed, for instance, most people viewed it as a separated out *virtual* world, able to facilitate the coming together of groups with specialist interests. There was also much concern with new kinds of social relations made possible by anonymity.[12] By contrast, with regard to social media, the issue of anonymity has reversed into a concern over lack of privacy. Similarly the emphasis upon separate special-interest groups on the internet has also reversed into a concern with the way in which quite disparate social networks of friends, family and work are now juxtaposed in the same space on Facebook. Rather than being seen as a virtual 'other' world, social media stands accused of being embedded in the most mundane toenail painting and lunch-eating aspects of the everyday world.

Obviously social media builds on prior uses of the internet for social and communicative purposes. Yet there are clearly as many discontinuities with prior uses of the internet as continuities. It might therefore be better to grant social media its own status as a topic for research, and allow for the possibility that it is often the very opposite of what was thought of as the internet, even while sharing the same space. For these reasons we have generally avoided an historical approach that makes social media the latest point in a narrative, then viewed as the cause of what it is now. As noted in the introduction, social media is not just a step away from the study of earlier uses of the internet, but is also more embedded in everyday social life. As such, it provides a new opportunity to bring media and communication studies together with other forms of social science such as anthropology.

Another way in which danah boyd stands out as a pioneer in the study of social media is her establishing of an online bibliography, in which anyone studying social media can post the details of their publications.[13] At the time of writing (April 2015) there were 669 entries. These represent a wide variety of disciplines and approaches. In examining some of these it is quickly apparent that they represent several quite distinct perspectives, often with little cross-fertilisation between. We do not want to dwell on this, but it is important to note that the bulk of studies come from disciplines that are more directed to methods and perspectives influenced by the natural sciences; they thus involve samples of users, the testing of hypotheses and models. This huge body of material is not dealt with here because the bulk of this book is concerned with comparison between diverse cultural contexts; evidence from one population cannot be extrapolated to the behaviour of any other population.

This volume should therefore be seen as complementary to and distinct from the dominant approaches to the study of social media.

The bibliography also provides a neat reason why in this volume we have concentrated on a comparative approach. The combined users of the Chinese sites QQ (820 million), QZone (625 million) and WeChat (355 million) are certainly comparable to Facebook (1.25 billion).[14] QQ is also older than Facebook. Yet the titles of the 669 studies listed in boyd's bibliography do not include a single mention of QQ, QZone or WeChat, while there are 157 references to Facebook.[15] Even taking into account the language issue,[16] this shows that exposure to the Chinese material for those working in English is limited. Such a discrepancy forms part of the justification of our study. Natural science is based largely on the study of substances with universal and unchanging properties that allow for such generalised extrapolation, so it really may not matter where the study is carried out. Social science is another matter entirely, however, and this book is a plea for greater sensitivity to regional and social differences and their consequences.

Furthermore there is a danger that natural science-based studies may proliferate investigations of platforms such as Twitter because the material is publicly available, and so potentially usable as large data sets. It is far more difficult to make use of platforms such as WhatsApp, since you need to know someone very well before they will grant you access to their private conversations. boyd has a very extensive additional bibliography of work on Twitter, but as yet neither of these sites features a title that makes reference to WhatsApp. We do not wish to disparage any approach. All genuine research provides valuable evidence. If our suggestion that some conventional methods produce their own biases and problems of generalisation is valid, then hopefully these concerns will be shared by those who regard themselves as involved in studies of social media modelled on the natural sciences.

History and culture

Although boyd and Ellison provided a genuinely global perspective,[17] boyd's bibliography suggests this may not have been sustained by the bulk of subsequent research, at least in the English language. This may also apply to the history of social media. As anthropologists our primary concern is not with the invention of the technology or the commercial launch, but with platforms that became established as significant within particular societies. Bearing this in mind, the history of social media probably begins in Korea with the success of Cyworld. The platform was launched in 1999 and became the first to reach effective ubiquity among the young people of a significant population. By 2005 almost all young Koreans used Cyworld.

One of the characteristics of Cyworld was that it operated its categories of friendship as a series of concentric circles. Academics then noted that this was analogous to the way kinship systems traditionally operated in that country.[18] If one agreed to be a *Cy-ilchon* – a very close relation – then you became socially bound to principles of reciprocity, such as commenting upon each other in a manner that evoked these kin relationships. In short this implied a specific cultural alignment between the particular society and the particular platform – a possible reason why Cyworld was so successful in Korea, and not particularly successful anywhere else.

The trouble is that it is very hard to mobilise evidence for such an argument. Cyworld has largely been replaced by Facebook in Korea. Yet this may have nothing to do with either functionality or cultural alignments; it could be simply a desire to follow global dominance. There are other instances in this book of an association between the characteristics of platforms and the regions they are associated with, mostly through examples from China which has its own distinctive social media platforms. Given the political prohibitions on using other platforms in China, however, it seems sensible to be cautious in interpreting these cultural associations as causative.

This cultural chicken-and-egg is a common problem in the analysis of social media. For example, it is often argued in journalism and popular psychology and sociology[19] that social media is associated with individualism and is primarily used for self-expression or ego-centered networking. Approaches from critical studies[20] may go further in suggesting this is linked to our contemporary political economy, which itself is an expression of neo-liberalism.[21] Social media companies are among other things capitalist corporations, and therefore likely to promote such values. However, most such research takes places in North America, a region where writers such as De Tocqueville[22] laid great stress upon individualism as the dominant cultural character at a period prior to modern capitalism, while perhaps the most successful capitalist region for much of recent history has been Scandinavia, an area usually characterised as comparatively collectivist in terms of values. Although one would expect anthropologists to highlight issues of culture, we therefore intend to be just as cautious about cultural determinism as about technological determinism.

Generally speaking, it seems unlikely that a set of new media whose primary use was to develop and maintain social connections is best characterised in terms of individualism. Indeed it is possible that some social media platforms first developed in the rather more individualistic climate of the US only fully flourished when they migrated to more group-oriented societies. For example, one of the most successful early platforms was Friendster. This was started in the US in 2002, but it achieved a greater hold on countries in Southeast Asia, eventually being bought by a Malaysian business and re-established there. Similarly Orkut was first developed by Google, but achieved its primary impact through massive popularity in countries such as Brazil and India; indeed later it became re-established in Brazil. Today the most deeply established social media platform in China is arguably QQ (founded 1999, though initially as an instant messaging service);[23] it also dominates in terms of numbers of monthly active users. Renren, a Chinese platform with strong similarities to Facebook, is a much smaller component of the Chinese social media world.[24] As will become clear QQ is a much broader platform, with more functionality and greater integration into people's lives than are found in any of the Western social media platforms.

More important than any alignment with cultural propensities has been the tendency for more peripheral areas to emulate those regarded as more metropolitan. For this reason the more standard history of social media does not start with Cyworld, but focuses upon developments in the US. Within North America the first social media platform to achieve this degree of social penetration and influence was MySpace (founded 2003), which from 2004 quickly established a vast teenage base. As time passed it became more specialised in its orientation to music. Other specialist sites such as Friends Reunited (started 1999), whose purpose is self-explanatory, and LinkedIn (founded 2003), used for professional and business networking, also showed the potential for niche variations – as did dating sites such as Grindr (founded 2009) and now Tinder (founded 2012).[25]

It was probably because of the prestige of the US, along with the development of Silicon Valley as a high-tech incubator, that platforms such as Friendster and Orkut, although more successful in other parts of the world, initially came from the US.[26] The very same factor may well have led to their demise, as for a while Facebook looked set to devour its siblings and run the pack. At that point it seemed likely that Facebook would have represented world domination but for the political intervention of the Chinese government. Our project thus started at a moment that looked like the end of social media history, but over the last two years such a conclusion has turned out to be premature. Instead we now see several alternative sites for young people including Instagram (founded 2010) and Snapchat (founded 2011), while Facebook has shifted to be of greater interest to an older user base, also important to the spread of Twitter (founded 2006). The dynamism of this sector is best illustrated today by the remarkably swift rise of sites such as WeChat (founded 2011) and WhatsApp (founded 2009). While Facebook has 1.25 billion users, WeChat reached 600 million and WhatsApp 800 million at much faster rates.[27]

As noted above, arguing that cultural alignment is a primary reason for a platform's success is just as difficult as arguing that this is the result of technological affordances. However, anthropology offers an alternative explanation. In this book we see cultural alignment not as a cause, but as a consequence. In other words we observe how a platform becomes localised, which also reflects our greater interest in content rather than the platform itself.[28] Once it becomes populated by local content then cultural alignment follows as a consequence.

While a platform may have a consistent identity with respect to the company that owns it, or even a consistent infrastructure, it is still subject to constant change. Facebook is a good example. Even as early as 2007 boyd and Ellison pointed out that many of these platforms were started with quite different functions and intentions. Is Facebook the initial platform (with a different name) intended to help male students rate female students, or is it the platform investigated in 2015? Furthermore the main changes that have taken place, such as the platform's recent migration to older people, may be largely a result of users' activity rather than anything intended by the company – just as earlier sites such as Friendster and Orkut attained traction in quite different regions than those for which they were invented.

The same issue raised by changes over time applies to differences over space, and these are the primary concerns for anthropology. When we study Facebook in Trinidad and we discover that it is significantly different in its content from Facebook in India, what is it that we have discovered? If we say this is a study of the way Trinidadians have appropriated Facebook, then it sounds as though there is a more authentic Facebook located somewhere else that has now been changed by Trinidadians. However, the point illuminated by our anthropological approach is that Facebook only ever exists with respect to specific populations; the usage by any one social group is no more authentic than any other. The same problem applies to the word Trinidadian as to Facebook. In some small measure the people of Trinidad have been changed by their use of Facebook, but then they have always been changing. The issue is thus not how either of these changed the other. One should instead recognise that we study culture, which is always dynamic as a result of the mutual interaction of people and the world in which they live.[29]

These questions laid the foundations for our comparative study, which has to balance evidence for global homogeneity (everybody/thing becoming more similar) and heterogeneity (everybody/thing becoming more different). In brief, to the degree that everyone uses the same platform it might look as though social media is an instrument of global homogenisation. Yet to the degree to which users turn that platform into something specifically local, social media seems to be an instrument of global heterogenisation.[30] Much of this volume is concerned with giving flesh to that skeletal observation. First, however, we offer a brief review of some of the main concerns of the academic literature, moving from media and communication studies through to sociology and anthropology.

Defined studies of social media[31]

We cannot pretend to cover the vast number of publications and specialist journals that emerge from disciplines such as computer, internet and communication studies and that can therefore define the study of social media as the latest iteration of what was already established as their tradition of study. In particular, as already noted, this survey will not include research conducted under the auspices of methods that emulate the natural sciences.[32] Our concern is only with observations made of social media as derived from qualitative observation of everyday usage. However, that still leaves a huge amount of research.

Many core debates developed quite early on. One concern[33] was with the relationship between online and offline sociality, and an appreciation that, unlike earlier internet practices primarily used to contact strangers with common interests, social media was more focused upon existing social relationships. As boyd and Ellison noted: 'What makes social network sites unique is not that they allow individuals to meet strangers, but rather that they enable users to articulate and make visible their social networks.'[34] Partly to confront public debates that claimed otherwise, such scholars were insistent that users did not confuse 'friends' as a term on, say, Facebook with offline friendship. The academic discussion also tried to reflect the growing popular concern over social media as a threat to privacy, especially among younger users.[35] Addressing public concerns over privacy, and the extent to which children understood what they were doing, was supplemented by observations on the norms of usage that seemed to be developing. Gradually a series of journals came to pay increasing attention to such studies of social media. A proper perusal of these debates would require going through the recent issues of *Computers in Human Behaviour, New Media & Society, the Journal of Computer-Mediated Communication* and the new *Social Media + Society*, to name but a few.

Another popular concern has been with social media as a resource used by people to present themselves, leading to the question of how this online persona reflects or differs from their offline persona. Other themes are the number of friends or followers that seem appropriate to each platform, and how this reflects the judgements people make about others. A further concern, following from earlier internet studies, was whether networking constituted any sort of community.[36] There is also an obvious desire to explore how social media impacts upon people's welfare – whether, for example,[37] it makes us happy or unhappy. Because these are common and popular questions we have used them in order to structure this book, and show how our study can be used to answer them.

These debates and concerns do not form the foundation for our field work. The degree to which our own research focused upon a topic such as political activism was based on neither our interests nor its role in current academic or popular debates. It was dictated only by the degree to which we encountered such activity among the informants of our ethnographies. It is our informants who decide the focus of our research during ethnography. From that perspective the primacy concern of this project has been social media in the context of personal relations, since that is what usually dominates our experience as ethnographers. Fortunately there are two very clear and helpful books that examine this field: one by Baym,[38] with respect to media more generally, and the other by Chambers, with a more specific focus upon social media.[39] These books provide extensive bibliographies for topics such as intimacy, dating, friendship and identity. In addition to this comparative volume the present book series includes nine individual monographs, one for each field site, which all devote their Chapter 4 to the impact of social media upon personal relationships – reflecting the way in which these dominate not only the usage but also the consequences of social media.

Perhaps the majority of social media studies in the main journals are concerned with various psychological and sociological terms, including social capital, gratification, wellbeing and status. However, some of these shade into correlational analysis, which we tend to avoid because of the level of generalisation usually presumed within such analysis. A typical example of such studies would be that of Al-Deen and Hendricks,[40] but there are a host of others.

A major initiative was the establishment of the Pew Center for the Study of the Internet and American Life in 2004. This centre has published a continuous stream of important surveys and reflective discussion, providing the best available guide to both the extent and the nature of usage, as well as a sense of users' opinions, at least as reflected through survey questionnaires.[41] Once again, however, the regional bias will be evident from the very title of this project.

One observation that clearly emerges from this Pew Center research is the ever-increasing trend towards ubiquity. Teenagers now look at these platforms and apps daily, if not constantly, and generally keep up with several different ones simultaneously, mainly through mobile access. Some of the Pew reports reflect the same trends found in our own project. Their findings that females dominate the more visual sites, for instance, was also noted in our study of English schoolchildren. Yet, as this book will show, generalisations become more precarious when one examines places such as Turkey or China. Indeed some of the Pew studies are also helpful for showing quite specific US tendencies, for example the degree to which US users share their religion online on any given week (Pew 6/10/2104).

There are many approaches that understand their own perspectives as predominantly critical studies. These continue a tradition that harks back to what came to be called the Frankfurt School[42] of social theorists, and are also prominent in what are generally called Cultural Studies today. A clear example of this kind of perspective is the work of Fuchs,[43] although there are elements of his approach in more mainstream studies.[44] Much of this work is directed at criticism of the companies that own social media as capitalist corporations and favour arguments that link the consequences of social media to the interests of such companies. The other major concern of these writings is with the state use of private information following the revelations of WikiLeaks and of Edward Snowden.

At the other end of the spectrum are a somewhat larger number of studies whose primary concern is to help people to make money using social media or which are fixated on the share value and rise of the companies themselves. If critical studies tend to presume the malign, commercial studies tend to presume the benign.[45] Our project results will engage with both sides of this equation, including how people make money from social media and how social media companies make money out of them. However, our primary concern is carefully to assess the consequences of the ways people use social media, though hopefully reflecting the clear concern for their welfare that comes with living with each population over an extended period.

Another important approach that provides a considered body of detailed evidence comes from linguistic-based research, often including very detailed examination of the specifics of posting such as the nature of language and norms of usage. A good example of such a study is that of Lomborg.[46] While his main concern is with communication theory, he shows how cultural genres emerge through detailed study of social media usage seen as part of everyday life. This means recognising that genres (i.e. particular styles of use) represent a balance between many factors such as entertainment, information and intimacy. Such a study shows how, even in a newly emergent platform, the content reflects a whole series of different genres. Yet individual users very quickly learn to negotiate quite easily and comfortably around these spaces. Also attractive to an anthropological perspective would be studies that examine the violation of norms.[47]

As social media has become more ubiquitous, the tendency has also been to study specific phenomena rather than write about the nature of social media *per se*. Today a comprehensive survey of the literature on social media would soon find itself exhausted by the time it had tried to cover its impact on religion, economic life, state institutions, the practice of science and so on. The point is that there are very few topics which could not now be considered under the title 'the impact of social media on . . .'.[48] Since this volume includes separate chapters on several of these topics, for example gender, inequality, politics, education, the visual and commerce, there is no review here of the literature on these now highly dispersed topics and interests, which may be found within the relevant chapters. There are a plethora of other usages, for instance health work, specialist marketing or disaster relief, which are not covered anywhere in this book because this study can only really speak to that which was actually observed in the nine field sites.

Instead of trying to be comprehensive, this review of general studies of social media will close with a suggestion as to 'best practice'. One area stands out as the exemplary case of extremely high quality and effective research that could be a model for how such research might develop in the future. It is the work on how social media (or, more properly, new communication media more generally) impacts on education, and especially on the broader notion of learning. Such work has tended to be multi-disciplinary, including some from the anthropological field. It complements long-term, ethnographic-style qualitative work with large-scale comparative surveys, straddling quite academic concerns but also applied, policy-directed reports. Perhaps it reflects the fact that academics usually also have some experience as teachers. These publications will be discussed in more detail in our chapter on education, but include work by boyd, Clark, Ito and her colleagues and Livingstone with her colleagues.[49] For readers wanting to engage in their own research on the use and consequences of social media, this is the literature we would unequivocally recommend. We would hope that our main additional contribution is through our comparative perspective.

From communication studies to social studies

While most of the initial academic interest in social media arose from communication studies and internet studies, this is complemented by an increasing interest from studies of sociality, as we come to see social media as a place within which people associate. The obvious disciplinary base would be sociology. As noted in Chapter 1, a founding figure for both sociology and the study of sociality was Georg Simmel,[50] who extensively and systematically discussed the issue of how people associate with one another. Contemporary sociology is a broad discipline, but probably the two most relevant writers to studies of the internet have been Castells and Wellman. Both in different ways have focused upon the idea of a network.

It is not possible to avoid some jargon in considering Castells's influential book, *The Rise of the Network Society*. Castells[51] places the logic of our new political economy within the global forms of organisation, in which the role of 'informational capitalism' is increasingly critical. He describes this process by making a systematic distinction between the 'network' and the 'self'. These new information systems create innovative forms of powerful networks that align with others to develop new forms of political economy. The network is said to impose a higher and implacable 'culture of real virtuality' onto the latter. Thus 'we are not living in a global village, but in customised cottages, globally produced and locally distributed'.[52] Our research will contest these broadbrush generalisations. From the evidence presented in this volume, as well as from previous work by anthropologists,[53] it is not at all clear that the local use of media and internet are to this degree the product of global forces such as political economy, rather than the localised and very specific cultural features we identify in popular genres of communication.

A similar emphasis on the radical change brought by communication technologies is found in the recent book *Networked* by Rainie and Wellman.[54] In a much clearer argument they contend that the Social Network Revolution is a third revolution, after the Internet Revolution and the Mobile Revolution. The authors examine a series of shifts both in how people network and in the constitution of the groups with which they network. This is a book we certainly would suggest interested students would want to read in full, although the authors' primary argument is one that our own evidence would contest. The authors see a continuous trend through the rise of the internet, the mobile phone and now social media which leads to a decline in people's relationships to groups and the rise of the individual-based network. We will present a summary of our own evidence within Chapter 12. There are instances where our evidence would support the arguments made by Rainie and Wellman. In certain cases of extremely tight traditional social control, as in rural China or southeast Turkey, we also see social media in terms of this shift to individual-based networks of the kind they predict.

However, there are many more occasions when we find evidence that would suggest a different or even the opposite trajectory. This may be partly because they situate social media as a continuation of trends that had developed around the rise of the internet. By contrast we will argue that it is better to regard social media as most commonly a *reversal* of those trends. Social media marks a return to the significance and viability of groups such as family, caste and tribe, and a repudiation of the prior trend towards individually-based networks. For example, families that have been divided by migration or transnational employment use social media to repair that rupture.[55] The concept of scalable sociality and the rise of platforms such as WhatsApp clearly relate to groups, not just to individual networking. It will also be apparent in Chapter 7 that much depends upon contextual factors such as social status and gender, with the online being used sometimes to strengthen and at other times to complement different elements of offline sociality.[56] At the same time, Wellman with his colleagues[57] conducted much of the systematic research which demonstrated that social media is not a virtual world. In particular he showed that relationships online were not at the expense of relationships offline: if anything, people who were more connected online had more connections offline. It would therefore be misleading to reduce this sophisticated theoretical approach to this single trend towards individual networking.

The contribution of anthropology

Anthropology would align with other social sciences in having a long tradition of studying both human sociality and communication, the obvious foundations for the study of social media. With respect to sociality, perhaps the best known contributions associated with anthropology are on the one hand the study of kinship[58] and on the other the role of gifts, debt, exchange and reciprocity as often what constitutes a social relationship.[59] However, we see as the foundation for anthropology a word that we do not usually use every day – the normative.[60]

What does 'the normative' mean? We believe that people grow up from infancy to be socialised into what for their given group or society will be regarded as appropriate or inappropriate behaviour. When a child does something a parent may say 'that is not how you are supposed to behave' or 'what do you think people will say if you do that in public?' With praise and punishment we 'teach' proper behaviour. Much more is absorbed simply through observing what those around us do and refrain from doing. The reason people grow up to be 'typical' Kenyan farmers or Siberian nomads is not genetic. A child adopted at birth will become 'typical' of the society he or she is socialised into, not the one into which the child was born. These norms of appropriate and inappropriate behaviour are not fixed rules; they can be imaginatively interpreted or indeed flouted. In our ethnographies we try to present characteristic ways in which people in Trinidad, for example, use social media, but also give a sense of the wider range and exceptions surrounding this, since no one is merely 'typically Trinidadian'. In this manner anthropology studies norms not as rules, but as the analysis of what people actually do and why, including the variations from these norms. In anthropology this is generally called the study of 'practice'.[61]

If the spine of anthropology is the study of normativity mainly within social relationships the discipline also has many limbs, one of which is a flourishing anthropology of media. In 2002, prior to the spread of social media, two collections helped to consolidate what had developed as a sustained tradition of media studies;[62] there are now various groups and associations dedicated to anthropological research on media.[63] More recently two attempts have also been made to summarise the contribution of anthropologists to the study of digital media, and more specifically of social media.[64] One of the foundations for our study was the establishment at University College London of the first MSc in Digital Anthropology, which several of the authors of this book previously took as students.

Other than media studies and sociality per se, perhaps the main drive towards a specifically anthropological study of new media has come from the latter's importance for migrants and diasporas, often the results of political disruption or the requirements of our modern political economy. Examples include an edited collection concerned with indigenous populations and their diasporas,[65] and Bernal's[66] research on the Eritrean diaspora. Other disciplines have similar concerns, for example Greschke's study of South American migrants in Spain.[67] More recently we find anthropological studies that look specifically at the impact of social media itself on these diasporic groups, whether Brazilian, Filipino or Uyghur.[68] One small caveat to the growth of such a focus within the study of social media is that it can lead people to simplify the prior experience of offline communities in contrast to those online.[69] In reality we have always been subject to various forms of rupture.

More generally for anthropology, as with every other discipline, when social media became ubiquitous research fragmented into diverse and more specific topics. These range from Coleman's[70] work on Anonymous and Hacker groups to Uilemon's work on arts students and visual identity in Tanzania.[71] Relatively few anthropologists have tackled the issue of cultural diversity in itself.[72] There is an obvious overlap with studies of life online, such as that by Boellstorff and others,[73] and further overlap with studies of development and especially movements such as ICT4D,[74] which also focuses upon the impact of media.[75] Many of these approaches unite around a concern with global inequality, which we share with approaches from sociology and elsewhere.[76] Particularly helpful has been the work of Graham within the neighbour discipline of human geography, serving graphically to illustrate the inequalities of internet, communication and information geographies.[77] Other contributions focus upon issues of politics[78] or work.[79] Most characteristic of anthropology, however, would be the rise of studies with a regional focus.[80]

Curiously, though, it has been hard to justify one of anthropology's strongest claims, which is to comparative studies. Despite discussion and advocacy for comparison,[81] and the tradition of small regional comparisons on topics such as African divination systems or honour and shame in Mediterranean societies, this is largely an unfulfilled promise. Anthropologists have been better at cultural relativism[82] and the claim that each place is unique, while ceding generalisations to theory or other social sciences. This proved to be the main challenge for the research outlined here. Could we somehow manage the kind of genuinely comparative study that the discipline sometimes claims is the very definition of anthropology?

The problem is that a comparative study of many sites should not be at the expense of the depth of commitment to each individual site represented by ethnography. Indeed to characterise properly the research discussed in this volume, the emphasis would be as much on ethnography as anthropology. Chapter 3 provides an outline of our ethnographic approach and our methodology more generally. Yet anthropologists are not the only people to use ethnography. Many of the studies that are discussed in this chapter come from a broader qualitative approach. Those that we most respect, such as Nancy Baym, danah boyd or Sonia Livingstone, may also employ a mix of methods that are ethnographic, interview-based and also quantitative. The main difference is that our approach, coming specifically from the discipline of anthropology, has a focus upon the comparative study of cultural diversity, which may be present in these other studies but usually features as a smaller component. This book also contains a chapter (Chapter 4) about our quantitative results. It will indicate not only why the project embraced quantitative methods, but also why the results have been treated with far more scepticism than has evidence that is primarily qualitative.

The aim of this chapter is not to argue that any one approach can possibly suffice for a comprehensive understanding of the use and consequence of social media. All approaches have their advantages and commensurate disadvantages. Anthropology provides depth and comparison, but presents considerable problems with respect to generalisation and tends to be relatively ahistorical. If we have emphasised that approach, it is because this is a book that presents the results of an anthropological enquiry. Yet clearly the more that our findings can be situated alongside historical, linguistic, communication and other studies, the broader the understanding that may be achieved.

3
Our method and approach

Succeeding in failing

If this project is ultimately regarded as at all successful, the main reason will paradoxically be because again and again our individual projects failed. Failure was a major component of many of our studies. Those failures represent the single best body of evidence to support the claim that there is an integrity and scholarship to what we do. In claiming that our projects failed, we simply mean that they were unable to realise certain intentions of the academics involved. We can start with four cases.

Costa had written a PhD about online journalism, digital media and foreign correspondents in Lebanon, and her prime interest was social media and politics. A comparative case in Turkey would clearly benefit her career. The field site she chose, Mardin, was not far from the Syrian border and in what had become an autonomous Kurdish zone. Mardin itself comprised a heterogeneous population of Arabs, Kurds, Syriac Christians and Turks. Surely this would be an ideal site for her study of politics? In the end Costa did write one detailed chapter about politics in her book.[1] However, politics ultimately became an element – rather than the foundational focus – of her enquiry. She instead gave a more central role to the importance of gender and family relationships. This is partly because of the sheer gravity of any overt political engagement – an involvement which had previously caused the death of many of her participants' relatives. This meant that they largely avoided discussion of politics on social media. The exception were supporters of the government, or some in opposition who used fake and anonymised accounts. Meanwhile the same adoption of multiple and fake accounts had facilitated a radical transformation in gender relations, especially as interactions between young people, which actually became the big story. In her approach Costa followed the material she found, rather than the topic that she had initially thought to be of greatest importance and that may have best served her personal or career interests.

By contrast Wang chose her field site carefully because she wanted to study family relationships. She found a population that had just come from very close-knit families where everything was bound up in kinship. Now, however, they had travelled far to work in factory towns, thus becoming what people in China call a floating population of rural migrants. It therefore seemed certain that the main use of social media would be to retain links with their families and home villages, as users sought to repair the rupture of migration. Yet that is not at all what she found. Actually these migrants simply do not use social media that way and just do not seem to want to. A major reason for migration is to see the outside world, and the young generation of migrants from rural areas use social media to keep away from traditions of family control in order to gain autonomy as factory workers.

The situation was even worse for Venkatraman. He chose a field site in southern India that had until recently been a scattering of rural villages in a rural area. Then, as part of ambitious development plans, numerous IT companies and 200,000 IT workers were relocated there. This location seemed ideal, presenting a stark contrast between what might be regarded as the most modern population in India juxtaposed with the classic tradition of India's vast rural hinterlands. His prime interest was social media and work. Surely the basis of his book would be the extreme contrast between these two populations? Everything was set up for this to be the case.

Yet in reading Venkatraman's book this contrast is, to quite a remarkable extent, muted. Instead there is consistent emphasis on the specific features of traditional Indian society and the ways in which they have impacted upon the local use of social media, involving factors such as gender, caste, inequality and the extended family. Taken as a whole, these factors actually unite the IT workers and the villagers: what social media reveals is that almost everyone remains characteristically south 'Indian', bounded by these issues of kinship and caste notwithstanding the extreme differences in their circumstances. Certainly this juxtaposition highlights the issue of social hierarchy, but then for anthropologists this principle has always been seen as central to the organisation of South Asian society. So once again, to a remarkable extent, the initial plan could not be followed through because the evidence spoke to a different conclusion.

Perhaps the most abject failure was that of Haynes. She accepted a position at the Interdisciplinary Center for Intercultural and Indigenous Studies, housed at the Pontifical Catholic University of Chile in Santiago and funded by a Chilean government grant specifically to study the indigenous populations. Since her PhD focused on urban indigenous people in La Paz, Bolivia, it was natural for her to gravitate towards northern Chile, which includes significant Aymara and Quechua populations. For the study of social media we did not want a very small village, however, and the demographics of Alto Hospicio seemed to suggest it was of an appropriate size with a reasonable percentage of people who identified as indigenous, at least for census purposes (about 18 per cent). The problem was that her study of social media showed very clearly that most people of indigenous origin did not actively identify as such. Only quite late on in her study did some of her close friends happen to reveal their indigenous ancestry. Ultimately her book is extremely informative as to why this should be the case for the population in this town, being consistent with a similar suppression of a whole series of other potential points of differentiated identity. Nevertheless indigenous identity simply could not be the primary focus of her study of social media, even though that was the source of her funding.

Not everything went wrong. McDonald chose a site in a rural Chinese hinterland, close to the birthplace of Confucius, and then actually encountered the degree of tradition that might have been anticipated. Sinanan had already worked in El Mirador in Trinidad where she has relatives, so things were less of a surprise.

So what is so great about failure? Most of these anthropologists would have benefited personally if their studies had gone to plan, since the sites were often selected with regard to their particular academic interests. They would certainly have experienced fewer sleepless nights. However, this is where anthropology differs from many studies. Anthropologists get rather frustrated when writing grant proposals that expect clear predictions of the results of their proposal. The reality is that often the very reason anthropologists like ourselves carry out research is because we simply do not know what we will encounter; the discrepancy between what we plan to learn and what we subsequently discover is, by definition, a major part of our original findings. Failure for us is at least the guarantor of the integrity of our project. It is the main reason we believe that by the end of 15 months of field work each researcher had allowed himself or herself to be re-oriented to the actual use and consequences of social media. So while for us failure may be disappointing, its silver lining is that it suggests the quality and success of our scholarship. This does mean, however, that you cannot read our evidence as a reflection of our opinions. When we argue that social media has this or that impact, it does not mean we either approve or disapprove.

Is ethnography a method or an end?

In some disciplines[2] the word ethnography has come to mean any direct observation of what people do in their 'natural' habitat – rather than, for example, what they say in response to a questionnaire or a test. However, within the discipline of anthropology a central tenet of ethnography is time. A person must be present in the field site for an extended period, typically more than one year. All of our researchers were present in their field sites for at least 15 months of field work.[3] The anthropologist should have sufficient proficiency in the local language so that they can understand conversations between other people, not just conversation directed at them. Anthropological ethnography is often described as 'participant observation'. Rather than observing from a distance with a clipboard, anthropologists get involved: they help look after children, serve drinks, sell in a mobile phone shop and make genuine friendships. When Miller undertook his earlier ethnography of shopping[4] some readers were shocked to find that he often gave advice to his informants about what to buy. His point was that when people go shopping with friends they expect those friends to have opinions about how their figure looks in a dress or whether they have heard something tastes good. It is the failure to engage as a participant that makes the work artificial, not the engagement.

There is an additional way to define ethnography which does not focus upon the way we behave, but rather on the ends that it is supposed to achieve. The crux of anthropology is perhaps better described as a commitment to 'holistic contextualisation'. While we start with an object of study – in this case social media – our premise is that we simply do not know what factor in people's lives will be influenced by this object. It might be gender, religion, work or family. Furthermore none of these can be isolated to make statistical correlations, because in real life they are not isolated. A real person on any day in their life confronts these, and a multitude of other factors, simultaneously. An individual might be a woman, a Hindu, a mother, a factory worker, an introvert, a lover of soap opera and a devotee of Bollywood film stars on Facebook – all at the same time. It is not that we anthropologists are trying to be complicated and difficult; it is just that we believe this is a more truthful description of how people actually experience the world. No one lives inside a topic of research. Holistic contextualisation means that everything people do is the context for everything else they do. As a method ethnography cannot really get at every aspect of a person's life, but in trying to achieve this we at least gain a broader sense of what these aspects may be.

So, armed with the requisite language skills and sufficient time, the commitment is made to live among a range of different people within the field site, so that one can participate and observe as fully as possible. The specific aim is to gain enough understanding of all these factors – gender, religion, work, leisure and family – that we feel we can make an argument as to which seem more or less important in understanding how and why people use social media in the manner we observe. In sciences, which deal with universals, a negative case can disprove a hypothesis. In a society, however, there may be nothing that every single person does the same way or for the same reason. A negative case is just one more case. The method is not anecdotal, because we are seeking typical behaviour that is constantly repeated. Yet anecdotes, that is, individual stories, are used to convey our results. We often provide an extended example so that one can see how many factors and contextual features were relevant for one specific individual. We then often add other shorter stories, though, which show that there are many variants – to the extent that no individual stands for all members of that society.

What we did

Why these nine sites? Why no sites from Africa or the ex-Soviet bloc or Southeast Asia? We call this a global study, meaning that we include sites from all around the world, but clearly that does not mean it is a comprehensive study. There was an initial desire to include the biggest populations and emergent economies such as Brazil, China and India. We never intended to work in North America, simply because that area is already hugely overrepresented in the study of social media. Beyond that, however, much of the selection had to depend on whether there were suitable people available to carry out this research. We could only employ people trained in anthropology who could also make a commitment to this time frame. The initial proposal included a study in Africa, for example, but the designated person was not available. So logistics ultimately determined the specific nine sites. Another important factor was funding. Through the generosity of a government-funded research centre in Santiago and the Wenner-Gren Foundation, we were able to include two additional team members beyond the original generous ERC funding, providing the project with one study in Chile and a second study in China.

Each anthropologist was responsible for the selection of the actual field site, so this generally reflected a particular interest that they wanted to pursue – for instance Costa on politics or Wang on migration. Once committed to a field site this implied working with the entire population and not just a selected element: wealthier and poorer, religious and secular, young and old, male and female. Fortunately most of these field sites have a strong tradition of open social life, so Nicolescu could hang out in the town square as Italians expect to do and Haynes could frequent the market or children's afterschool activities as her neighbours would. When there are divided communities the field workers had to make separate groups of friends and networks, as Costa did with Arabs and Kurds in Mardin. Even that was not enough, however. Because there are no 'typical' Kurds, Costa had to make sure she included friendships with well educated and sophisticated Kurdish families where the men worked in the public sector, as well as with poorly educated, unsophisticated Kurdish families who had recently migrated from farms into the city. Wang had to make sure she maintained a good relationship with factory owners while studying the workers, which meant being discreet and cautious. On a number of occasions female researchers employed local male research assistants and male researchers employed female research assistants in order to ensure better access.

Perhaps the most difficult field site was in England, because English people may not be especially friendly to strangers, or even know the names of their neighbours. Many people in the village commute to work elsewhere and do not attend local social events. If one simply attended the 'community' events one would meet only the fraction of local people who are community minded. For the first six months Miller thus walked door-to-door,[5] striving to persuade people to let him into their homes. Only that way could he be sure of including people who are anti-social or lonely, as well as others who may not be community-minded. He also worked with schools, since everyone goes to school; and with a hospice, since everyone equally will die.

Participation generally means just that. Visiting McDonald in the field, it was evident that children would shout with glee the moment he appeared, but adults smiled just as broadly. He really did seem to be everyone's best friend, but that was partly because he lived in extremely ordinary quarters, sharing an outside toilet with other families and struggling with irregular water and electric supplies in the same way that they did. For an academic such as Wang to spend 15 months with factory workers whose primary interests, after a hard day's work, consisted of playing endlessly repetitive games, and who were often too tired to say anything particularly sensible, was (to be honest) extremely tedious. In the village where Spyer lived gossip seemed untrammelled, and had in effect become the major form of entertainment. Not surprisingly this included speculation as to who this intruder might 'really' be. Rumours spread that he was working for the CIA. This was not too problematic at first, but when people started suggesting that he was investigating local drug lords he began to worry, since many people in the town had been killed because of the drug trade. The situation grew more serious still when personal threats started to appear. Fortunately the arrival of his wife seemed to allay local people's fears.

Haynes experienced a turning point in her research when an earthquake measuring 8.3 on the Richter scale devastated buildings in Alto Hospicio. There was no water or electricity for over a week and the highway that connects with the larger town of Iquique was fractured by the earthquake, so that the city was cut off. This created quite a bit of community cohesion, allowing Haynes a new sense of being part of the social fabric of the town, as well as providing bonding moments even a year later. In her last week of field work, even with two new acquaintances, when the earthquake came up in conversation all three admitted with a laugh that they thought they were going to die at the moment it struck, and a deeper friendship was born.

An important component to participant observation is learning about what behaviour is considered appropriate. A gradual adaptation to the ways people in each particular site make friends is thus integral to this method. In Trinidad making and staying friends with one group of people requires constant partying; for a different group living in the same area, one becomes friends by constantly attending religious services and life cycle ceremonies. An ethnographer has to be a chameleon, able to change his or her manner, appearance and language for each of the different groups, with the aim of making everyone equally comfortable in his or her presence.

One important area in which we commonly fail, and thereby learn, is our own appearance. Venkatraman may be an Indian from the region where he undertook his field work, but he still had lessons

Fig. 3.1 Venkatraman dressed inappropriately

to learn. When he started his field work in south India he wore a T-shirt and jeans (Fig. 3.1). Practically no one would speak to him. When he tried to go to the other extreme and conduct field work wearing a formal shirt and trousers, he found that most people thought he was trying to sell them something because he looked like a businessman. In one case, after patiently explaining to a school the nature of our project and the research he would like to conduct, the school teacher apologised but said firmly that the school was not really interested in purchasing this 'anthropology'. Eventually Venkatraman took further measures. He pierced both his ears and started wearing traditional Indian hand-spun *kurtas,* supposedly 'intellectual-wear', to clearly position himself as an academic. After this the field work went just fine.

Spyer found his field site to be a split between evangelical Christians and others interested in some very non-Christian activities. He thus needed to look neither like a 'person of God' nor a 'person of the world'. Instead he went for a European style that managed to be a neutral 'gringo' look, enabling him to talk with people from both sides. Sinanan, by contrast, had to take off most of her clothes and adopt Carnival costume (Fig. 3.2) in order to gain a rapport with people who worked on the creation of a Carnival camp. Costa found that she had to shave her legs and underarms more carefully than usual since in this

Fig. 3.2 Sinanan unveiled

part of Turkey even to show a single hair where the legs or arms are not covered could be seen as shameful. She also found that she had to keep the house immaculately clean and sometimes wear a veil (Fig. 3.3).

Even when we had questionnaires or an agreement to study a particular question, it is often simply too artificial to put this question directly. Wang's factory workers were quite suspicious of formal questions; they would only talk with her if she was a friend helping them to deal with the emotional aspects of their relationships. For example, these were three formal survey questions:-

- Do you have your partner's social media password and, if so, could you tell me why and how did you get it?
- Will you remove your ex-partner's photographs on your social media profile? If so, why? And why do you think some people keep their ex-partner's photographs on social media?
- How do you deal with your partner's ex-partner's photographs on social media?

Fig. 3.3 Costa veiled

In practice the conversations through which she obtained answers would be more like:-

- 'Oh gosh, how come? That's totally outrageous, I just can't believe it. But…hey you are great, how can you know his password? My boyfriend never told me his!'
- 'Relax, you are strong, and I hope he will learn a lesson. By the way, did you give him any warning or at least a hint about this?'
- 'Really?! So…which means he knew you looked at these photos? I do not get it, what's wrong with men? Why do they think we can accept those ex-bitches…with a big smile?! I just do not get it!'

The point is that people should feel comfortable with, and ideally enjoy their engagement with, the anthropologist. Otherwise they will not give us their time. In addition all the field workers included formal recorded interviews, made mostly after researchers had built trusted relationships. These allow us to include the exact words of our informants in our books.

It is impossible to name a definite sample size of participants – a question we are often asked. Sometimes it was just a casual conversation over a drink, and sometimes it was people we saw every day for months. Not surprisingly, ethnographers tend to draw most heavily from the close friends they make after ten to 15 months. Such friends may admit that the things they said at first were intended to impress or disguise. Eventually they then provide much richer insights into what they really think is going on around them. Anthropologists are constantly making judgements about the validity of what they hear, being open but also sceptical about gossip. Rather like a detective we constantly try to check on our sources, always looking for further or better evidence.

In one respect this study had a distinct advantage over most such ethnographic encounters, which came from our topic of social media. Prior to starting the ethnography we agreed that all field workers should aim for around 150 people whom they would follow online ideally for the entire course of the field work. However integrated he or she feels in a community, an anthropologist will worry about the extent to which people's behaviour has been altered by his or her presence. But it seemed clear that just being one more person on Facebook or QQ along with hundreds of others was not likely to impact upon people's online behaviour, and in that sense posting online seems an ideal example of the possibilities of direct participant observation with regard to the topic of our project. For this purpose each field worker created a unique account on the major social media platforms. There was some discussion as to whether our presence online should be passive or active. Sinanan found very quickly that people were only comfortable if the anthropologist was at least as active as a typical 'friend' would be, making occasional 'likes' and postings of their own.

The other component of field work was our more systematic questionnaires, which are discussed in Chapter 4. As noted there, our first questionnaire was intended as an exploratory effort which some of us used to try and ensure that we engaged with the entire spectrum of the population, since this was organised according to estimates of the income range of participants or in some cases caste or education or religion. The second questionnaire was carried out towards the end of field work and is more reliably comparative, which is why it forms the basis of that chapter. It certainly helped that Venkatraman is a professional statistician as he was able to organise and process much of our material. We have a good deal of material derived from simply counting what people do on social media sites, or in one case calculating with whom they most interacted and then finding out through discussion who these people actually were, but this material has not yet been analysed.[6]

During this first year of field work we realised that, although we invested a great deal of time in sharing monthly reports, when someone could actually visit another person's field site so much more would become evident. This was a problem since unfortunately you – the readers – cannot visit all the field sites. So we decided that in addition to writing, everyone would commit to making ten short videos. One would be about their field site and one about how the work was done, with the remainder being stories or cases that illustrate the researcher's findings. Several of these, such as those in south India and north Chile, were made by others who generously agreed to collaborate with us.[7] These films are all on YouTube and our Why We Post website[8]. We suggest that if you want to appreciate our evidence fully it is a good idea also to 'visit' the sites through these films.

This discussion remains brief as a description of ethnography as method. To give a more detailed account would compromise the intention of this publication also to reach non-academic readers. Fortunately a recent book gives an excellent introduction to this topic in terms of planning and carrying out field work and all the different considerations from ethics to data storage that are involved.[9] Although it is directed to studies online, which makes the context rather different in some ways from our own approach to holistic contextualisation as described above, the discussion of ethnography itself – in terms of topics such as research design, observation and interviews – would stand for both approaches.

Comparative and collaborative work

The vast majority of anthropological and ethnographic work is highly individualistic, with a single person isolated in their field site. So this project is unusual, even within anthropology, in its commitment to both collaborative and comparative work. This is also perhaps unprecedented because it is only recently that cheap digital communications have made it much easier to stay in touch while conducting field work. Most of the team assembled as a group by September 2012. Following our preparations we all went to our field sites in April 2013 (except Haynes, who started later). Each month of field work we all worked on the same topic and then circulated 5000 words on that subject, which we then discussed via video conferencing. At first this followed an initial plan: the first month describing our field sites, the second talking about the social media landscape. As time went on we adapted to unexpected findings. For example, we had intended to work more on death and memorialisation, but most sites had relatively few older people on social media, making it less useful to spend a month observing and writing about this topic. On the other hand other subjects, such as education, which we had not originally planned to focus upon, were clearly becoming important across all the sites, and so we included a month on this. From the beginning we agreed that everyone would also have an individual topic, because obviously there could be issues of considerable importance to one site but not others. For example, Spyer would work on social mobility and Sinanan on the visual.

It might seem that all of us working on the same topic would lead to similar results and repetition, but in fact we found the opposite. It constantly kept us aware during field work of how distinct each site was. Normally, in conducting an ethnography, at first everything seems very strange and in need of explanation. After a few months, however, there is a danger that we take things for granted and they become obvious to us, so we forget that we need to write about them and explain them to others. For this project, constantly reading each other's work reminded us of the differences that need to be explained. Sometimes there were regional comparisons: the dualism of Pentecostalism against the underworld in Spyer's field site seems like an extreme version of the dualism of Carnival values against Christmas values in Trinidad – possibly because both sites include some common history, such as slavery and religious conversion. McDonald's site was always expected to show both similarities to and differences from Wang's. His site represented the long-term stability of values and residence, while hers represented the rupture of moving to factories. There were, however, still surprises – for example, the extreme difference in the attitudes towards education, which was of significant importance in the rural site and of very little importance in the industrial site.

Again and again we learned how we could not generalise from any one site. Sinanan found the concept of 'Facebook Fame' of considerable importance in her Trinidad site where people would do all sorts of things in the hope that they might go viral (e.g. schoolchildren fighting), but Haynes found that in her site in north Chile people did not have the slightest desire for that kind of fame; they would have been embarrassed by such attention. This degree of variation is most clearly expressed in our list of discoveries on the Why We Post website (www.ucl.ac.uk/why-we-post). In each case our main generalisation or question is tempered by nine comments from each of our field sites. If you read these you will see that almost inevitably at least one of the field sites will completely disagree with any particular generalisation. Such an outcome is also evident in our answers to the ten questions that constitute most of this book. For example, we shall find that in most cases social media does not represent the rise of individualism; but in a few field sites that is exactly what it does represent.

Mostly we could see more similarities if we looked at genres such as memes, selfies, indirects[10] and so forth, but then we saw more differences if we asked what exactly terms such as privacy, friendship or selfies meant for people in each site. The common language of English may exaggerate the degree of similarity. For example, even though the word friend is used throughout this book, it does of course stand for different terms with different meanings. In the Brazilian field site locals used the term '*colegas*' to describe relations between peers of the same age and socioeconomic background; *colegas* implies a level of competitiveness among the young people that does not fit the idea of solidarity carried by the Western definition of 'friend'. So the problem of the meaning of the word 'friend' did not start with Facebook; it started with the Tower of Babel.

After completing one year of field work the team spent May 2014 in London, consolidating and planning. They then returned to the field for the final three months, which ended in September 2014 (other than Haynes, who started and finished a bit later). We then decided to continue explicit comparison by writing individual books that contained the same chapter headings for all but Chapter 5, which represents each person's individual topic. In addition we noted how often works on social media are bereft of visual illustration, so each book contains a Chapter 3 that is largely devoted to directly illustrating and analysing what people post.

Most academic books within social science are expected to be in large measure a dialogue with other academics. However, the problem is that this is usually of very little interest to anyone who is not an academic or is from a different discipline. Other subjects such as history often keep these debates with other academics within footnotes and endnotes in order to retain a clear narrative for readers. We followed their example. In our nine monographs we have left our main text free to be as clear a description and analysis of our 15 months' ethnographic field work as possible. In order to achieve this, most of our citations and discussion of other academics are in our endnotes, or will be in future journal papers. Several of us also plan to write second monographs. We have always seen our topic as a telescope. We can use our ethnography to focus in on the nature of social media. We can also use social media to expand the focus outward to an enhanced and expanded ethnography. The books published so far represent the first strategy. Subsequent books will emerge from the second.

Ethical issues

There were two strong ethical commitments regarding the dissemination of this research. One was that we should make our material available in the languages of the countries in which we worked. Another was that people with low incomes in these countries should not be prevented from reading them by reasons of cost. We chose to work with the newly established UCL Press because it was set up with a commitment to offer free digital copies under Open Access with a Creative Commons Licence, as well as print copies for sale at cost. We were also delighted to be given an opportunity to create a free online lecture course (known in jargon as a MOOC) on the FutureLearn platform, developed by the UK Open University, as well as a website (ucl.ac.uk/why-we-post) containing our audio-visual material. These are also the places where we hope to develop an active social media presence, providing further avenues for discussion and for viewing our findings. Here you can comment and contribute to this project. Through the combination of these disparate forms and levels of publication we have also tried to develop a holistic vision of research dissemination to match the holistic nature of ethnographic research.

Other ethical issues raised by this project have led to a mix of formal procedures and informal considerations. As stipulated by the original grant from the ERC, our research proposal had first to be approved by the ethics committee of University College London, and then by ethics committees in all the countries in which we worked, before being signed off by the ERC itself. This includes the need for written or oral consent from participants. That is the bureaucracy of ethics. In practice our main concern has been to ensure that we explain clearly to all those who took part the nature of our project and how any information we obtain from them might be used. Ultimately our basic ethical rule is quite simple: nothing we do should cause harm to the people who took part.

Actually the vast majority of material we obtained is unproblematic and most people have no reason to be concerned if other people know that they posted a meme or discussed what they had for lunch. In fact, our informants overwhelmingly preferred to be identified. However, we feel that informants may not always be aware of potential misuse of their personal details, and so we collectively have agreed to reject that preference, other than for film work where identification is likely. All of our books are instead based on anonymised material. That means we feel free to change details about an individual, such as the work they do or where they were born, but only as long as these alterations are in no way relevant to the particular point being made. In the case where the field site is a larger town such as Mardin or Alto Hospicio, we use the real name. In the case of smaller field sites we have used pseudonyms.

In the current age of Google and online searching it is entirely possible for a reader to find out the real name of our field sites, even though we would not confirm that identification; but clearly the only reason for anonymity is the protection of informants, so we cannot see why anyone would do this for other than malicious reasons. In any case we have introduced additional levels of anonymity at the personal level. The more we believe the actual information published could potentially cause harm to an individual, the more stringent we have been in our anonymisation. This includes both our concerns and those of our informants. For example, English people feel there is a risk in showing a picture of a baby, so all English babies in the *Visualising Facebook* text have been partially masked to ally such fears. People in other field sites had no such concerns.

Most writing about ethics is concerned with protecting participants from negative consequences. As a result few people seem to mention the other side to this coin. What are the positive benefits of research? The primary goal of this work is education, to disseminate knowledge about the use and consequences of social media around the world. As it happens, even at the level of field work, our experience is that almost inevitably people enjoy the opportunity to talk and spend time with visiting anthropologists; the informal nature of such relationships means that people feel free to ask questions of the anthropologist as much as to answer them. Sometimes, simply because we are *not* their family (or teachers or state bureaucrats), people feel able to talk cathartically at a deeper level about things they really care about, in a way that may not be possible with people they actually 'know'.

We all passionately believe in the positive benefits of anthropology itself. In a world where most people have little opportunity to find out about and appreciate the diversity of the world we live in, we tend to assume that other people are more like us than they actually are, and have little idea how odd we may appear to them. We hope that by reading this volume, and all the other books in the series, readers will gain a better understanding of social media and what it has now become through its differential usage around the world. Above all, however, we hope that in reading these books people from around the world are able to gain a better and more empathetic understanding of other people, and that positive imperative is the core to our ethics and those of anthropology itself.

4
Our survey results

The survey questionnaire presented here contained 43 questions in total, of which over 80 per cent were in the format of multiple choices; the remaining were simple numeric answers, enabling a respondent to complete it within ten minutes with ease. It was tested multiple times to try and make sure that it adhered to local meanings within each field site. The intention was to administer the survey to at least 100 respondents per site, though in practice this varied from 99 (north Chile) to 229 (Brazil), producing a total of 1199 responses[1] across all of our nine field sites. We also tried to encompass the entire range of economic levels relevant at each field site. More details and further background to the survey are given at the end of this chapter. In all cases the percentages presented in this chapter are relative to the people who responded to that particular question, rather than to the total surveyed. The results are intended to be illustrative of how people answered a particular question and should not be interpreted for statistical significance.

We have only presented those results that are common to all nine field sites.[2] They are organised according to five different themes. As throughout this volume, the country and regional labels are used for convenience of recognition. They are never intended to make claims that homogenise populations. For example, our site labelled as southeast Turkey mostly consisted of either Arab or Kurdish people, with relatively few Turkish informants. In most cases we highlight figures that came out as especially high or low, which we then try to account for.

Theme 1: social relationships

As ethnographers we found that the results presented in Fig. 4.1 generally reflect the views expressed by our informants during the ethnography regarding their more general patterns of sociality. People in Trinidad, Brazil, Italy and north Chile tend to see themselves as highly sociable offline, as compared to people in England or rural China.

While McDonald writes extensively about the importance of strangers as a category within social media for the rural China site,[3] social media contacts of this type are not numerically significant. By contrast Wang points out that, for highly mobile factory workers in industrial China, their online social connections are generally more stable than those with their offline neighbours and the temporary colleagues whom they encounter at their work place. Given the restrictions these workers face in their offline lives,

Fig. 4.1 Average number of friends on primary social media – QQ in China, Facebook in all other sites

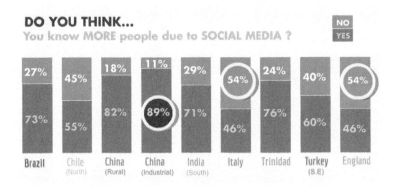

Fig. 4.2 Distribution of responses to question on whether users thought they knew more people due to social media across all field sites

social media becomes the core space in which they socialise. They often value these online contacts more than their offline connections. Also, since most of these migrant factory workers are under 30, social media for them becomes the place to express themselves better and to explore 'modern' lifestyles. These results are also confirmed by the independent survey[4] that Wang conducted in her field site. In England, by contrast, people tend to be cautious and wary of interacting with people who they do not already know offline, partly as a result of many stories about the problematic consequences of friending strangers that circulate in the English media. The exception to this will be dating sites such as Tinder.

The Italian respondents were highly sociable offline and saw social media mainly as an extension of the fact that they already knew the people in their home town. In fact 54 per cent of the respondents from Italy suggested that more than 60 per cent of their Facebook friends were from their home town. Apart from the highly educated fraction who were more connected with Italians from other regions, these users also did not expect either that social media usage would bring them many new connections or that a large number of offline contacts would necessarily translate to more online contacts (Fig. 4.3).

Respondents in Trinidad, on the other hand, did equate having more offline friends to having extended networks outside town – for example, those who had attended university or worked outside town, or had family and friends overseas. In general the Latin American and Trinidadian field sites were those where people expected to expand their social networks by using social media, specifically though the mechanism of friending the friends of friends. Such a belief is also reflected

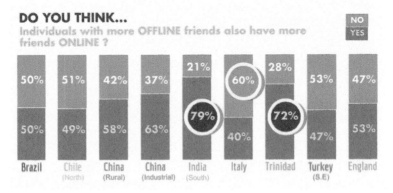

Fig. 4.3 Distribution of responses to question on whether users thought having more friends offline resulted in more friends online

in the larger number of their online friends found in Fig. 4.1. There is a gradation here. In south India friends of friends whom the respondents have not met offline are seen to be closer to a category of strangers, but there is no clear desire to make contact with strangers as found in the rural Chinese field site.

The differences in responses to this question (Fig. 4.4) provide us with one of the strongest examples of why we feel these questions often teach us quite different lessons from those we expected. In Brazil Spyer was anticipating a very different answer, since his ethnography had clearly shown that people in his field site do not ask for permission from family or friends before they friend others. However, the answer made it clear that while they do not seek permission to add friends, they often *turned* to family and friends in order to find out who the person sending them a friend request actually was.[5] While it is also true in both north Chile and Trinidad that people accepted that a friend of a friend was a potential friend, they did not see this as equating to consulting with others as asked by this question. What this indicates is that, although we took measures to try and phrase our questions the same way in every case, in practice people interpreted the implications of that question differently. The variation in their answers thus reflects that difference in interpretation, and not necessarily a difference in practice. Yet one can only appreciate this by already knowing the informants' practices very well through the wider ethnography.

The next section of the survey comprises three questions to help establish further the level of involvement of family and friends in our respondents' social media use.

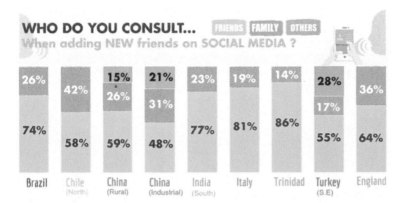

Fig. 4.4 Distribution of responses to question on who users consulted when adding new friends on social media

Table 4.1 reflects the technical competence of the respondent. In our English field site all those people who let others set up their account were older people, as can be seen from the fact that one of the main groups (six per cent) that assisted them were their children. Younger people might be ashamed to suggest that this is not something they could do for themselves. By contrast the people in industrial China, with very limited education, might expect help from an internet café, already an important hub for learning about the internet. Wang notes how mobile phone shops are gradually taking on this role as access to the internet is increasingly mediated via smartphones. Both strongly contrast with our Brazilian site. Here the social nature of social media is reinforced by making the setting up of an account itself a social project, intended to deepen and broaden existing friendships.

In the Chinese case the figure within this table represents the percentage of people who interact with you most regularly on social media, since direct posting on another person's site is not a feature of Chinese platforms. Nevertheless it is hard to imagine a more unpredictable result than the highest figure for posting from siblings coming from a rural Chinese site that is subject to the Chinese government's family planning restrictions of one child per family. McDonald suggests this is a combination of two factors. Firstly those who do have siblings perhaps share a very close relationship with them, but secondly this figure represents a practice in China whereby it is common to refer to one's cousins as siblings. This is thus a further warning about the presumption that it is possible to prevent local interpretation of questions that strive to be common to cross-cultural settings.

WHO set up your FIRST SOCIAL MEDIA ACCOUNT?

	myself	friends	parents	siblings	partner	children	other relatives	Internet Cafe worker
Brazil	41%	39%	1%	7%	4%	3%	0%	6%
Chile (North)	74%	6%	1%	9%	2%	6%	0%	1%
China (Rural)	48%	18%	1%	19%	5%	3%	5%	1%
China (Industrial)	20%	41%	0%	15%	1%	2%	9%	12%
India (South)	48%	23%	3%	17%	5%	4%	0%	1%
Italy	65%	12%	2%	9%	6%	6%	0%	0%
Trinidad	62%	25%	0%	7%	3%	2%	0%	1%
Turkey (S.E)	74%	17%	0%	6%	0%	2%	0%	1%
England	83%	7%	1%	1%	2%	6%	0%	0%

Table 4.1 Who set up the user's first social media account?

WHO posts regularly on your SOCIAL MEDIA ?

	parents	siblings	partner	children	friends	nobody
Brazil	5%	32%	14%	2%	47%	0%
Chile (North)	9%	13%	23%	7%	49%	0%
China (Rural)	10%	40%	7%	2%	41%	0%
China (Industrial)	4%	25%	1%	11%	59%	0%
India (South)	3%	15%	9%	5%	68%	0%
Italy	4%	18%	10%	6%	62%	0%
Trinidad	6%	15%	15%	4%	60%	0%
Turkey (S.E)	1%	8%	13%	1%	49%	28%
England	19%	10%	14%	12%	45%	0%

Table 4.2 Who among the respondent's family and friends posts regularly on his or her social media?

In Italy social media is considered a very public platform, and is principally viewed as a connecting platform for friends rather than family. The Italian term for friends, '*amici*', is broad, encompassing best friends, friends from the town, schoolmates and colleagues from work. Similarly in Trinidad the figures seems to reflect the earlier finding that people have a relatively high number of friends on Facebook with whom they socialise online and offline. In south India daily posting on friends' social media profiles is seen as extending sociality, while most communication to close family members is routed through other media such as phone calls and messaging services. The anomaly here is the figure (28 per cent) showing no one posting on the social media sites in southeast Turkey. This is plausible since it reflects the local problem of public display, which traditionally has been highly controlled with infringements seen as an affront to modesty. Costa found that many people generally preferred just to post on their own walls because they were anxious about how the recipient would feel about what has been posted on their profile by others.

In Brazil it is commonly assumed that social media has led to more infidelity and suspicion. Here, as in Trinidad, social media is seen as a means for partners to 'spy' on each other. There was considerable ethnographic evidence for the use of social media for quarrelling among school pupils in the English field site. Given that friends were central

With WHOM do you have arguments over their use of SOCIAL MEDIA ?

	parents	siblings	partner	children	friends	other relatives
Brazil	24%	17%	38%	3%	18%	0%
Chile (North)	30%	8%	28%	16%	18%	0%
China (Rural)	24%	21%	8%	10%	29%	7%
China (Industrial)	26%	2%	48%	7%	11%	7%
India (South)	25%	16%	12%	6%	41%	0%
Italy	26%	15%	11%	7%	41%	0%
Trinidad	18%	15%	24%	4%	38%	0%
Turkey (S.E)	14%	13%	32%	0%	41%	0%
England	22%	16%	18%	4%	40%	0%

Table 4.3 People with whom respondents have arguments over their use of social media

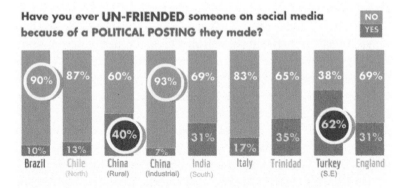

Fig. 4.5 Distribution of responses to question on whether user had unfriended someone because of a political posting he or she made

to social media use in most of our field sites, we also wanted to understand whether the respondents had unfriended anyone from their social media profile, and to relate this to the much discussed topic of politics on social media.

The answers to this question provide a good example of why our two Chinese sites should not be lumped together as 'Chinese' – the site in rural China has one of the highest numbers and the industrial

China site has the lowest numbers for the act of unfriending because of politics. Wang was surprised that even seven per cent had unfriended someone on these grounds, and suggested that these were most likely the factory owners and managers rather than the factory workers. This is partly because people refrain from postings about politics in the first place. The exception would be posting about corruption, local regulation, pollution and unequal social status for rural migrants, injustice and poverty, since all of these are ways of bonding with other migrants. By contrast informants in rural China will unfriend those who post about any kind of politics, which is seen as inappropriate. People there feel that social media is a place for sharing happiness, in the form of baby photographs, romantic memes or pictures of tourism, rather than complaining about things with which one is dissatisfied. The problem for them is not a fear of retribution from the state, but of disapproval from their own friends. In our Brazilian site politics is also seen as something best left to the politicians and really not worth discussing on social media, but it is rarely a reason for unfriending anyone.

However, our field site in southeast Turkey was altogether different. Politics not only mattered here, but was also hugely important and sensitive. The political divisions in this site are quite neatly demarcated. Given the history and presence of the Kurdish conflict, people here supported either the Kurds or the government. Many of Costa's informants had relatives who were arrested, tortured or killed by the police or the army during the 1980s and 1990s. People supporting different political groups were often friends on Facebook, in the same way in which they shared the same buildings, neighbourhoods, schools and work offices. Given the strong political undercurrent, they consciously avoided discussing topics (both online and offline) that could create disagreement and conflicts. However, when they did share political posts on social media, it was very likely to cause conflict; unfriending someone from Facebook was probably the easiest way to manage the conflict.

Finally, under this theme of social relationships, we wanted to understand the possibility of dating through social media across all the nine sites.

As we have already noted earlier in this chapter, social media in both Latin America and Trinidad is strongly related to the making and breaking of relationships. The first story in Miller's book, *Tales from Facebook*,[6] centres on the jealousy Facebook created in a relationship in Trinidad. This is less common elsewhere. Tinder became important in

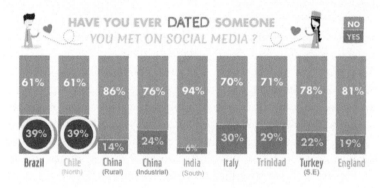

Fig. 4.6 Distribution of dating on social media

England mainly after the end of our field work, while Grindr was already well established for homosexual males (though not everyone considers Grindr or Tinder to be social media platforms). Momo is used in China, mostly in urban areas rather than in our field sites. One reason the people in our north Chilean field site would try and find partners in this way was, as they joked, simply laziness. It was easier to chat with someone online than to approach them in person, as there was less chance of rejection. Moreover this field site in north Chile has very few social spaces such as bars or activity clubs where one might meet a potential partner – although even here people were more comfortable meeting friends of friends than complete strangers. As Miguel, an informant from north Chile, explained:

> People do not trust things like dating websites, or something like Tinder. You do not know who the person is. You can't see their friends... If you're looking at someone on Facebook, you can see your mutual friends, and you can see where they are from and maybe their hobbies. So you get a sense of the person, who they really are. You know they're not fake.

In south India men generally would have liked to find dates through social media, which might happen among the middle classes or IT employees. However, even if a lot of flirting on social media does occur, this very rarely develops into any kind of offline relationship, let alone marriage, because many restrictions are placed on the behaviour of women.

Theme 2: activities on social media

One of the main activities on social media is posting visual materials such as photographs and memes. Our first question under this theme specifically addresses this aspect.

Fig. 4.7 suggests some marked contrasts between the sites. While 67 per cent of the respondents in north Chile post less than 20 per cent of their photographs on social media, 20 per cent of those from southeast Turkey post over 60 per cent of theirs. On the other hand 32 per cent of the responses from the rural China field site indicate that none of the photographs that are taken ended up on social media.

The reasons lie in differences regarding what visual material is seen as appropriate for social media posting. The key criterion in many places, including northern Chile, is humour. People share items such as pictures which are funny, and attract comments for that reason. Social media is viewed as a form of entertainment. For example, a 'meme war' is where people post memes in the comments section. These will often generate hundreds of responses, whereas someone's photograph of food, their afternoon activity or a selfie will generate at most 15 comments. Thus while users here continue to snap images for their own personal enjoyment and posterity, the emphasis in social media is on visuals that generate a large amount of social interaction.

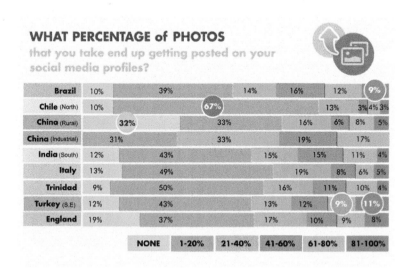

Fig. 4.7 Distribution of percentage of photographs posted on social media

This is even more true for our rural China field site, where people generally do not share their own photographs on social media – the exceptions being teens and young women who share selfies. Generally they prefer to share memes and funny postings. McDonald thinks that here, just as in northern Chile, such postings are thought to be of greater general interest. Another reason is privacy. For many the few photographs of oneself or one's family that are shared online are often kept in password-protected galleries, accessible only to those who know them personally.

Our next question on activities looked at playing online games.

The stand-out figure here is from industrial China. This is probably the site where people's working day involves the most unremitting labour in factories. It is therefore not all that surprising to note that they use gaming as a means to relax and to separate themselves from work. In fact this reflects a wider emphasis upon the use of smartphones for entertainment more generally, a feature that clearly emerges in this additional survey conducted by Wang[7] on smartphone usage among 200 handset-owning respondents in her field site. These workers usually do not have the spare time, money or energy for extra social life after long hours of heavy labour. At the same time, in addition to the relaxation that such games provide, gaming is also viewed as a major way of hanging out with friends online, especially among the young men.

Online gaming is also a very important aspect of social media (especially Facebook) in southeast Turkey. The most common games were *Candy Crush Saga, Ok* and *Taula*. Gaming is a way to socialise with new and old friends. People play these online games not only with known friends but also with strangers. There are possibilities that these strangers might also become new friends through gaming. Online

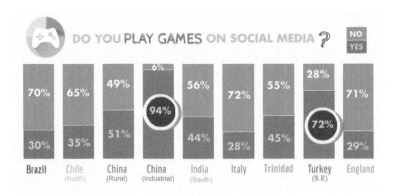

Fig. 4.8 Distribution of online gaming on social media

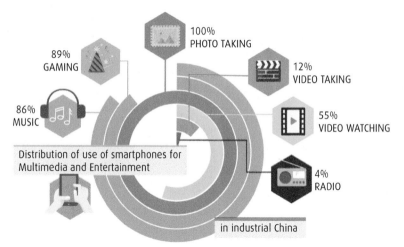

100%
PHOTO TAKING

89%
GAMING

12%
VIDEO TAKING

86%
MUSIC

55%
VIDEO WATCHING

Distribution of use of smartphones for
Multimedia and Entertainment

4%
RADIO

in industrial China

Fig. 4.9 Distribution of use of smartphones for multimedia and entertainment in industrial China

gaming is also used to flirt discreetly with people of the opposite sex. For the very young (i.e. children in primary school, aged 8–11 years) gaming is probably one of the main reasons for using social media. In fact many actual farmers in Turkey played Farmville, the first really successful Facebook game. In contrast home gaming (Xbox, PlayStation, Wii) is still important in Italy, where it works as an element of bonding within the family group.

Theme 3: privacy

A third broad area in which people often see an impact from social media and which we thus explored was privacy.

It is evident from Fig. 4.10 that respondents across different field sites have different views about sharing their social media passwords with others. As we can see, this varies from the one in five who do this in north Chile to the four out of five who do this in our rural China site. However, we learn more when we look in detail at whom they are prepared to share their passwords with.

Most field sites recorded high percentages when it came to sharing passwords with partners, which can be explained by the perception (in some of our field sites) that social media use can easily lead to infidelity, through being able to friend strangers. Sharing passwords between partners thus allows for the security of monitoring of a partner's account.

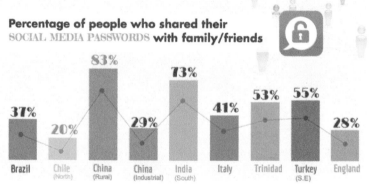

Fig. 4.10 Distribution of people who shared passwords with family/friends

WITH WHOM DO YOU SHARE YOUR SOCIAL MEDIA PASSWORD [?]

	partner	parents	siblings	children	friends
Brazil	48%	7%	19%	6%	20%
Chile (North)	50%	10%	10%	5%	25%
China (Rural)	30%	10%	22%	10%	27%
China (Industrial)	12%	38%	50%	0%	0%
India (South)	30%	3%	11%	8%	48%
Italy	42%	4%	18%	24%	11%
Trinidad	46%	6%	11%	7%	30%
Turkey (S.E)	46%	7%	17%	6%	24%
England	75%	4%	0%	7%	14%

Table 4.4 People with whom users shared their media passwords

In sites such as south India couples sometimes maintained just one social media profile between them, making sharing passwords inevitable.

In our northern Chile site the entire extended family, from nephews to grandparents, may well share use of the same computer. The mobile phone may therefore be the only piece of privacy a person has. While many couples experience jealousy over their partner's use of

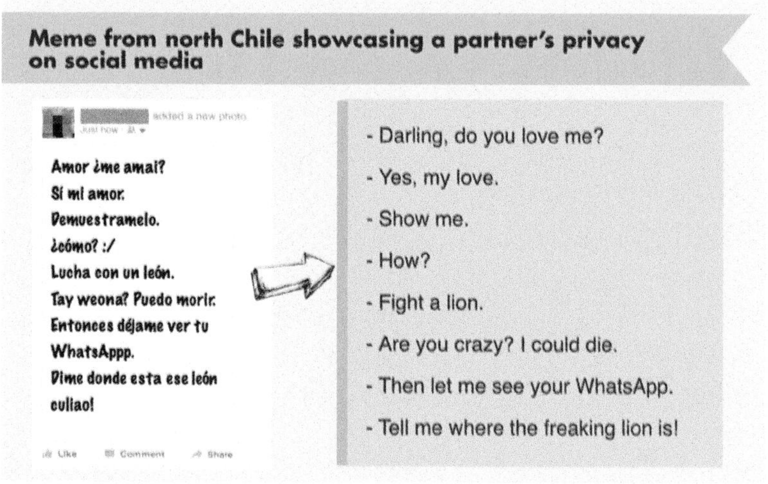

Meme from north Chile showcasing a partner's privacy on social media

added a new photo
Just now

Amor ¿me amai?

Sí mi amor.

Demuestramelo.

¿cómo? :/

Lucha con un león.

Tay weona? Puedo morir.

Entonces déjame ver tu WhatsAppp.

Dime donde esta ese león culiao!

Like   Comment   Share

- Darling, do you love me?

- Yes, my love.

- Show me.

- How?

- Fight a lion.

- Are you crazy? I could die.

- Then let me see your WhatsApp.

- Tell me where the freaking lion is!

Fig. 4.11 Meme from north Chile showcasing a partner's privacy on social media

social media, sharing a password is rarely considered obligatory. People respect their partner's privacy, with many reporting that they preferred not to know if their partner occasionally speaks with an ex or flirts online. A meme sums up this feeling, illustrated in Fig. 4.11 above.

In rural China many share passwords with their friends while in school – not only in order to establish trust, but also so that their friends can help them look after their QZone profile (by logging in and maintaining any games that need care to ensure continued accumulation of levels).

Fig. 4.12 shows that, with the exception of the English field site, there were groups of people in sites who used fake or anonymised profiles. The Chinese situation is very different since social media is not generally based on the use of real names. Real names are mainly used for work-related accounts, since many factories use social media for communication with workers. For 'private' social media most used an anonymous QQ name, since anonymity provides a huge space for freedom of speech. People also have multiple accounts for purposes of playing games or being able to use several different sites, as is evident in Fig. 4.13.

McDonald's participants generally felt that, if someone was a true friend, they ought to be able to recognise you from your avatar/screen name. As such this convention also acted as a way of 'testing' friendship. Chinese social media platforms such as QQ and WeChat also allow you to 'label' a friend's account with a nickname of your own in cases where

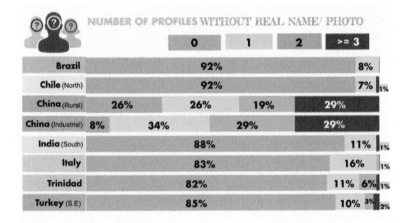

Fig. 4.12 Distribution of social media profiles without real name/photograph

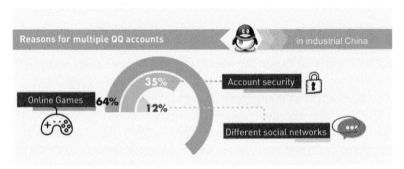

Fig. 4.13 Reasons for multiple QQ accounts in industrial China

you do not recognise the account owner. Avatars also helped to facilitate friending of strangers, providing a 'mask' from behind which the initial interactions could occur.

The main problem with this question is that people who use multiple fake accounts are quite likely not to want to reveal this to a survey. Certainly Costa felt that her result was unlikely to be accurate for her site in southeast Turkey. Admitting to fake profiles could damage one's reputation. For a man to acknowledge this was almost an admission that they were actively hunting and harassing women, while for women it was tantamount to declaring openly that they were hiding something.

A different source of anxiety was the possibility of photographs being uploaded onto social media by other people, without their knowledge/permission. This topic is investigated in Fig. 4.14.

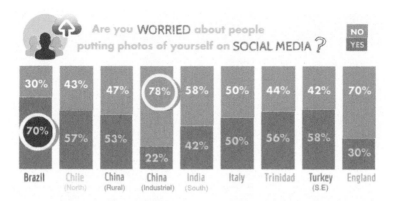

Fig. 4.14 Distribution of responses to question on whether users worried about people putting photographs of them on social media

In industrial China people are generally happy to see others posting their image – something they took as a sign that they were valued by others. These factory workers were usually in the position of being 'attention givers' in their daily lives, finding that as a disadvantaged group attention was rarely paid to them. However, some young women might be concerned that photographs of themselves posted by others might not look as good as those they chose to post themselves. This was also a consideration in Trinidad.

Our Brazilian site is both sociable and given to sharing, but there may still be several factors that mitigate against this practice. Teens are very careful about placing photographs online, and avoid those that carry information about their relationship status. Villagers typically are careful about whom they are seen with, as any sign of proximity (for example, a man and a woman speaking on the street) can and often will become gossip, as locals will imply they are having an affair. In our English field site there was a radical difference between young people, who hardly ever removed such tagged photographs unless they were particularly damaging to their reputation, and older people, who often systematically removed all such images.

Theme 4: commerce

We also explored the use of social media within the commercial sphere, starting with a question as to whether people click on advertisements.

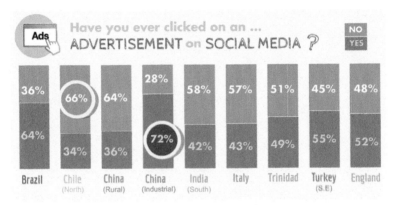

Fig. 4.15 Distribution of responses to question on whether users had clicked on advertisements on social media

The evidence from our site in northern Chile is consistent with a general tendency to avoid consumption. The town of Alto Hospicio in northern Chile has remarkably few shops and also of offline advertisements. In general, consumption, brand loyalty and even displays of upward mobility are considered here to be somewhat crude and superfluous. While the city is considered 'marginal' it is not 'impoverished'. Many residents financially benefit from working in industries connected to the region's abundant natural resources such as the copper mines. What drives this lack of conspicuous consumption is a sense of solidarity with neighbours and of fitting into an unassuming form of normativity. While individuals very often 'like' or 'follow' local businesses on Facebook, they rarely consume national or international products of the type that place advertisements there. By the same token Facebook is not used as a site for expressing conspicuous consumption. The situation is entirely different in our Brazilian and Trinidadian field sites.

If this is a case where we cannot lump together sites from Latin America, it also reveals a clear discrepancy between our rural and industrial China sites. Conducting business via WeChat is very popular in the industrial China field site. Wang suggests that only around seven per cent of people 'proactively' engage with e-commerce, such as setting up one's own online shop or selling goods through one's social media profile. Others engage with social business more passively, mainly through clicking on advertisements which were shared on their friends' social media profiles. A frequently mentioned and practiced activity related to potential consumption is '*Jizan*' ('collecting "likes"'), a practice on WeChat to earn a free gift or discount. Even local restaurants use *Jizan* to promote their businesses. People will frequently forward sales promotions on their personal WeChat pages and urge their online contacts to 'like' the retailer's official WeChat account in order to get the discounted commodity. All of these encourage people to click on the advertisement on their social media profiles. More generally merely noting that one has ever clicked on an advert may not mean a whole lot. Most of our evidence is for a quite limited impact from social media on marketing.[8]

We then looked to see if social media extended the way people influence each other socially with respect to consumption, asking whether respondents had ever bought something because they saw a friend with it on social media. Although 30 per cent is not that high for this event occurring at least once, Miller was surprised to find the English site had the highest percentage. The ethnographic evidence was entirely different. He found older informants were quite proud to declare that they were not susceptible to advertising, either on or offline. It is possible that they took this question to show how they were being influenced by friends as opposed to being influenced by social media. The issue in Italy is possibly not that users refuse to be influenced by images on social media, but that those influential images will be those of Italian celebrities as role models rather than of their local friends.

We then looked at whether people actually made money through social media. The figure for our northern Chile site should again be seen in the wider context. Since this is a place where people largely avoid contact with the formal commercial sphere, which is remarkably absent from their town given the incomes generated by mining, an informal use of social media for local selling on a small scale has become a substitute for such formal commerce.

In industrial China many social media games were designed to encourage people to spend money in order to gain advantages in the

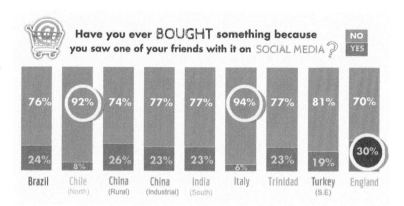

Fig. 4.16 Distribution of buying behaviour

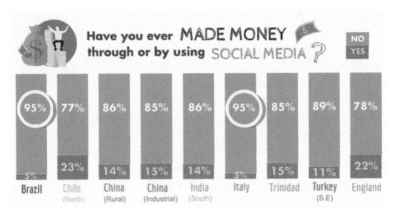

Fig. 4.17 Distribution of responses to question on whether users had ever made money through social media

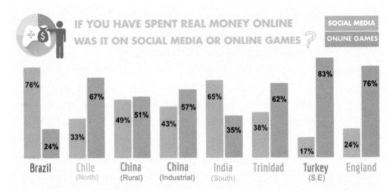

Fig. 4.18 Distribution of amount spent on social media/online games

games. This is discussed in detail in the books written by McDonald and Wang.[9] This may be especially appealing among factory workers since even the status of having achieved a higher level in games can become important when one's status is so low in the offline world.

Once again problems arose with the way in which people interpreted the question. In south India responses to this question reflected two categories: 1) spending on pay-as-you-go internet data plans with the intention of using the data for social media; and 2) money spent on buying things through advertisements that appeared on social media, which respondents also regarded as spending on social media.

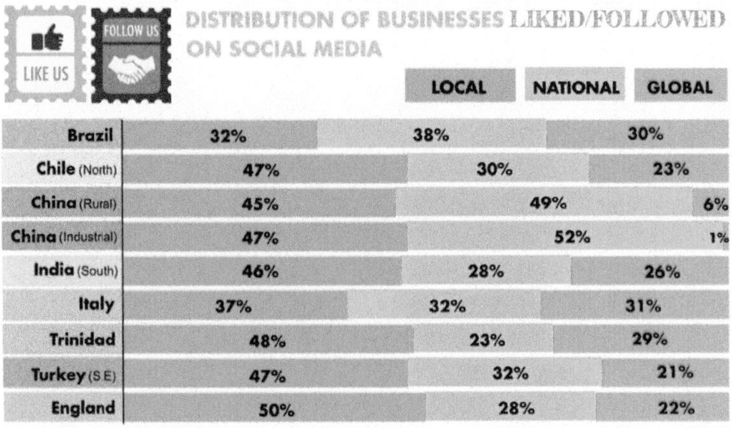
LIKE US
FOLLOW US
DISTRIBUTION OF BUSINESSES LIKED/FOLLOWED ON SOCIAL MEDIA
LOCAL
NATIONAL
GLOBAL
Brazil 32% 38% 30%
Chile (North) 47% 30% 23%
China (Rural) 45% 49% 6%
China (Industrial) 47% 52% 1%
India (South) 46% 28% 26%
Italy 37% 32% 31%
Trinidad 48% 23% 29%
Turkey (S.E) 47% 32% 21%
England 50% 28% 22%

Fig. 4.19 Distribution of businesses 'liked'/'followed' on social media

As social media has become a channel of marketing for local, national and global businesses, we enquired as to whether people 'liked' or 'followed' businesses on social media.

There are several factors behind these responses, the first being that this represents the distribution rather the extent of such influences. Prior to this study Miller had already noted the degree to which Facebook had become integral to local businesses in Trinidad.[10] Sinanan observed promotional activity on social media by local businesses such as bars, where image and reputation were particularly important. Furthermore, with regard to the relatively high usage of global commerce in Trinidad, respondents who purchased items from global businesses usually arranged for relatives in the US to courier their items to Trinidad.

We would not have expected the Chinese sites to have global links since the Chinese internet is essentially internally directed. In China Taobao is the biggest online shopping site, along with WeChat; both of them are largely focused on domestic markets. In other areas people interpreted the question in various ways. Brazilians may consider Coca Cola as local because it is present locally, though a global brand, and Nike may be seen as national, through its association with well-known Brazilian footballers. As noted above people in south India regard any money they spend in response to advertisements within social media as money spent on the social media companies themselves. A better understanding will come from our qualitative work as described in Chapter 6. Analysis of this suggested that in most sites social media marketing was limited in its impact other than for businesses where personal relationship are involved – in which case it does seem to be important.

Theme 5: attitudes towards social media

Other than knowing how people use social media, we wanted to explore people's attitude towards social media and its impact on various aspects of their lives. Our first question on this theme, presented in Fig. 4.20, concerned people's views on the appropriate age for a child to start using social media. The responses range from 13 in the rural Chinese site to 17 in south India, but compared to many of our questions the range is relatively small.

We then enquired as to whether people have access to social media at their workplace and/or at their site of education.

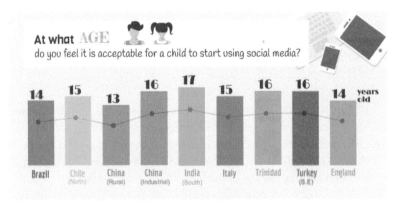

Fig. 4.20 Distribution of responses to question on what age is appropriate for a child to start using social media

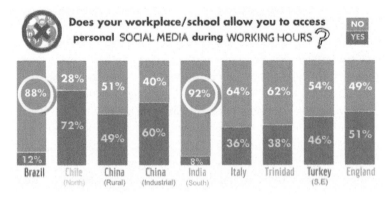

Fig. 4.21 Distribution of access to social media in workplace/ educational institutions during working hours

Fig. 4.21 illustrates that in south India and Brazil access to social media was restricted/not permitted during working hours at workplaces/educational institutions. This was not surprising as in our Brazilian site people mostly worked in hotels, often as cleaners and waiters, with strict supervision of their work. However, our qualitative work on whether people would actually find ways around these restrictions and use social media would reveal quite different patterns. This was particularly true of south India, where often the modern workplaces and educational institutions were most restrictive. Yet equally in both these settings smartphones make it extremely difficult to regulate and enforce such restrictions.

We then asked if people felt social media was good for education. This question receives considerable attention in the next chapter, because it was a contentious issue in several of our field sites. Here we will see how in south India schools with lower-income intakes were very encouraging of social media usage as an educational tool, while upper-class schools were the most concerned about banning it as a distraction.

A similar question was asked about the impact of social media on work as well. As illustrated in Fig. 4.23, the responses of Brazilians echoed the perception held by managers that social media was a distraction in the workplace. However, even here managers also recognised that it could have positive uses as well. For example, when a domestic worker

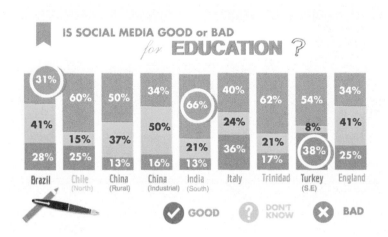

Fig. 4.22 Distribution of responses to question on whether social media has a good or bad effect on education

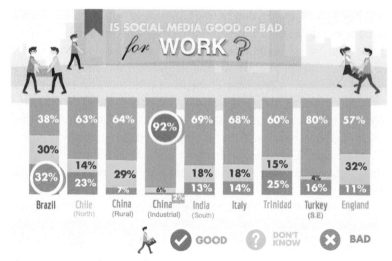

Fig. 4.23 Distribution of responses to question on whether social media has a good or bad effect on work

sees that her employer needs a professional to fix an electrical problem, she uses WhatsApp to contact a friend or relative to do the job. Most seem to see the positive impact of social media as outweighing its distracting nature.

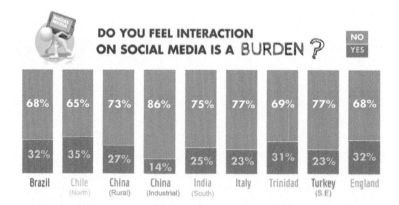

Fig. 4.24 Distribution of responses to question on whether users felt interaction on social media was a burden

The next perspective was a more general enquiry as to whether people felt social media had become a burden. Several of these questions, as with the titles of several chapters in this book, reflect our desire to respond to popular questions posed to us, rather than expressing only academic interests and concerns. In this case the answer is mainly interesting as a contrast to the dominant representation of social media in popular writing.

The next question also follows from such popular discussion in journalism and elsewhere.

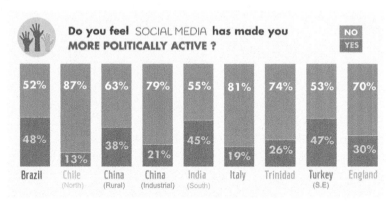

Fig. 4.25 Distribution of responses to question on whether social media had made users more politically active

There may be a time-specific component to these results. The two highest positive responses came from our Brazilian and Turkish field sites. These were also the two countries that saw high-profile popular demonstrations during the time of our field work: against the President Dilma Rousseff in Brazil and around Gezi Park in Turkey. In both cases the use of social media was closely associated with these events. It is worth noting that, in practice, Spyer felt that there had been almost no direct comment at the time on local social media, so this survey result seems to be more an association that had left its impression rather than a reflection on what people actually do. In south India this was a period where people were coming to realise that some issues (such as abuse of women) had become more prominent through social media in particular, emerging from that base into greater visibility on traditional mass media such as newspapers and television.

Finally the survey echoed another very general question that we tend to be asked outside of academia, and that is reflected again in Chapter 13. It is whether social media had left the respondents feeling happier, had made no difference at all or had left them feeling less happy.

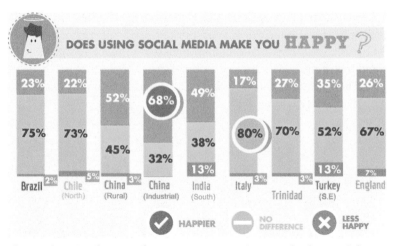

Fig. 4.26 Distribution of responses to question on whether social media made users happier

This last question, rather like the first, was one that actually did make some sense in relation to the general qualitative research. It is in the more conservative sites of south India and southeast Turkey that we feel social media has made the most difference to people's lives by opening up new possibilities. Factory workers in China, on the other hand, became most dependent upon social media for realising their aspirations and for compensating for the sheer degree of their unhappiness with their offline conditions. However, the clearest finding is the relative paucity of negative feeling throughout as compared to journalistic reports (see Chapter 13).

Conclusion

It may be rare that a set of figures has been published with this number of caveats and self-criticisms. In the case of almost every question in this survey at least one of the researchers has suggested that the results have to be understood in the light of the context of that field site; the responses may have more to do with the way people interpreted the question, rather than anything that reflects on their actual behaviour. As noted at the start of this chapter, we do not regret the exercise of conducting these questionnaires and attempting to make sense of the results. The sheer range of answers to most questions also supports one of the central points of our entire project, which is that an assumed extrapolation of quantitative results from one place to another is problematic. At least these results provide a visual impression of the extent of regional difference in social media usage.

The other reward of this exercise is that it raised many questions that were productive. Researchers had to ask themselves *why* people answered in the way they did, which is especially helpful when the results did not accord with what we knew from our 15 months of field work. The results of the quantitative exercise directed us to look deeper into our qualitative insights. One example was Spyer's discovery that respondents in Brazil actually meant that they had just consulted with others before adding friends, not that they had asked for their permission to do so.

The material from this chapter is taken from a single questionnaire with 1199 respondents across all of our nine field sites. We have resisted any temptation to look for correlations. These are in any case problematic with such material, but would have been particularly so when our respondents spanned a range of age, gender and income differences. We hope it is clear from our discussions why we remain cautious in using quantitative findings. None of the issues and problems we have pointed out with respect to interpreting these figures relate to the small size of the questionnaire. They would have remained exactly the same if we had asked ten times this number of people. Our overall emphasis on the greater authority and reliability of qualitative findings, therefore, is not because we never carry out quantitative surveys: it is because sometimes we do.

Background to the study

Questionnaires are commonly employed within an ethnography.[11] As is typical in the service of anthropology, those who use them hope to accomplish other tasks in addition to generating statistical data. During the course of our 15 months' field work we conducted two separate questionnaire-based surveys[12] (we will call them Questionnaire A and Questionnaire B) common to all of our nine field sites. In addition to these common surveys, each of us also carried out our own independent questionnaire-based surveys. These were specifically designed to cater to our individual field sites. For example, in England we undertook a survey of 2496 schoolchildren; in Italy we conducted a survey with 750 schoolchildren aged 16–18 years old; and in industrial China we conducted a survey of 238 rural migrants. The results from several of these surveys are included in this chapter.

For many of us these questionnaires acted as tools in building rapport with a potential informant. Often starting with a questionnaire put our informants at ease and provided a means of getting to know them more informally later on. In a few sites people expected the researcher to pose direct questions, and this helped to assure them that we were genuine researchers.

Other than collecting response figures, a primary purpose of Questionnaire A was to include representative sample proportions of people across approximate income categories in each of our field sites. The survey thus helped to ensure that from early on we actively engaged with people across the entire spectrum of income groups within each site; it was helpful for pushing us into a more representative engagement with our populations. Questionnaire A was administered to at least 100 respondents from each field site, including people who did not use social media. As it was administered at the start of our field work we had not yet worked out how to ask each question in culturally appropriate wording across all nine sites. A direct comparison of these results would therefore be misleading. Instead each researcher has used these results within their own individual ethnographic studies.[13]

By contrast this chapter is based on Questionnaire B, our second survey, directed entirely to users of social media. This exercise was undertaken during the last three months of our field work. After a year in the field we hoped to create a more directly comparable set of common questions.[14] A particular challenge we faced was that the rural and industrial Chinese sites use entirely different social media platforms compared to the other sites, and these have different functionalities. This chapter thus only includes those questions that we felt could be reasonably compared across all nine field sites. We also wanted approximate parity in gender, though in practice this varied from 67 per cent female respondents in England to 61 per cent male respondents in industrial China. Overall 55 per cent were women and 45 per cent were men (see Fig. 4.27).

There was more variability by age, since usage of social media was more established with the older generation in our European sites (as shown in Table 4.5). Overall approximately 73 per cent of our respondents were aged under 29 years.

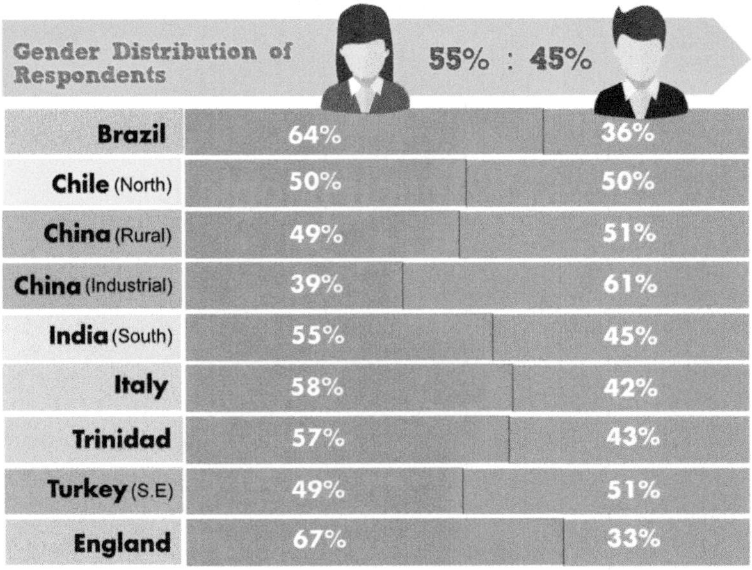

Gender Distribution of Respondents	55% : 45%	
Brazil	64%	36%
Chile (North)	50%	50%
China (Rural)	49%	51%
China (Industrial)	39%	61%
India (South)	55%	45%
Italy	58%	42%
Trinidad	57%	43%
Turkey (S.E)	49%	51%
England	67%	33%

Fig. 4.27   Gender distribution of survey respondents across field sites

AGE DISTRIBUTION OF RESPONDENTS

years old	13-19	20-29	30-39	40-49	50-59	60-69	70-79	80-89
Brazil	49%	35%	12%	2%	3%	0%	0%	0%
Chile (North)	24%	51%	14%	9%	2%	0%	0%	0%
China (Rural)	57%	21%	15%	6%	1%	0%	0%	0%
China (Industrial)	9%	57%	22%	6%	6%	0%	0%	0%
India (South)	18%	64%	7%	7%	3%	1%	0%	0%
Italy	24%	29%	18%	20%	6%	2%	1%	0%
Trinidad	39%	47%	10%	2%	2%	0%	0%	1%
Turkey (S.E)	30%	42%	20%	8%	1%	0%	0%	0%
England	19%	32%	24%	8%	10%	6%	1%	0%

Table 4.5 Age distribution of survey respondents across field sites

5
Education and young people

If there are two topics in the general study of social media that stand out as having already received considerable attention, they are politics (see Chapter 10) and education. The latter tends to pique interest because social media itself is so closely associated with young people, and is seen by many as being where youth now spend much of their time. There is also considerable uncertainty and anxiety over the broader impact of social media on young people's education and welfare. There are those who believe that social media is destroying the educational system and will lead to a dramatic fall in grades, which can only be solved by banning access to phones and other Information and Communication Technologies (ICTs). Others see social media as potentially re-energising the experience of education and believe that, by forcing formal education to embrace new forms of informal and interactive learning, the use of such technologies will inevitably benefit all concerned.

This chapter steers clear of such polarised positions, instead focusing on the actual practices of social media use as they occur in our field sites. It will first examine the distinction that often persists between formal and informal learning, showing how social media is challenging these boundaries in several of our field sites. In some places it is even facilitating a retreat from formal learning.

This chapter also pays more attention to how social media is reshaping the key relationships that education encompasses: those of student–student, teacher–student and teacher–parent. Examining each of these relationships reveals key themes shaped by social media – specifically intimacy and conflict; surveillance and engagement; and mediating understandings of duty respectively. All of these highlight the important social dimensions of learning, which are increasingly being conducted through online spaces.

Prior literature and research

As noted in our review of academic studies of social media, the research on education is often exemplary. This is a field in which social scientists have managed to produce balanced and systematic research to inform public debate. Much of this research is influenced by the concept of 'media literacy'. This child-centred policy project emphasises equipping people with skills enabling them critically to analyse and skilfully to produce media messages. In so doing the project stresses an awareness of production, language, representation and audience.[1]

One example of this was the project on American teens' new media use by Ito and her colleagues.[2] The authors showed how teenagers use new media to create opportunities for friendship driven by peer-to-peer learning, and fostering media literacy. The authors argue this works best within a general environment of 'hanging out' and 'messing around', as well as giving young people partial access to wider public spheres. This theme is taken up here, where social media is found to make a more positive contribution if we consider learning more generally, rather than a narrow sense of formal education.[3]

In these studies social media is considered within a wider context of new media. The anthropologist Lange,[4] for example, has examined the creative ways in which young people use YouTube through the production of 'personally expressive' spontaneous, ephemeral videos made collaboratively with peers. Michael Wesch[5] leads a long-term ethnographic study on video blogging; his emphasis is upon learning, the wider interactivity, new forms of community[6] and the skills and knowledge acquired through this process. The concept of 'connected learning', which stresses continued interactivity and 'active' learning, represents the vanguard of educational theory more generally[7]. These studies also show how often denigrated 'geek identities' are increasingly central to young people we would otherwise regard as being within the mainstream.[8]

Both boyd[9] and Clark[10] demonstrate how problems relating to social media use are often unfairly attributed to young people's behaviour, while highlighting how the behaviour of the parents in managing and using social media is a factor of equal – if not greater – influence. Understanding that parental pressures on young people are often contradictory, inconsistent and unhelpful is an important complement to the narrow focus on young people themselves. In our English field site it is surveillance by their parents, rather than by social media companies, that children worry about. The importance of paying attention to this wider context also emerges in a forthcoming ethnographic book by Livingstone and colleagues.[11] Based on an ethnography of one school class in England, it also included time spent with these children in their homes.

For boyd and for Clark this is especially important since teenagers want (and also need) a degree of autonomy from parents and other senior figures in order to develop their own experience of managing social interactions, especially among their peers. So 'media literacy' is also a form of social literacy that potentially could be facilitated by social media, providing parents gave them the space to develop this.

Clark highlights the underlying class dimensions to this proviso. In the main it is better educated and wealthier parents who appreciate how possession of such digital communication skills will enhance their offspring's life chances, thereby exacerbating prior class differences. Others note how social and new media have become symbolic of cosmopolitanism, or even a force for increasing cosmopolitanism.[12] This is especially relevant in many of the small places that constituted our field sites. Here new ICTs may widen the gulf between these new cosmopolitans and poorer, less well educated families, who end up facing yet another barrier to social inclusion.

Others have conducted research beyond the parent–child relationship to investigate the impact of groups such as governments and education systems that have authority and represent infrastructures, including the law and the school system itself. This is what makes the work of Livingstone and her colleagues so important. They have undertaken extensive surveys on the state of new media use in schools and by children, presenting their findings as balanced, sensible and easily understood advice that can feed directly into policy areas such as education, law and child protection; this in turn allows for better informed and more sensitive interventions. Livingstone and her colleagues also respond both to the anxieties of parents about their children and the anxiety of boyd and Clark about parents' behaviour. They advocate a delicate negotiation between respecting young people's autonomy and remaining aware of the dangers posed to young people by the exposure that new social media platforms create.

We have no desire for our project to detract from these contributions by new academic research, which unusually is based on extensive qualitative ethnographic studies of the same form that we advocate (in the case of Livingstone in particular this is supplemented by extensive, cross-country comparisons).[13] This chapter's contribution is really a lateral one, recognising that for most children in the world the experience of both school and parenting is very different from the North American and European setting that informs these studies. The emphasis on context that they promote will become even more evident as we now turn to very different situations in places such as Brazil, China, India and Turkey – though we shall also find marked differences between ostensibly similar sites such as an English village and a southern Italian town.

From 'formal' to 'informal' learning: mitigating for perceived failings in education

Parents from the least economically developed field sites (Brazil, China and the rural component of our south India field site)[14] are beset by marked financial inequalities. They often expressed a general frustration at the failings of local schools to equip students properly with the skills and knowledge required for success in formal education, work and life more generally. In response many young people were inventively appropriating social media to provide supplementary means of learning and networking that they believed would contribute to their education. On occasion they saw these as more useful and relevant to their lives.

In the Brazilian field site Spyer noted that parents viewed their children's interest in computers as positive for their future, believing it would help them to become better informed and more connected with the world. By contrast teachers saw social media as the 'bad internet', distracting children, having a detrimental impact upon their studies, undermining professional authority and causing disruption in class; Google on the other hand was regarded as the 'good internet', a reliable source of knowledge. Students felt that social media helped them to improve their reading and writing skills, partly to avoid criticism of their misspellings from peers, something which was acknowledged neither by parents nor teachers. Social media also provided some autonomy from parents, who often had significantly poorer reading ability.

The south Indian field site mapped this variety in attitudes onto social class and the type of schooling received. Venkatraman noted massive variation among middle schools (students aged 11 to 15) in both environment and teaching quality. Children from wealthy and middle-class families attending private and international schools tended to use social media with comparatively high levels of monitoring by their parents – the result of parental concerns regarding the effect of such use on educational achievement. In contrast children from poorer families who attended state schools generally held far more positive attitudes; their parents perceived social media sites as educative in and of themselves, regardless of how they were used.

Similarly lower class parents – whose children attended schools that lacked comprehensive ICT facilities and teaching – tended to encourage their sons in particular to use social media, hoping that this would give them ICT skills and thereby employment in the enormous IT park being developed in the area. Unmarried women from lower income families were prohibited from owning mobiles, mostly because of fear that its use might lead to marriage outside of caste prescriptions. However, many young women circumvented these restrictions, accessing social media through the phones of school colleagues or by taking an office job that required having a mobile phone with internet access.

In industrial China Wang found that migrant factory workers showed little interest in their children doing well in formal education or continuing into higher education – a marked contrast to standard generalisations about education in China,[15] this highlights the radically different value systems held by these groups. The factory workers saw their children's withdrawal from school in favour of manual labour as inevitable. This was compounded by segregation of these children from local residents in separate schools. Wang noted that, given this disengagement from formal education, factory workers and their children often used social media for reading extensive articles on topics they regarded as useful, for instance self-help, nutrition, health and financial advice. They seemed less concerned with sharing or communicating these with friends. Instead they archive such postings on their own profile page so that *they themselves* could return to view them later. This appropriation of social media for storing and reviewing knowledge exemplifies the way populations convert particular platforms into tools for learning.

The situation was quite the opposite in the rural China field site. Here parents placed great importance on their children's education, believing that academic achievement would help their children obtain a secure and comfortable life. In this context social media was largely understood (not only by parents, but also by students themselves) as having a negative impact on educational progression and learning. Students spent long hours in school each day. During the summer holidays they often attended expensive private tuition classes in the town. Parents wanted their children to reach university, but had little understanding of what skills students needed to do well in exams or what life inside university was actually like.

All of these constituted considerable restrictions, despite which students found ways to access social media. They made extensive use of 'QQ Groups', instant messaging groups whose membership often corresponded to their physical class groups. Apart from allowing for continued socialising with classmates outside of school time, students used these to share homework answers and get help from other classmates. Asking for help from peers was especially important given that parents often lacked knowledge relevant to their homework and physically meeting with classmates outside school time was often difficult in this rural area.

If the Brazilian, Chinese and south Indian field sites feature considerable disparities in wealth, some families in the comparatively more equal south Italian field site had similar reservations regarding the ability of schools and colleges to equip their offspring comprehensively for the job market. Nicolescu notes that while teachers typically prohibit the use of mobile phones in classes, many students, especially those from vocational schools, felt entitled to use these devices in the classroom. They felt it was the traditional forms of kinship and solidarity, fostered by social media, which would prove more useful than formal education in helping them to find work. As a result the teachers stood out as the only group not advocating social media use by students.

Economic status was also a factor in differentiating attitudes to social media in Trinidad. Prosperous families prefer to enrol their children at prestigious private schools and pay for after-school lessons. Such students typically use the internet and social media to undertake research and complete school assignments. By contrast lower income families, often headed by adults with very little exposure to formal education, place less emphasis on social media use for children. Similarly in the field site in southeast Turkey affluent and elite families favour social media as beneficial to education.

To summarise, this study found that in some of our sites it is wealthy families who have positive views on the use of social media for education. More commonly people who value and trust formal education are worried that social media might detract from this, while those who feel let down by formal education hope that social media will provide an effective entrée into informal education – and these are generally low income families. Factors include whether social media is seen as an instrument of social mobility or not, and also whether usage is seen as an accessory or alternative to formal education. Some of the more affluent populations also possessed more confidence that children would make positive use of social media. For example, in the English field site most secondary schools (for students aged 11 to 18) set up Twitter accounts aimed at specific year-groups to keep those students informed about school-related activities.

In all these cases, however, widespread use of ICTs has transformed the relationship between formal and informal education. The most significant consequence was for our field sites in rapidly developing economies such as Brazil, China and India, where people often hoped that social media and other ICTs might mitigate for what was perceived to be inadequate provision of formal education in certain areas. However, the perception of the educational value of these services related to a broader desire for achieving prosperity. This broader perspective on the impact of social media on education also emerges from our ethnographic context, which in turn reinforces one of the main lessons from our initial review of the literature: that understanding the relationship between formal and informal learning depends on acknowledging the social context of both. While prior digital technologies, such as search engines, may have impacted more directly on autonomous learning, with social media the key factor is likely the way the new communications facilitate more subtle shifts in the relationships between students, teachers and parents, thereby highlighting the critical social dimensions inherent to all kinds of learning.

Relationships between students: intimacy, drama and bullying

In all of our field sites we observed a common trend with regard to how students used social media to manage their relationships with each other: social media allowed these relationships to become increasingly persistent, on-going and personal in nature. In many cases students appreciated the greater intimacy fostered by these platforms; however, this close and persistent contact between students also formed the basis for cases of taunting and bullying. Often intimacy and intimidation are seen to be opposed to each other, though the evidence from the various field sites emphasises the way they both reflect particularly strong relationships which are fostered by social media.

There were many examples of closer friendships being forged by social media use among students. In our rural China field site social media was seen to be extending the sociality of the classmate group beyond the physical confines of the school. Despite the fact that students already met in school for long periods of the day, class groups were spending increasing periods of time together online, away from the school grounds and outside of normal school hours. The use of QQ Groups to organise regular reunions amongst former classmates further facilitated the Chinese tradition of retaining the class group as a social unit into later life.

In both the rural and industrial Chinese field sites social media was a space that was typically free from parental surveillance (in contrast to other field sites, to be discussed later); it was seen as an easier place for conversing with peers, especially with regard to intimate or embarrassing topics. In the rural China site, around half of the middle school students surveyed responded that instant messaging would be the most appropriate means of declaring one's affections for someone. University students were increasingly using social media networks for the purposes of finding partners on campus.

The intimacy of social media communications was not a pre-given – rather it was selectively and intentionally applied. For example, in the English field site the range of social media platforms corresponded to different grades and levels of intimacy within friendships between high school students. As noted in Chapter 1, Snapchat was considered to be the most intimate social media platform, with most pupils maintaining around 10 to 20 contacts with whom they regularly shared images. Sending ugly self-portraits relies on but also creates trust that these will not be forwarded outside of the group.[16] By contrast Twitter was predominantly used for whole-class communication.

This intensity of social media communications could also be employed for negative purposes. Although taunting and banter occurred prior to social media and are in themselves well-researched phenomena,[17] social media allowed these kinds of behaviour to assume new forms and also, increasingly, to occur beyond the school gates. In Brazil, for instance, participants explained that young teens challenged each other to be daring – for example by submitting indecent images of themselves to WhatsApp groups. This content might eventually be circulated by one of the members of the group as a form of 'revenge porn'. Although this usage is particularly vindictive, it implies an initial sharing as a token of trust more in common with the English example of Snapchat.

Other changes directly attributable to social media in the study of English school pupils included the extension of taunting from school time to 24/7, the way pupils felt more inclined to indulge in such taunting when 'hiding behind a screen' rather than face to face and an increasing use of 'indirects' as status updates which leave their intended subject or recipient uncertain as to whom these are directed. Such indirect postings often sparked conflicts and arguments resulting in considerable distress, especially for teenage girls.

Sinanan shows how in her Trinidadian field site the increased visibility provided by social media directly impacts upon such school conflicts. Sharing self-made videos of fights between students within school grounds has created a new form of 'evidence' that was understood to be especially truthful, despite being particularly open to misinterpretation or fabrication. Some people posted these fights in the hope that their video would 'go viral'.

All of these examples show how social media facilitates both greater intimacy and greater friction between the school pupils themselves, but these relationships are never entirely independent of the associated connections with parents and teachers to which we now turn. Indeed some school teachers in England feel that the larger problems from social media come not as a result of students' inappropriate behaviour online, but rather from the behaviours of parents. Because social media allows parents directly to see quarrels occurring between children online, they naturally desire to support their children, often resulting in situations where the parents (rather than the children) become the ones found quarrelling at the school gates.

Yet it is the same parents who insist that these are problems for which the school is responsible, and which it should be solving. In general much of this usage of social media, and the tendency of young people to conduct their social relationships online, appears alien to many teachers and parents alike, often fuelling significant concerns over social media's ability to arouse such passion among young people. In response we also see a reconfiguration of important teacher–student and parent–child relationships as both these groups try to appropriate social media, in turn redefining and re-shaping their relationships with young people.

Teacher–student relationships: between surveillance and engagement

In many of the field sites a persistent belief that young people's social media use hinders their educational achievement creates particular ambivalence among teachers. The growing field of 'New Literacy Studies' (NLS) is useful in highlighting the tendency of political and theoretical approaches to construct a great divide between school and out of school, often relegating all pleasurable activities to non-school contexts, but also assuming they are frivolous and not conducive to learning.[18] Teachers are often tasked with policing these boundaries by enacting bans on social media and ICT use within schools. However, they are frequently acutely aware of the importance of social media for communication between young people, and therefore perceive its potential role in young people's education and development. Nonetheless our Italian site was entirely and our Brazilian site partially contrary to this generalisation.

Several studies informed by NLS[19] have advocated the necessity of teaching approaches that incorporate the skills of technology use developed at home by students into school curricula.[20] In so doing they challenge assumptions not only that the schools are best qualified to judge what technology should be taught, but also that the knowledge taught in schools is useful for life while knowledge attained at home is incidental. This chapter does not attempt to recreate these important debates regarding pedagogy. Rather, in line with our study's focus on sociality, it concentrates instead on the shifting relationships between students and their teachers that social media is helping to facilitate.

Many teachers are also conscious of the possible role social media may play in redefining the relationship between student and teacher. A key issue for many teachers seems to revolve around deciding whether being friends with their students on social media is appropriate; and if so setting and maintaining the appropriate boundaries and distance between themselves and their students through social media profiles.

The clearest example comes from the south Indian field site. Here there exists a particularly high degree of ambivalence and uncertainty regarding the best way of aligning the fairly egalitarian friending that social media facilitates with the strongly hierarchical system felt to typify student–teacher relationships. Venkatraman notes how in this context teachers often end up caught between their roles as protectors of the students in their care (which necessitate engagement with and monitoring of students) and the official ban on social media use (by both students and teachers) within many of the schools.

One of the key repercussions of this apparent contradiction is how the appropriateness of online teacher–student relationships becomes influenced by factors such as the age and gender of students. It is middle school students (aged 11 to 15) who are generally the keenest to friend their teachers on social media. Venkatraman describes how these students typically feel immense pride upon successfully 'friending' their teachers on Facebook, and are particularly keen to make their friends aware of this new online relationship. Venkatraman attributes this to the fact that middle school students see their teachers as commanding a great degree of authority, with which they are eager to associate themselves. Equally many teachers were willing to friend their own students because they felt that it allowed them to monitor their students' activities online, and thus fulfil a duty of care towards pupils.

By contrast Venkatraman notes that precisely because of such monitoring, older high school students (aged 16 to 18) were often less enthusiastic with regards to friending their own teachers on social media. Many (particularly male) pupils expressed concern that friending their teachers in this way would infringe upon their privacy. This caution was also felt by teachers, who themselves were reluctant to 'friend' their older students through social media, citing concerns that these students would be able to observe elements of the teacher's own personal life through social media. Venkatraman argues that in these cases it was the degree of closeness and trust that *already* existed in their offline relationship with such students that dictated whether teachers would become friends on social media.

The south Italian field site arguably had even greater barriers between students and teachers friending each other on social media. In this case it was largely informed by teachers' own reluctance to use social media, describing themselves as outmoded and reticent to engage in these platforms. They also feared that social media would potentially undermine what they perceived to be the 'classical model' of education, in which knowledge is transmitted from learned teacher onto unknowledgeable student.

The most notable exception to this trend of teachers being reluctant to friend pupils came from China. This is likely to be due both to the specificity of domestic platforms and to local norms regarding what kinds of postings ought to be shared online through them. First, the most popular platforms such as QQ and WeChat do not allow posting on each other's walls, and have limited or no photo-tagging features respectively. This strengthens the user's own controls over what appears on their profiles and limits the opportunities for others to make potentially embarrassing postings on people's social media profiles. Hence the most outward-facing aspect of social media, which concentrates on sharing posts among small groups of friends, is generally less contentious in nature here than in comparison to many other non-Chinese field sites. It consequently poses far fewer problems in terms of students and teachers seeing each other's posts. Although in China teachers appeared to be less anxious about friending students than in our other sites, a significant barrier still existed in that some teachers saw little reason to go online. Students appreciated those teachers who did use social media, and sometimes found it easier to approach teachers for help with home-work this way.

The use of social media to overcome anxiety in student–teacher interactions was also seen in Trinidad. Sinanan noted that within school people tend to use more formal English, but when communicating on social media pupils are more comfortable using local dialect. As a result some of the less confident students, who are reluctant to speak formal English in class, prefer to ask teachers questions on social media outside of school and in dialect. In this way they are able to engage more fully both with the teachers and with their school work.

The examples in this section have shown that social media has redefined student–teacher relationships in all of our field sites. By pro-viding stronger on-going links outside of the school space, new modes of visibility and monitoring have become possible, creating concerns for both students and teachers alike. Conversely these new social media have created new avenues of communication, modes of engagement and, in some cases, more egalitarian student–teacher relations than existed previously.

Parent–school relationships: mediating study

The third side of this triangle – and the one that has become increasingly central to the core studies of social media in the US and Europe through the work of Livingstone, boyd and Clark, among others – is the relation-ship of parents to the schools as well as to their own children. Here the defining theme is the moral obligation that parents feel to raise their offspring in a particular way, how this envisioned education may differ from that imagined by the school and its teachers and the role of social media in mediating such discrepancies.

The most notable (and arguably most successful) case of teacher–school interaction via social media in this study came from the English field site. Here one primary school (with pupils aged from 5 to 11 years old) had started a school blog and Twitter account, posting images of the work that their students had produced each day. The blog was an immediate success among parents. It provided a solution to the age-old problem that many parents find it difficult to get detailed accounts from their children about what they have done while at school, often causing parents to worry that schools might not be structuring students' time properly. In this case posting students' efforts (for example, pictures painted or poems written) online allayed parents' fears, allowing them to reconceive the act of sending their children to school as a fulfilment – rather than a dereliction – of parental duty and improving teacher–parent relations immeasurably. [21]

In the north Chilean field site local schools similarly post photos of events within the school, such as workshops and special activities. Haynes notes a perception among parents that, as children in the town grow older, education – apart from learning practical skills – matters less and less; most women are expected to become pre-school teachers or work at the local supermarket and men to take up manual labour in the mines or the port. Facebook engagement by local schools is an effort to re-involve them in a way that rekindles interest in their children's education.

A final example of schools actively appropriating social media to manage their relationship with parents came from the south Indian field site. In this instance a higher status school was reacting to the damage that social media use was perceived to be doing to its reputation. In this case the problem was caused by parents, who believed their duty towards their children extended to affecting change within the school. They set up their own Facebook groups together for discussing potential changes in education delivery and their children's homework, as well as to provide more general support. However, before long the tone of conversation on the pages became more inflammatory, shifting to gossip and pointed criticism of several individual teachers from the school.

These Facebook groups soon came to the attention of the school head teacher, who sought to exert control over them in response. The head teacher encouraged certain parents to form a single Facebook group managed by a number of parents who were on the school's Parent-Teacher Association[22] (PTA), with representatives from the school lending an extra level of oversight to the group. Venkatraman mentions how one parent felt that this new, more tightly regulated group with active participation from the school brought a greater sense of community to their online activities. For the school, opening up one channel of communication on a social media platform was beneficial; however, they also remained keen to discourage teacher–parent communications through platforms such as WhatsApp because of fears that sharing a teacher's personal phone numbers with parents would result in teachers becoming subject to incessant parental queries. The south Indian example gives a sense of the efforts schools go to in using social media to channel parents' sense of duty towards their offspring and investment in their children's education in ways that these organisations feel to be conducive.

Conversely in the south Italian field site there appears to be quite limited school–parent communication via social media, such that parents are often left to discuss issues of education among themselves. This was tied into the heightened role parents have in arranging their child's education: helping their children with homework and engaging in extracurricular activities for children are very common here; Nicolescu notes that they are seen as part of a mother's moral duty in providing for her child. Given this, Facebook became a particularly important venue in which the different achievements of children were shared by mothers, and subsequently commented on by their female friends.

Nicolescu notes that these practices also lead to parents actively desiring their offspring to use mobile phones from around ten years of age and social media from the age of 13. This runs counter to school bans on ICT and social media. Parents nonetheless felt that their offspring's social media use would be helpful because it fulfilled desires that their children should be afforded a similar life to their peers – not only in terms of access to specific ICTs, but also in having access to the kinds of opportunities that these technologies were seen as providing.

The downside to this, as noted in some field sites, is that social media is increasingly being used by parents to assess their own proficiency in child raising, leading to parents feeling competitive about how their children compare to their peers. In England parents traditionally compared children within family groups that contained children of different ages. The growth of ante-natal classes and baby and toddler groups has created a situation where comparisons between children of the exact same age start from birth (or even pre-birth) and continue into the education system. In turn this relates to a highly entrenched class system in England, increasingly expressed through which particular school a child manages to gain entrance to (or for wealthier families which private school they can afford). Variants of such systems of differentiation also exist in China and Trinidad, though these depend more upon competitive examination to get into the best schools. However, all of these tend to exacerbate the tendency towards competition between parents, now fostered by proclaiming their children's achievements on Facebook and constantly monitoring the progress of others.

In this section we have seen how social media can mediate discrepancies between different understandings of what a child's education is supposed to be. In some cases, schools in our English, north Chilean and south Indian field sites have attempted to engage with parents through social media. In Italy, and in a separate case from our English field site, these visions of parental duty may create standoffs with representatives of formal education or increase competition between parents respectively.

Conclusion

With respect to the impact upon education and young people, our project was able to make use of an exemplary literature that developed very quickly in relation to government and general concerns about whether social media was destroying or facilitating education in countries such as the US and in Europe. Livingstone's work has often been government-funded, while Ito's research was funded by the MacArthur foundation with a strong commitment to educational research. As a result this is one domain where research was already well established. As was seen in their work and also in that of boyd and Clark, it was becoming very clear that social media by its very nature drew attention to the wider social context of learning – including especially the role of parents, but also factors such as social class.

This provides an ideal doorway onto our own ethnographic research results. In every case we have found that it is these wider social relations between students themselves, teachers and students, and teachers and parents that have proved central to understanding why social media in some cases is felt to mitigate certain inadequacies in formal education provision, by offering an alternative informal route to knowledge, while in others it is seen as a distraction from learning, or even a direct cause of negative interaction amongst school pupils.

6
Work and Commerce

Since so many individuals and companies have a vested interest in speculating on the future share values of social media companies, it is no surprise that journalism focusing on the use and potential of social media within commerce is often enthusiastically read, shared and commented upon. However, there is also a clear popular interest in questions such as whether social media is helping communication at work or just distracting workers, and whether it is worthwhile for companies to invest much time and money in social media marketing – as well as how far social media extends the ability of commerce to manipulate and entice customers.

Venkatraman's research in the south Indian field site specifically focused upon how social media impacts on the relationship between work and non-work. We follow this with four other topics. Our second section examines how individuals use social media for obtaining work. Our third section considers the social media companies themselves and the impact of social media advertising, an increasingly common strategy by which they seek to fund themselves. The fourth section concerns the potential of social media for the development of e-commerce, trade and small entrepreneurial activities. The final section contributes an anthropological analysis of the very categories of work and commerce, and explores the varied ideas people have about money and its relationship to the family and other values.

The relation between work and non-work

One of the most dramatic and significant consequences of the internet has been a radical transformation in the relationship between workplace and home. Ever since the beginning of the industrial revolution in

England those in control of work have sought to impose a strict dichotomy, trying to isolate the workplace entirely from social and personal considerations and contacts.[1] An important breach in this wall was made by email and then mobile phones;[2] more recently social media and smartphones have in many cases left this separation in ruins, though the degree of destruction varies by region and according to the type of industry. We tend to see commercial innovations as naturally aligned with the business interests that produced them, so it is important to acknowledge instances such as this where technology has dramatically undermined a previously hallowed principle of capitalism – the separation of work from non-work.

This is particularly important for an anthropological perspective, since the discipline has always been committed to understanding work within the wider context of people's lives, and is thereby also opposed to such a strict dichotomy of work and non-work.[3] Furthermore many anthropologists study parts of the world where such regimes of work are not as fully established. In India, for example, work such as weaving was traditionally delegated to families working from their own homes, while the factory system has a much shallower presence than in Europe. Even within factories, workers in India continued to try to exploit kinship links in recruitment and retain traditional associations with caste.[4] However, in some sectors Western practices of separation between family and workplace were eventually established.[5]

As in most other regions social media has broken through these barriers and facilitated non-work communication at the workplace relating to romance, hobbies and socialising. Office chat systems or WhatsApp were used between workers, their friends and partners to give reassurances of love, to chat about cycling, cricket and new films, and to organise essential family responsibilities. A husband might plan with his wife in another company who would pick up their daughter from school. A young working mother sent a WhatsApp voice message to her mother's phone for playing to her infant at home.

In several of our field sites there were debates as to whether social media represents a distraction from work or something useful. In the Italian field site there was a pragmatic acceptance that certain jobs are just plain boring. For a shop assistant with no customers social media seemed a reasonable antidote to boredom, meaning that he or she was less likely to quit their job. Workers such as Spyer's Brazilian informants found the survey question of whether social media was good or bad for work too simplistic: clearly both were true. It can be an efficient solution to share information about work opportunities and can also be useful for fighting boredom – such as that of security guards working nightshifts – but it equally has a negative effect for work in terms of draining attention and time.

A similar ambivalence within work places was noted in the English field site. Workers in one medium-sized firm felt that it had now become too big for constant face to face encounters; it no longer felt like a 'family'. They used Facebook to resurrect some of that earlier closeness; this gave them unprecedented access to fellow workers' private lives. As a result the topics of football and television could now be supplemented with conversation about the family and home life. Although this afforded a greater degree of intimacy between workmates it could also become intrusive; for example, when a boss had access to more personal information than workers liked or employees were made uncomfortable by a colleague's political opinions as expressed on social media.

Our most significant example of the re-integration of work and home life came from the Chilean field site. The city's major industry is copper mining, which primarily employs men; they work week-long shifts, inhabiting dormitories at the mining site. During this time they use social media to maintain family communication, keeping workers integrated into domestic life; conversations range from planning children's birthday parties to paying the electricity bill.

Social media also has a major impact on women's relationship to their families where they have become a significant part of the workforce, raising issues of child care. In England women now form 47 per cent of the workforce, but in the English field site they commonly take extended maternity leave, often a period of intense social media use.

Our comparative survey included a question about whether social media is permitted in the workplace (Fig. 4.21), but the answers were quite specific, making generalisation difficult.[6] For example, in Brazil use of social media is not permitted by managers for hotel workers – a major part of the village population. Nevertheless, as in most of the sites, even when social media use is officially not allowed most people find ways around such regulations.

Finding and getting work

The single most obvious connection between social media and obtaining work is the platform LinkedIn. With claims to 380 million users,[7] this platform is primarily used in commerce and especially for work recruitment. In our English site it was never mentioned outside the commercial sector, but for some working inside commerce it was by far their most important social media platform. One person always checked how active job applicants were on LinkedIn as a key criterion in deciding who to hire. People working in small-scale local business enterprises showed a strong collaborative rather than competitive ethos, often meeting face to face but also well aware of the role of LinkedIn. After the US the country with the largest LinkedIn user base is India, followed by Brazil. It was, however, never likely to impinge upon the kind of low income, poorly educated workers studied by Spyer, though it is certainly known to the Indian IT sector.

So LinkedIn is important in some sites (mainly the English site), but in fact people creatively appropriate other forms of social media in order to develop work opportunities. Nicolescu's field site in south Italy proved a revelation in showing how social media can help people to find employment. Locals felt that formal education was of limited value in obtaining work. Traditionally people tended to find employment through family and social networks, partly since this area is famed for its more artisanal work, as in high-quality food and expensive tailoring. Such work is now in decline, however, and new forms of employment are less susceptible to influence by such family networking.

As it happens, social media such as Facebook favours visual rather than just textual modes of expression (see Chapter 11). On Facebook people learn to craft stylish and clever postings, echoing the role of style in more traditional artisanal work. With more than 200 different cultural organisations, 437 artisanal[8] businesses and 116 bars and restaurants present in the south Italy field site there are many opportunities for visual promotion such as designing posters, alongside an expansion in related commercial sectors, including advertising and public relations. Inadvertently, therefore, Facebook has become a training ground and exhibition space for the skills that were becoming an increasingly important route to work. This suits people with high cultural or educational capital since, although poorly paid, these are reasonably prestigious occupations that highlight their more artistic skills. As Nicolescu shows, this has done nothing for people with less educational or cultural capital – but people with the right background can capitalise on social media in this shift from older artisanal skills to this new, more international world of online design.

In other areas the key to employability remains education. As noted in the previous chapter, Venkatraman found a clear distinction between the more privileged schools, which tended to forbid the use of social media, and schools serving lower-income pupils. The latter encouraged social media use, partly in the hope that it would prepare low income school pupils for jobs in the IT sector. As such they become rather more liberal than the norm in more developed countries,[9] although it is unclear whether using social media ultimately helped secure this kind of employment. More generally the Indian IT sector has in recent times tried to recruit more through apparent meritocracy, focusing upon educational credentials[10] rather than family or caste connections. Yet even in this modernised sector Venkatraman found that WhatsApp played a significant role in returning the recruitment processes to these more customary avenues; existing employees passed information on vacancies or company details back to qualified friends and extended family members, often before the job was officially advertised.

Spyer uses the term 'emergent class' in his book title, since in Brazil employment is one aspect of the recent experience of more than half the population of increased social mobility, together with the aspiration to achieve a decent level of income and consumption and at least some educational and cultural capital. The term emergent could equally well apply to our China and Indian field sites, two regions that represent perhaps the majority of the population of the world today. In this context work is not just labour and a source of income: it connects people to a wider formal world including not only banking, regulation, timetables and the state, but also often literacy and mobility. For those in Brazil who manage to go to college, social media becomes the place for sharing work opportunities or tips for success in a job interview. Social media thereby becomes the mode of solidarity for this emergent class. It can also be used to link related work opportunities. Similarly to Brazil, a plumber in our English field site will use social media to connect with carpenters or house painters, since an opportunity for one can often be turned into work for them all.

The significance of the social media companies

Our project is not concerned with the social media companies themselves as employers. The numbers employed are small, and we would have been very surprised to have met a single such employee in any of our field sites. We were more interested to gauge how far users worried about the influence of these companies on their lives – for example, whether they were concerned with the potential use of the vast amount of personal information to which these companies now have access.

We found little evidence of such concern. When Miller pointed out that Facebook had lost its cool for the young,[11] he argued that this was not because they cared about what Facebook as a company might do with their data, but because of what their parents might do with their data. The fact that Facebook as a company owns both Instagram and WhatsApp has not changed the public discourse. In our field sites people compare, contrast and differentially use Instagram, Facebook and WhatsApp as alternative or complementary platforms quite irrespective of their common ownership – a matter of which most people seem generally unaware and uninterested.[12]

In determining the significance of the companies, it is worth reflecting back on their histories as described in Chapter 2. How much difference would it have made, for example, if Facebook had never been invented? In China it is not used anyway. In other major populations such as Brazil and India it was Orkut that popularised social media; the reason for the switch to Facebook was mainly emulation of metropolitan regions. If things had gone differentially and Orkut had wiped out Facebook and become the major global player, most people would hardly have noticed. At the same time the demise of Orkut (which was owned by Google) and the relative lack of success of Google+ also indicated the limits of corporate power. Even huge, cross-commercial ventures such as QR[13] codes can fail. Our evidence is that users might care about adding a video component to communication, for example, but have much less concern as to whether this is achieved through Skype, FaceTime or Facebook, or whether a message is WhatsApp, Facebook or just their phone. Given the environment of polymedia, it is likely to be a cultural significance that has been allotted to the contrast between these options – something that matters far more to our informants in every region than a platform's technical properties or its ownership. There is clearly an interest in Apple as against Android or Microsoft. However, this may again be for cultural purposes, such as showing off one's new phone, rather than a concern about the companies themselves.

With regard to issues of surveillance or the power of companies, the sense of monopolistic control may be greatest in China given the dominance of the company Tencent (who own the two most popular platforms, QQ and WeChat). In China this control is also associated with a monopolistic state, which although separate from Tencent nonetheless does interfere in people's social media use, most noticeably through preventing access to Facebook and Twitter. As Wang notes, much of the commercial development of the social media companies in China came about as a result of a government initiative in 1999 to expand this sector, appreciating that China was many decades behind other countries in terms of communication technology. The promotion of ICT as one of four 'modernisations' was spectacularly successful. In 2003 China surpassed the US as the world's largest telephone market,[14] and in 2008 the country had the world's largest number of internet users[15].

Furthermore the impact may be more pervasive. As McDonald shows, social media users in his rural Chinese field site were increasingly reliant on the Tencent News Centre, which delivers in-app new updates, as their main daily source of news. He failed to find a single user who had deactivated this function. His analysis also shows the difference between social media news compared to central state news networks. The former is dominated by crime, followed by general topics of romance, marriage and sex. Crime here includes many stories of corruption, thus while censorship is not challenged the critique of corrupt politicians remains significant. However, on social media this critique tended to centre on discussions of figures from other areas. By contrast people were more willing to talk about local concerns in informal face to face settings. Outside of China there is no parallel suggestion that, as yet, Facebook controls news content to this degree, while Twitter is seen more as a route to news than a content creator. Again if we turn to southeast Turkey the main issue for people is the state rather than the company, and the threat by the state to limit access to sites such as Twitter.

Another way in which commercial activity can impinge upon users is through social media advertising. In her study of the commercial usage of social media in both her factory town and Shanghai, Wang found relatively few people who claimed to have bought things directly because of social media advertising, but many who have been influenced in their purchases by the opinions of other people they know on social media (Fig. 4.16). Mostly this is indirect, such as people mentioning a restaurant where they liked the food. While earlier forms of advertising may have had less impact on social media, small businesses found new forms of advertising, for instance through collecting 'likes' on WeChat which they use to approach customers.[16]

The topic of advertising highlights a major concern with surveillance by social media companies and how much the companies know about the individual. This was a common topic in the English field site, where the evidence suggests there may be a flaw in what many companies hope will be a sustainable business plan. For commerce there is now a huge stake in the increased use of targeted advertising, largely because social media companies, like most other digital companies, have singularly failed to find an alternative business model. The problem is that while people in England may not have worried too much about the abstract idea of surveillance, or even the political issues arising from the exposures by WikiLeaks in 2010 and Edward Snowden in 2013, these concerns become very real when they personally experience targeted, sometimes quite inappropriate advertising that can only come from a source with a good deal of intimate information about them. Examples were advertising that showed the companies knew that they had cancer or had reached retirement age. It seems that companies may be ignoring evidence that such targeted advertising may well put people off rather than build a closer relationship to the company. Even if targeted advertising initially succeeds in occasionally persuading people to buy those goods, it is entirely possible that the negative side effects of this constant reminder of how much the company knows about you may be more detrimental.[17] Certainly it was a complaint often voiced by informants.

Entrepreneurship and networking

In several field sites social media and e-commerce more generally are becoming seen as a promising instrument for developing small-scale local businesses. In our Chinese factory field site we meet A-mei, a female factory worker. She used her kinship networks and images from the commercial shopping site of Taobao to establish a make-up business on WeChat, only to find there were already too many people doing the same thing, partly because with social media there is such a low barrier to entry into commerce. By contrast a free-range chicken and egg business in the same area succeeded, but mainly because the customers were mostly friends, family and work colleagues. Mainly such ventures are set up by young women as a supplement to formal work rather than as a full-time occupation. More generally McDonald and Wang argue that personal recommendations have far more influence over what people buy in China compared to Western countries, and this is fuelling the growth of e-commerce on platforms such as WeChat.[18]

McDonald notes that the lack of dedicated business profiles on Chinese social media platforms makes it harder to establish a business presence, but even in his town people do use social media to promote businesses that rely on personal custom such as restaurants or a photocopying shop. For example, they might use the company name and shopfront photograph as their ID photo on their user account. However, the key to commercial usage in China is not the direct use of social media platforms. More important is the way in which the commercial platform of Taobao has developed social characteristics distinct from equivalent non-Chinese sites such as Amazon. This is a case of a hybrid development, where e-commerce websites allow features of social media to be embedded within them. On Taobao buyers and sellers are enabled to chat directly together. Prices can be set individually for a specific customer, allowing for haggling. Even in McDonald's rural town, at least one woman operated her own Taobao store selling clothing online. A bricks-and-mortar Taobao store had also opened in the town; it helped people with their online Taobao shopping by organising delivery, otherwise a significant barrier to e-commerce. This also could provide personal assistance to help people learn how to shop online, or for people without bank accounts.

Similarly there is a stronger development in China of online payment services (often referred to as 'digital wallets'), which result in a more effective monetisation of social media platforms. Sometimes this means young people spending more directly on social media, unbeknown to their parents. All of the above suggests that rather than looking for an autonomous effect of social media on commerce, we should see social media as simply part of a new fusion of personal, commercial and communicative developments.

In a slightly different way, the same conclusion follows for our south Italian field site. Here entrepreneurs also represent the most overt examples of social media use. They seem to be always on the phone. They might have two smartphones and regularly update both their personal and business profiles on Facebook. Yet again it is not so much the direct use of social media, since the limited evidence suggests that even for business such as hairdressers Facebook advertising is not especially effective. Rather this heavy usage by business people has more to do with Italian expressivity and the desire for visibility and display. Generally people here are comfortable mixing business and personal use with a common sense of their style. This is partly because business has traditionally been based largely upon personal relations, but more because often the primary motivation behind business is not the profitability – rather the way it displays social position and facilitates socialising as an end in itself. It is also the way people represent themselves as good citizens and obtain local prestige. Particularly active are businesses that are trying to cultivate style and a sense of cool, such as bars and restaurants. By contrast the more abstract and distant uses of social media such as e-commerce are far less well developed.

The situation in Mardin in southeast Turkey helps us to refine this focus on personal connections. Costa argues that Facebook has had a considerable impact on small businesses, for example shops, musicians, estate agents, cafes, restaurants and private schools. In some cases this particular form of business might not have been viable otherwise. For example, an estate agency used Facebook to create connections with people not living in Mardin, including its diaspora population, and helped civil servants elsewhere in Turkey to invest in property in the city. In addition to this national dimension, social media allowed local musicians and artists to get in touch with people in Europe, to ask for and buy musical instruments and technical equipment, or simply exchange impressions on the best way to play a song. The visual power of Instagram was starting to become important in fashion advertising. However, a caveat was that social media was making age an important factor – it was mainly people under 30 who saw these opportunities, and economic activities by older people were barely affected.

One of the remarkable things about our north Chilean site of Alto Hospicio is that, aside from a few supermarkets and one home construction store (owned by Home Depot), there are only small, family-owned shops. The *feria* ('market') probably makes up for more commerce than all of these formal businesses combined. It is where people buy new and used clothes, home goods, prepared foods, foods for cooking, pet supplies, electronics, auto parts, tools, appliances, etc. Nevertheless it is striking that one of our largest field sites, with 100,000 people, has almost the least amount of commercial activity. It is hard to even find an advertising billboard. By contrast to the lack of formal business, dozens of pages have popped up on Facebook with names such as 'Buy and Sell Alto Hospicio'. This basically acts like the US site Craigslist, where people post pictures of whatever they want to sell (used goods such as clothing, appliances, cars, homes, houses for rent, tools, prepared food—sushi being the most popular, etc.).

Other people open up their own businesses entirely through Facebook, selling homemade food or imported clothing and shoes. Most people do not have credit cards and do not trust the mail system, so ordering things online is very rare. However, Facebook has opened up a whole new kind of online commerce that is entirely local. People say they trust social media more than other forms of e-commerce because they can see who is selling them something. This is consistent with the more general ethnographic observations about trust, personal connections and suspicion in this site.

As we move across the different field sites we can see that in all cases social media create new forms of entrepreneurship. However, the precise way in which this happens tends to depend upon local factors, and especially on whether the personal side is seen as a good or bad aspect of commercial relations. For example, in Trinidad using social media for commercial use is quite specific. One example is a photographic firm whose main work is taking pictures at Trinidadian parties in order to post these on Facebook; the presence of these photographers has become one of the ways in which the firms that promote such parties attract the crowds.[19] In addition a social market advertiser explained in an interview how during the course of the day the promotions on Facebook will reflect the time of day, relating to when people are having meals, for example, or when they might go to the gym.[20] Similarly there were some businesses, such as bars and hairdressers or nightclubs, that depend upon personal relations and therefore make use of social media. For example, one bar in Trinidad that was trying to market their business to a more media-savvy crowd updated their events and news regularly.

More generally, however, Trinidad and England were the two sites that revealed clear limitations in the commercial use of social media in areas of business less dependent upon personal connections. Many of the shops and other commercial outlets in our English village site had tried using social media such as Facebook, but one can see how many of these online sites were abandoned as just not worth the time they took. Once again, unless there was a strong personal element, most local commercial interests saw little benefit in using social media. This was also true in Trinidad, but the reasons are diametrically opposite. In the case of Trinidad people still prefer face to face communication or gossip as their means to obtain information about the quality of goods or services within the town itself. In their quiet country community they may have known the shop keepers all their lives. By contrast, in the English village field site this may be true of the baker or the butcher, but otherwise shops and services that merely sell goods are judged by price and efficiency rather than personal relations; they are often run by minority ethnic groups who are kept at a distance. Here it is the desire to keep money and social relationships separate that makes social media ineffective in commercial transactions.

Finally in south India Venkatraman found WhatsApp being used to turn personal networks into a mode for coordinating entrepreneurial activities. A few educated young mothers (aged 35 or below) previously with well-paying corporate careers now wanted to run part-time entrepreneurial activities from their homes. These could range from cooking freshly prepared snacks to producing colourful fancy jewellery or providing home-based tuition for children. These were mostly targeted at other mothers with children. All of their advertising went through WhatsApp, preferred because it was cheap, almost synchronic and easily accessed through mobiles.

However, for independent entrepreneurs in service-oriented businesses who want to cultivate a more extensive project, Facebook acts as the platform of choice, providing in effect no-cost marketing. Usha is a professional paid storyteller in her late forties. Usha was clear in her aim to establish herself as the most sought-after storyteller, reviving the culture of storytelling from its roots as an informal tradition and making it available for educational purposes within the home. As a self-employed entrepreneur she saw technology as the key to both marketing and organising her day-to-day operations. In turn she used Yahoo groups, then Orkut and now Facebook.

Usha had recognised a potential because of the growth of nuclear families, often without grandparents. She therefore offered to coach parents on the skills of storytelling. She also could see that companies were placing an emphasis upon corporate executives becoming good storytellers, Usha then created a Facebook page for herself, separating out her personal profile from her public, work-related page. She posted stories, links to pages on storytelling and storytelling for sharing through Facebook. She then posted pictures of her storytelling sessions, where she appears in action with a variety of audiences. Usha felt that pictures of her in action created far more of an impact than any text. Overall she was happy that Facebook provided her with a no-cost advertising platform, enabling her to market herself as an independent entrepreneur.

The south Indian field site also demonstrated the particular issues facing certain consumers. Venkatraman found that several men from lower socio-economic castes used e-commerce websites such as Flipkart to shop for T-shirts, shoes, slippers and similar items, as they found it socially awkward to shop at bigger stores for branded goods. Workers in such stores may discriminate against men from lower socio-economic classes. Without credit or debit cards, they made use of the cash-on-delivery payment system that this portal permits. Furthermore they came to know about Flipkart only through its advertisements on Facebook, which they accessed through their smartphones.

These anecdotes from south India remind us that commerce is a huge and diverse practice; we can find stories reflecting an astonishing range of uses for social media across our nine field sites. It is possible, however, to proffer some generalisations. Overall there was little evidence from our research to support the massive drive within commerce itself to promote social media as the key to modern marketing. Apart from LinkedIn, these platforms were largely devised, and are mainly used for, communication outside of commerce, consisting of small groups and personal connections. So not surprisingly we find social media has been mostly useful for those commercial enterprises that are themselves based on personal connections and small-scale sociality. As far as our informants are concerned, the impact for larger-scale business operations was much more limited. This is the area where people become anxious about the spread of targeted advertising as a sign of unwelcome intrusion into personal life.[21] At the same time younger people in many regions are now quite adept at using online commercial outlets such as Amazon and Taobao, where the latter is gaining social media-like attributes.

Wider values

One of the core roles of anthropology is to question what we sometimes call 'Western' categories. We tend to see these as rational, scientific and natural, while by comparison when we read a description of Chinese people burning fake money at funerals we might find this relationship to money 'weird'. Yet it is something that can be readily explained through the concept of differing cosmologies.[22]

Underlying this examination of the relationship of social media to commerce, therefore, is a need to consider what people actually understand by things such as money, value and exchange. As an example we will examine first the contrast between ancient and traditional Chinese ideals, and then the beliefs of contemporary young people in places such as the UK and the US. An example to consider is the monetisation of WeChat through the 'red envelope'. This is based on an ancient custom of giving money in red envelopes during festivals such as New Year and Weddings.[23] However, in this case the money is digitised and, in a very Chinese fashion, an element of luck is introduced. 'It is reported that from Chinese New Year's Eve to 4pm on the first day of the Chinese new year (31 January 2014), more than 5 million users tried out the feature to deliver in excess of 75 million digital red envelopes',[24] all of which further tied users to WeChat itself. While traditional red envelopes were from the older to the younger generation, the WeChat version became more peer to peer oriented.

We need to appreciate that in the West the domain of the private and domestic life has traditionally been defined partly by its opposition to the realm of money and finance.[25] Gifting money feels less personal than other gifts. In China money and finance have always been seen as an integral aspect of, rather than an opposition to, intimate and domestic life. Money in many Asian societies is regarded as the proper and perhaps the best way for people to demonstrate love and care in families, and to show that their feelings are genuine.[26] In some cases cash may be seen as more appropriate for presents between people who are close than a gift.

Furthermore it we turn instead to young people in the UK and the US we find an interesting parallel. Social media has facilitated a whole series of practices such as Kickstarting, Crowdsourcing and Couch Surfing that admittedly were almost entirely absent from our research project. While some of these are linked to the potential for making money, mostly these are quite the opposite. They rely on altruistic concerns, encouraging people to give both money and services without expecting any immediate return, and relate to other trends, such as Open Access and Open Source, which are important to the ethos of new digital practices.[27] In this sense they are not like the de-commodification of music or entertainment, where pirating or getting things for free is clearly in the interests of the people involved. In some of these other new movements, narrow self-interest disappears into what anthropologists call 'generalised exchange or generalised reciprocity',[28] where it is hoped that if we are all generous in the short term everyone benefits in the long term, including ourselves. In these new movements people invest in ideas and developments that might not otherwise be funded. Social media in this case has brought out forms of altruism in young people, based on shifting ideals about the public domain.

The point of ending with a consideration of the WeChat 'red envelope' on the one hand and Open Access or Couch Surfing on the other is that they represent quite significant uses of social media for purposes that relate to exchange, money, de-commodification and value. These are wider concerns, however, than traditional ideas of commerce. One of our conclusions is that for work and commerce, as with all the other topics we discuss, social media results in this wider contextualisation, with particular reference to the social relationships which are the principal content of social media.

A second conclusion is that if the primary determinant of social media usage in commerce had been formal economic rationality then we would have predicted relative homogeneity in the impact of social media between field sites – at least those at a similar level of economic development and with similar histories and forms of market capitalism. However, that was not the case. Rather in south Italy commerce was seen as something that could positively expand social relationships and sociality: being involved in commerce was part of being social, public and visible. By contrast in England we found that people prefer abstract, impersonal e-commerce. Only very specific businesses utilise the personal element in their relationships with customers, while the main impact of new advertising is seen as an affront to a highly regarded privacy.

So the point of this final section is to remind ourselves that the way in which social media impacts upon commerce depends upon a wider set of values – for example, how money or business is understood in some places as integral, and in others opposed, to proper and intimate social relations. The generalisation that seems to survive this caveat and therefore our third conclusion is that by and large people associate social media with commerce mostly when that commerce is aligned with small-scale, personal and group communication.

7
Online and offline relationships

With the growing popularity and ubiquity of social media worldwide comes the notion that there is a new generation of so-called 'digital natives',[1] who were born and grew up in the digital era. Social media seems set to become an ever-growing foundation to many of their everyday relationships. As a result much of the world is struggling to make sense of this new phenomenon and its impact. Precisely because social media is now so embedded in young people's lives, anxiety is rising that these are replacing offline interactions and offline relationships.

However, a comparison between two kinds of relationships designated as online and offline may imply either that they are mutually exclusive or opposed to each other. Yet throughout our research we have approached relationships as created, developed and sustained through integrated online and offline interaction. The entire range of offline relationships, from family through school and work to social relations in the wider neighbourhood, may also be present online in a manner that is rarely separated out from one's offline life. The popular perception of online relationships as things which can be contrasted with a 'real world' – inhabited by one's real or more authentic offline relationships – seems therefore simplistic and misleading. This corresponds to an earlier critique of the concept of the 'virtual', a term prominent during the early years of internet use.[2] In short our study treats social media in much the same way that everyone treats the landline telephone, never described today as a separate 'online/on-phone' facet of life.

It is, however, essential for us as researchers to recognise that whatever misgivings we may feel as academics about this dualistic terminology, it remains a primary mode by which people around the world understand and experience digital media. Our informants constantly do speak about a separate online world. Furthermore we need to acknowledge that people give different meanings to these terms 'online' and 'offline'. For example, in the south Indian field site, when asked about the privacy of photographs, many people responded: 'I won't share it online, we only share it offline.' As Venkatraman noted, by 'offline' people actually mean sending photos to their close friends via WhatsApp. Technically WhatsApp is 'online' in the sense of being sent through a smartphone app, but 'offline' in these people's understanding because that is not for them 'the internet'. 'Offline' also here refers to the very private nature of the sociality, whereas 'online' is understood to be the public-facing aspects of the internet. Yet the same informants in other contexts refer to WhatsApp as social media and thereby online. So even if we want to respect the fact that the participants in our field sites commonly use the terms online and offline, both their and our use of these terms is often inconsistent.

This chapter will first deal with the popular concern that increased digital mediation leads to less authentic relationships than offline ones – a belief that can lead to people regarding human societies as becoming less 'real' when relationships are mediated by digital technologies. The chapter then moves closer to our own approach, which examines sociality in the age of social media through the lens of ethnography. The final part of the chapter will further explore the new possibilities for human experience and social relationships that have been created through global uses of social media in different contexts.

'Authenticity' and 'mediation': the big concerns

Why do people feel that using digital technologies makes us lose something of ourselves? It is certainly not the first time societies have feared losing humanity in the face of a new technology.[3] As noted previously, anxieties can be traced back to when writing was adopted by ancient Greeks. The philosopher Socrates (as presented by Plato) warned people that this new technology was a threat to the oral traditions of Greek society; according to him, writing would create forgetfulness.[4] Ironically, without writing Socrates's remark may have been long forgotten.

No one today sees writing as making us less real or human. On the contrary, illiteracy may be seen as an absence of a fundamental capacity that every human being should possess. More familiar will be the accusation that television reduces us to 'couch potatoes'. Yet the idea of a family sitting together and enjoying television has become an object of fond nostalgia, compared to what is perceived as the more individualised, and still less 'real', domain of digital interaction.[5] We also find accusations today that echo those of Socrates. Among them is the idea that digital technologies reduce our capacity to think, by reducing our attention span through delegating cognitive functions such as memory to our digital devices.[6]

In all these instances digital devices are regarded as a form of increased mediation that leads to a loss of authenticity. However, anthropologists reject the idea of an unmediated authenticity, regarding all aspects of identity and relationships as intrinsically mediated by cultural and social rules, including gender and ethnicity.[7] It is axiomatic to anthropology that a tribal society is not less mediated than a metropolitan society. When we meet, face to face communication is thoroughly mediated by conventions and etiquette regarding appropriate behaviour between those in conversation. Rules of kinship can limit what someone is allowed to say just as effectively as technological limits. For anthropologists, therefore, communicating online can be regarded as a shift in cultural mediation, but it does not make a relationship *more* mediated.

There is a danger that our anxiety about the new technology will lead us simply to neglect the mediated nature of prior offline sociality – now assumed to be not only more real, but also more 'natural'. By contrast as anthropologists we want to use the study of social media to *deepen* our appreciation of the mediated nature of prior offline sociality. For example, there is increasing use of webcam as 'always-on', so that couples and other people living apart can feel as though they are still living together. By studying this practice we can come to understand the forms of interaction, avoidance and silences that people adopt when they were previously living together within the same domestic space, but learn to give each other autonomy and create agreed times and forms of interaction.[8]

In Spyer's field site in Brazil people use the term 'Facebook friends' to refer to acquaintances with whom one is only in contact through social media. In many cases, not only in Brazil, the so-called 'Facebook friend' carries the implication that 'friendship' of such a kind, even under the name of 'friend', is a lower category of friendship than 'real friends'. In China people use '*jiangshi*' ('zombie') or '*shiti*' ('corpse') to describe those social media contacts with whom one has never had any kind of communication (no 'likes', no comments and no one-to-one or group messaging); they are not even regarded as living human beings. Such phenomena were observed in other field sites too. For academic analysis, however, we need to recognise that people have always questioned their offline friendships to determine whether they were 'real' friends and to establish how much one could trust them or rely on them.

Although the terminology suggests a simple opposition between online and offline friendship, therefore, these questions about friendship are mainly being transferred from offline to online relationships. We can, however, still acknowledge that there may be unprecedented aspects to this experience of online-only friendship, and the ways in which we then use these relationships.

We found that in most places people now expect consistency between the two domains. If Brazilians have cordial relations offline, they are likely also to have genial relationships on social media. For a good friend social media is likely to help cultivate and enhance that friendship, whereas, if there is no bonding in the first place, being friends on Facebook may make little or no difference to the offline relationship. Most commonly social media may also be a space where friends of friends/relatives transform into one's own friends. This seemed particularly important in the regions of Latin America and Trinidad, and most likely reflects the way in which friendship there was previously understood. On the one hand online friendship may be seen as lacking the range of social cues[9] available in face to face interaction. On the other hand since the beginning of the internet people have used online anonymity to discuss issues that they may have found difficult to share with people who know them offline. The people with whom one shares the most intimate secrets may thus now be online strangers whom you will never know offline.

'Frame' and 'group': approaches to understand sociality

How then can we make more sense of social relationships in the social media age? The theoretical concept of 'framing', which derives from Goffman's[10] analysis of social activity, is also useful in thinking through the relationship between online and offline. Put simply, framing helps to set the boundary, establishing rules and expectations to guide behaviour. Being within the 'frame' of a theatre, for example, tells you that you should applaud at the end and not run on stage to rescue the heroine. There are myriad invisible but truly effective frames in social life, and our understanding of frames helps us to behave properly, in accordance with social expectations. For instance, the kind of conversation that occurs in an English pub is different from that at an office meeting because 'pub' and 'office' frame such behaviour differently, despite the fact that both are forms of talking. We should therefore also regard offline and online as two 'frames' in our daily life[11] that may trigger different attitudes and behaviours. That is also the reason why, in some cases, people feel that online environments induce some different aspects of certain relationships. Rather than opposing these contexts we can regard them as complementary frames which combine to provide a fuller picture of the person and their relationships.

In practice different social media platforms, or different groups and accounts within the same platform, serve as 'sub frames', enabling individuals skilfully to locate a niche within which to deal with various social relationships.[12] For example in Mardin, the field site in southeast Turkey, it is commonplace to find teenagers and young adults with multiple accounts on the same social media platform (e.g. Facebook); they can, and do, behave differently according to the groups with whom they share these. Costa shows how people switch easily and quickly from one platform to another, or to different accounts within one platform.

Different platforms or multiple accounts allow users to place their contacts into different categories such as 'classmates', 'colleagues' and 'others'– a useful way of exploiting social media to 'sort out' their social networks. These social 'categories' organised on social media again existed in offline social life long before social media existed; however, social media may make those categories more explicit. In our south India field site, therefore, people can retain the default setting on Facebook, so that users are not explicitly categorised, but they are well aware which contacts belong to the same caste – still one of the country's primary classification systems.

In contrast to Facebook, Twitter and Instagram, but like Google +, the Chinese social media platform QQ prominently features categories of friends. QQ encourages its users to sort their online contacts into groups, for instance 'colleagues', 'special friend', 'friend', 'family', 'stranger', 'blacklist' (used to block contacts), and any custom groups they may wish to create.[13] However, these are only visible to the user, not to their contacts. A popular expression among Chinese people is 'you will know your relationship better if you know which category your friends put you into on their QQ'. Such practices seem natural in China where (as would also be true of many places outside of China) sociality has long been characterised by diverse and overlapping circles and groups.[14] The main problem is that online categories cannot match the complexity of traditional networks of 'guanxi' ('social relationships'). The reason is that on QQ friendship categories are mutually exclusive, while in offline life we may well think of our friends as overlapping various groups. Here as in all field sites, therefore, social media may enhance social categorisation, but it cannot match the complexity of this practice in the offline world.[15]

From intimacy to anonymity: scalable sociality[16]

In Chapter 1 it was argued that the particular form taken by polymedia within social media can be termed 'scalable sociality'. The initial example from the English field site was based on school pupils. In our Brazilian field site many older people have limited access to the internet due to poor education and economic factors, so social media can be construed as a young person's space for creating peer-based collectives and displays of modernity avoiding the adult gaze. Here, as elsewhere, social media often becomes a place for designating intimate relationships (ties of kinship, close friends, couples), where it is relative intimacy itself which is scaled, experienced, maintained and reinforced. In the south Indian field site social media works like 'fictive kin', where many people come to be seen as 'aunties' or 'cousins' (even though not biologically related) in the tradition of extended families and caste. So kinship is used as the idiom to express how far up a person has travelled on this same scale of intimacy.

In Sinanan's field site in Trinidad many households have parents, children or siblings living abroad, and the use of social media is vital to the maintenance of basic family relationships. Indeed in some of our field sites social media has also allowed families who do not live in the same household to create more emotional bonds; they can spend more time together online than they might have done if actually living together. For example, teenagers in some Western countries may live at home, but sometimes with very limited family connectivity; for example, they may write notices forbidding parents to enter the teenager's room. Most of their sociality extends from the screens in their bedrooms, a space kept quite separate from the rest of the house. While they live in the same house as the rest of the family, therefore, it can be argued that these teenagers do not live 'together' – any more than they live 'together' with the people with whom they socialise online.

Haynes found in the north Chilean field site that WhatsApp has become incredibly important for mineworkers in negotiating periods of separation from families while they are working away. Yet while social media solves the problem of separation for some families, it may also bring problems for others. Some miners reported that social media increases feelings of jealousy among male partners of (the few) female miners; in other cases it may exacerbate already problematic family relationships. However, Haynes also reports that miners see social media as bringing an element of the outside world to the 'asylum' of the mine, giving it a sense of humanity.

In the industrial China field site some couples who maintained a long-distance relationship with each other even found that their partners appeared to be more caring online, free from the mundane concerns of physically shared everyday life. Some junior family members also reported that they found senior family members to be more easy-going and funny online, thanks to their use of cute 'emojis' on social media – whereas in face to face encounters with seniors these relationships were supposed to be far more serious and respectful.[17] Once again, so far from being separated from offline relationships, social media has become a primary mode by which traditional close-kin relations are in different cases sustained, retained, reinvigorated, but also in certain cases transformed. In all these cases scalable sociality encompasses the possibility that social media can be more intense and intimate than offline relationships.

Another reason this can become highly significant is when people become immobile. Miller included within his field work an extensive study of how a hospice communicates with patients, who mainly have a terminal diagnosis based on advanced cancer. He found that immobility has had a pronounced impact even in a rural area because of the particular nature of English sociality. Sociality in the village follows a general pattern in which people are highly sociable in public, but fiercely defensive of the private sphere; this combines with a strong sensibility among older people that they do not want to become a burden on their relatives and friends. As a result there is a surprising degree of isolation and loneliness. As an applied project, this led to recommendations to the hospice for encouraging the use of social media and easy-to-use devices such as the iPad, particularly at earlier stages of the disease in which people are more amenable to support and assistance. Having established that the cause of loneliness is the dualism of private and public sociality, the specific definition of social media as a form of scalable sociality that bridges between the private and the public makes it a particularly appropriate part of the potential solution to this problem of loneliness in the context of English social reticence.[18]

In some cases, the closer the relationship the more forms of different communication platforms and technologies are supported. Broadbent's[19] study shows that the proliferation of social media does not necessarily give rise to the extension of new social connections in the region (Switzerland) where she worked, 'but rather the intensification of a small group of highly intimate relationships that have now managed to match the richness of their social connectedness with a richness of multiple communication channels'.[20] As is often the case with our project, this generalisation works only in certain regions and not others.

Scalable sociality can be related to many other dimensions, such as the degree to which people want or feel they need the kinds of sociality made available by social media. Nicolescu found in the south Italian field site that for most residents their prior social networks were seen as both stable and sufficient. While the majority of people's Facebook contacts are also from the town, co-residence meant there was little need for social media as a mode for maintaining these relationships. As a result most people saw social media as making very little difference to their lives. However, Nicolescu also noticed that for a small group of people who had experience of higher education in big cities and had far more diverse social networks outside the small town, returning to the town often meant losing this extended social connectivity. For these people social media played a vital role in retaining such wider connections, often also seen as more important than everyday offline relationships.

Generally speaking, as found in our survey in Chapter 4, people view the way social media facilitates social relations positively.[21] For close relationships it is commonly a place where trust and affection are cultivated and expressed. At the same time people are aware of another side to this coin, in which the increased visibility of relationships leads to jealousy and surveillance.

Compared to these more common attitudes to the use of social media within intimate social relationships, we see a very diverse response to the potential of social media for connecting with strangers. The Chileans tend not to use dating websites or apps such as Tinder and Grindr, now becoming increasingly popular in England; here people sometimes seem to have less mistrust of strangers as potential sexual partners than as people who might view their social media postings. Instead the Chileans rely on friends of friends on Facebook when searching for romantic relationships online. In both sites strangers will not become online contacts without offline endorsement, for instance knowing the person offline or knowing someone who knows them well.[22] Otherwise strangers were a focus of suspicion.

This contrasts with our rural Chinese field site, where McDonald notes that prior to using social media interactions with '*mosheng ren*' ('strangers') were generally far less common. Now young people may friend '*luanjia*' ('large numbers of strangers') randomly, though others, especially married couples, maintain a comparatively cautious attitude toward strangers online.[23] Similarly Costa found out that in Mardin social media, especially Facebook, has been used to expand an individual's social networks to '*yabanci*' ('strangers') – whereas traditionally people's social relations mainly included either '*akraba*' ('relatives') or '*komşu*' ('neighbours'), and for some categories of people also '*arkadas*' ('friends').[24]

A transformation in attitudes towards strangers online was also observed in the industrial Chinese field site. Here many see entirely online friendships as '*chun*' ('purer') relationships, since they do not incur the pragmatic demands that often feature heavily in offline relationships and are less infused by social hierarchy. As Feige, a factory worker, put it:

> They [online friends] like you and talk with you because they really like you being you, not because you are rich so that they can borrow money from you, or you are powerful so that they can get a job from you. Here [online] everything is much purer, without power and money involved.

A parallel sentiment was expressed by some factory owners. They suggested that they sometimes avoided attending school reunions in fear of requests for financial help from their old classmates. However, they were happy to talk with online strangers on WeChat to release the stress that they believed could not be shown to their subordinates and family members. Although the factory owners and the factory workers represent the two extremes of income in this field site, they have similar reasons for wanting to friend and communicate with strangers online. In both cases online relationships are seen as more authentic compared to offline relationships, which in many cases are highly mediated (or 'polluted', as people say) by factors such as wealth and social status.

In the case of more public social media, the online exposure of relationships has also to be interpreted as an 'official verification'. In our south Indian field site, the relatively close and intimate communications facilitated by WhatsApp were used for communication between family members. On the other hand Facebook, as the most public platform, is the place where family and kinship ties are consciously performed to the audience of non-family contacts. For instance, a Facebook update of a new-born baby is usually followed by many 'likes' and comments from family members, even though all of them have already sent congratulatory wishes via phone calls or in face to face situations before posting.

Such social media performances are tailored for non-family and the wider public that share Facebook. Haynes explains that in north Chile a romantic relationship will only gain its 'official' validity by being published as a Facebook 'relationship update' or through informal posting of love notes on the wall of one's significant others. Similarly in industrial China young couples constantly need the online audience on QQ to witness their romance. In some cases young factory migrants even set up QQ groups which include all of one's online contacts in order to say 'I love you' in public (on the online group chat) to their girlfriend or boyfriend. Such confessions online are viewed as one of the biggest commitments in a relationship. In this way social media can make us more conscious and self-conscious of both our relationships and ourselves. In these cases offline relationships have now become dependent upon their recognition online before they are accepted as 'real'.

If we take these examples together, we see that social media has entirely contradictory consequences across the range of field sites. Yet this is partly because the term 'social media' conjoins a wide range of platforms. If we treat them as polymedia, that is as a general range within which each has its complementary niche, then a bit more consistency emerges. There is the use of platforms to create an opposition between more public and more private sociality, as well as the exploitation of either different platforms or different genres of usage within the same platform, to help organise one's social world into separated categories. This includes south Indian teachers' differentiated attitudes towards WhatsApp, depending on whether this is directed to school or family, the use of Facebook by Brazilian teenagers to gain autonomy from the control of adults and Chilean lovers gaining official verification from the widest public. From the maintenance of intimate relationships to the possibilities of forming relationships with strangers, social media can be seen as a form of 'scalable sociality' enabling people to better control their social lives. This may be through adapting existing social norms to different contexts or allowing for the creation of entirely new forms of social relations and sociality by exploiting this register of degrees of intimacy and distance.

Online identity: extended and new dimensions of daily life

This leads to our final issue with online identity: our tendency to regard identity as something constructed through social interaction rather than a given psychological state. Sennett's[25] work shows how identity in ancient times was almost entirely ascribed. A person was born into a particular class, occupation, social role and place of origin – whatever happened, you were likely to remain a butcher from Brittany for life. Giddens[26] argues that in the modern world, on the other hand, people typically have to deal with elements of identity that are no longer fixed and stable, but reflect the dynamics of people's situations, to the extent that now the struggle is to preserve a coherent narrative of self-identity. Both insights are complemented by Goffman,[27] whose previously noted concept of framing also pertains to how people manage multiple identities associated with various social roles and contexts: mother, worker, sportswoman. Going online adds additional frames to this mix. When this sociality becomes more scalable, it may also provide a greater flexibility to online identity.

One way to examine this is through the consequences of the greater visibility of persona and relationships.[28] This is especially important in Trinidad, which had already developed a fundamental association between the cultivation of the self as a project that can only be enacted through the mirror of social visibility. In short Trinidadians recognise that the truth of a person is not who they think they are, but who others deem them to be on the basis of their appearance. Historically this arose out of anti-slavery and resistance movements. Rather than being ascribed in status, as by slavery or social hierarchy, people could attempt to create an entirely different persona in the eyes of their audience through masquerade. Ideally people should be judged not on their birth or job, but their ability to craft themselves as attractive or powerful. The way you walk and talk and clothe yourself is not an illusion or just a performance; it is the only proper way by which you should be judged.

The same logic works for Facebook. Images such as photographs and memes dominate Trinidadian postings, because what is shown on social media is the curated truth of a person. Through that curating they show themselves to be someone who is international and cosmopolitan, or a family-oriented person, or a 'gangsta'. In Trinidad social media makes what is already visible about a person hyper-visible, further reinforcing their constructed identity. This is also why Miller referred to Facebook in Trinidad as 'The Book of Truth'.[29]

Trinidadian use of Facebook is perhaps an extreme example of how social media became a place where people create a visible identity that can be regarded as more real than their offline persona. Another would be the use of QQ among Chinese factory migrants – though in this case the result is entirely invisible to the offline world. In the industrial China field site tens of thousands of factory workers come from villages in inland China. In the context of China's developing economy, they migrate to factory towns for labour which is largely reduced to completing tasks also performed by machines. Migrant workers, labelled as a '*liudong renkou*' ('floating population'), are constantly on the move, providing temporary and cheap labour. They do not qualify for the increase in benefits and education targeted at more stable urban residents and tend to live and work in extremely substandard conditions. It is their offline life that these workers see as temporary. By contrast they regard social media as a far more stable and permanent place where they can keep contact with family and friends. By posting 'fantasy photos' (e.g. luxury cars, romantic holidays, images of princess-like women) and '*feizhuliu*' ('anti-mainstream') images (e.g. photographs of rebelling rockers), or by sharing 'chicken soup for the soul' (inspirational stories, such as 'you are poor because you are not ambitious enough'),[30] people actually build up their online identity. This is naturally quite different from the stigmatizing tag of '*di suzhi*' ('low human quality') worn in offline situations by Chinese factory migrants.

As noted in other research,[31] people who have difficulty in expressing or 'being' themselves in face to face interactions are more likely to craft what they regard as a 'real self' and form closer relationships with people they meet online. As one typical Chinese factory girl who dropped out of middle school suggested, 'Life outside the mobile phone is unbearable'. We might be tempted to dismiss images of the perfect wedding or being a princess as mere fantasy. Yet in this case the whole reason for taking on such employment is to provide a route towards a different modernity, the nature of which these people are trying to imagine for themselves. The scope for doing this offline is extremely restricted. It is online where people craft and enact a more permanent version of themselves, an image that they hope over time and with increasing income they may achieve. For them the wishes, longing and happiness that they express and clothe themselves in online are extremely real. In effect the migrant workers are part of a dual but simultaneous migration. The first is physical, from villages to factories in cities; the second is from offline experience to online. Social media is not simply a technology for communication, fantasy or entertainment. For these migrants social media is very much a lived place. They work offline and live online.

Conclusion

This chapter began by outlining popular concerns, at least in some Western countries, that social media, together with the supposed increased mediation of relationships, is somehow making human beings less 'real', or at least more removed from lived realities.[32] The last case study represented perhaps the most profound evidence as to why this is not necessarily the case. In the industrial China field site migrant workers, their lives dominated by manual labour, experience online as the place in which they can be *more* human, able to express individual aspirations and hopes for the future. The relationship between human beings and new technologies for these informants is not ambivalent: it is essential. The debate in Western countries makes assumptions about people's offline lives. Yet in this case factory workers sleep, work and eat offline, without many of them really having much of what we might call an offline 'life'. Instead they have an online life during the time when they are not sleeping, working and eating, a time in which they can become themselves and relate to others. We can also see how in some cases the denigration of social media as inauthentic may in part be the practice of elites. Such groups, secure in their power to construct themselves offline, may seek to dismiss the attempts by less powerful populations to assert the authenticity of their self-crafting online.

In a similar manner we cannot ignore the Trinidadian sensibility, which suggests that the visible appearance you have the power to create for yourself online is therefore more real than that over which you had no control; for example, the particular shape of nose you were born with, or the uniform you must wear for work. More commonly as we traverse the range of field sites the situation is less of a dualism. In most cases online has become simply another framed context aligned with the many prior framed contexts of offline life, where people always lived both at work, in families on holidays and so forth. Thus alongside a wide literature, including the work of Turkle,[33] Baym,[34] Hampton and Wellman,[35] Livingstone,[36] and others, the evidence from this project is a further call to progress from simplistic arguments based on oppositions such as virtual as against real, and to recognise instead that most people now engaged with a multiplicity of online and offline communications and identities with no clear boundary between them. At the same time we appreciate that almost all our informants employ a distinction that they refer to as offline and online, and that they exploit this to express a wide range of different oppositions, often using terms such as 'real' or 'virtual'. Further we also recognise that there are people who privilege the online as authentic and pure, as well as those who assume this is the natural condition of offline.

The central section of this chapter suggested a different approach to this issue. Instead of starting from a dualism of offline against online, our project began with a definition of social media as scalable sociality. In other words we constantly see gradations in people's spectrum of relationships – from more intense, less intimate, more private and so forth. From this perspective the distinction between offline and online is replaced by a consideration of many different dimensions of how we grade relationships. The distinction between online and offline becomes one aspect of this. Indeed many of our examples were cases where the online was higher on such scales than offline, in terms of parameters such as intimacy. These include instances where there is greater disclosure to strangers or preferring to open up to peers one does not live with than to parents one does. Generally, however, it is not that either is closer or more distant. Rather people recognise that they can exploit a variety of contexts for relationships as different frames, just one of which happens to be online as against offline. Finally it is possible that this new dimension of visible creativity in both relationships and identity is making us more conscious, both of our relationships and of ourselves.

8
Gender

In this chapter we will examine the influences that social media has had upon gender relations, gendered norms and identities across our field sites. By gender we refer to the socially and culturally constructed differences between femininity and masculinity, shaped by countless factors including the use of technology and digital media. Early internet research[1] often marvelled at the uniqueness of online social spaces in which personal characteristics such as gender, race, age and also apparent physical aspects of the body could seemingly be erased, as you could adopt an entirely distinct online persona. Feminist internet scholars[2] emphasised the role of digital media in providing empowering tools, enabling both women and men freely to perform selves and identities that they chose for themselves online, escaping from the oppressive gender norms of the offline world.

Donna Haraway[3] provides one of the best known arguments for this trend, emphasising the power of technology to transform gender relations and identity. Furthermore, because gender could potentially become erased or irrelevant online, this was seen as itself evidence that notions of gender were culturally constructed, created through interactions between the social world and the material culture (and technologies) around us, rather than being merely biological fact.[4] At that time other digital optimists[5] emphasised the internet as enabling the constitution of new forms of individual and collective gender identities. For them the internet facilitated a genuine expression of women's own agency rather than something imposed upon them.

In retrospect these notions of free-floating online identities, detached from real-world bodies, have proved short-lived. As social media has replaced more anonymous types of interactions such as chat rooms and forums, offline identities have become increasingly important in determining online identities – particularly in contexts where social norms and notions of respectability significantly influence or control social relations. In the 1990s some saw online as potential freedom from fixed gender identity. Others, continuing from debates in the 1960s and 1970s, tended to emphasise the role of technology in reproducing male domination. In this case the revisions came through recognition that digital technologies can destabilise gender differences.[6]

After these decades, which swung from one emphasis to another, most people today recognise that technology is neither patriarchal nor liberating in and of itself. Technology creates *potentials*, made manifest according to the contexts in which they are embedded. Some more recent studies have focused on the way in which social media has provided new tools for self-presentation and management of gender identities, especially among young people and teenagers.[7] Others have highlighted the dynamic of self-disclosure as the main element of this process.[8] However, what has remained unclear is the degree to which one could generalise beyond the Euro-American context in which most of the influential research was conducted.

This chapter uses ethnographic examples to investigate the ways in which social media has at times strengthened existing gender relations and dominant ideals of masculinity and femininity, but in other instances led to transformations in the way gender differences are imagined and practiced. A concern with cultural difference relates not only to the range of sites, but also to diversity within each site by considering regional, religious, class and urban/rural and ethnic variation. The chapter is divided into two main sections. The first explores the ways in which social media has facilitated the reproduction and the strengthening of existing gender norms, highlighting similarities between the online and the offline. The second section discusses some of the transformations brought by social media to gendered relations and gendered norms. The chapter concludes with a brief discussion of non-heteronormative – including gay, lesbian, bisexual and transgender – sexual identities and practices. It describes whether and how social media may give opportunities for people with such identities to expand their opportunities for private or secret interactions or, contrarily, to achieve more public visibility.

Continuities: gendered self-presentations

In all nine field sites of our study social media has reproduced and reinforced norms that regulate gender differences in the offline world, but in different ways and to different extents. In particular the reproduction of dominant ideals of femininity and masculinity in public-facing[9] social media such as Facebook is a common theme seen across almost all our sites. Public online spaces have emerged as often highly conservative, reinforcing established gender roles. Self-crafting on social media continues to have a gendered aspect, as one part of an individual's various intersecting identities, just as in everyday offline life.[10]

The field site in southeast Turkey perhaps best illustrates the conservative nature of platforms such as Facebook. Here men tend to portray themselves as successful professionals, while women emphasise their aesthetic qualities, or rather their adherence to Muslim values of modesty and purity; they all omit those aspects of their life that do not reflect the dominant values of female and male honour and Muslim moralities. For example, women's interactions with men are rarely represented in those spaces of Facebook that are seen by the general public of friends and relatives. Conversations between young women and men in secular and gender-mixed settings such as school and universities are routine, but this would not be apparent online. Also the gathering of gender-mixed groups of relatives for drinking coffee and tea together in semi-public spaces such as cafes and restaurants is rarely portrayed, as they can potentially result in gossip and misunderstanding.

Secular, well-educated women who are in premarital relationships known to their friends never make this public on social media. This is illustrated by the case of Leyla. Whenever some of her friends take pictures of her together with her boyfriend, she is always very careful to make sure that nobody will post these pictures on their Facebook wall. Fortunately people usually ask for authorisation before posting pictures on Facebook. Gender segregation and conformity on Facebook is thus even tighter and more extreme here than it is offline, simply because this space is subjected to continuous scrutiny, to a greater extent than most spaces offline. It is common for young women and men to receive phone calls from their older relatives demanding clarification and justification around the context of specific images they have seen on Facebook. People spend considerable amounts of time patrolling and speculating about their Facebook friends' walls. Any deviance from the norms can become an object of rumour and gossip, potentially resulting in shame and the ruin of the individual and family's reputation.

A young man named Fatih attended an event in a local restaurant with two special guests: female DJs from Istanbul who were performing that night. The women wore clothes that appeared completely shameful according to local standards. Although he and his friends spent the entire evening taking pictures of the two women, none of them posted any of these images on Facebook. On the online spaces visible to hundreds of friends and relatives these men strictly conform to moral rules that impose on them virtuous and pure conduct.

Dominant ideals of femininity are reproduced also through a contained online public presence of women's bodies: young unmarried women from more conservative backgrounds often use Facebook with fake profile pictures and fake names in order to avoid being seen by older male relatives. By doing so they reproduce current social norms that traditionally prevented them from having a presence in public spaces; yet this simultaneously also produces new opportunities to transgress these norms, by secretly maintaining spaces of representation outside the family's control.

The partial exclusion of women from the more public spaces of social media is not limited to southeast Turkey. In our rural Chinese field site several women who had recently married removed many strangers from their contact list; they had arrived there as a result of previous 'indiscriminate adding' sprees prior to marriage. Others might stop using social media altogether. Pregnant women often defriend many people and make themselves less visible on social media, representing a transition out of public life and into the private institution of motherhood. Women's lack of visibility on social media is thus heightened with the passing of certain life stages. Yet in contrast married women are particularly active and visible in offline public spaces, such as in organised dance troupes.

In this case it is the connotations of the online as an immoral space that discourages some women from overt online activities. Those women who are active online make considerable use of the greater anonymity afforded by Chinese social media.[11] It was rare for women to use their own photographs as their avatars or in their QZone profiles, and many women followed the practice of 'locking' their QZone albums, typically with questions such as 'What is my name?' so that only contacts known to them personally would be able to view these images. In rural China online normativity is expressed through a reinvention of traditional relationships based on traditional ideals. Women and men publicly share material which portrays what they see as traditional family relationships, including pictures portraying children and parents or happy spouses, as well as memes with romantic messages. The QQ platform has become an important place to express these traditional family and romantic values, often seen to embody ideals inflected by Confucianism.

In the Italian field site too the limited visibility of women's figures in public spaces corresponds to a lack of visibility on social media. It is extremely unusual for married women to post photographs of themselves on Facebook, and they limit these to special occasions, such as birthday parties, family reunions or specific events with female friends. The lack of photographic images that portray their bodies is balanced by abundant images of domestic objects, internet memes, artistic photographs or pictures of their own children. In this case the transformations over the course of women's lives replicate the shifts in visibility for women in the offline spaces of the town. Married women, especially after becoming mothers, are expected to change the way they appear in public spaces and to stress their roles as wives and mothers. As a consequence on social media they do not overtly display images of themselves, as these can be interpreted as signs of flirting.

By comparison adult men and friendships between men are more visible in the public-facing social media. In addition adult men share typical content conventionally associated with masculinity, such as politics, news, powerful motorcycles and sports. They are also relatively creative in posting. For example, they might edit photographs in order to create personalised, meme-like posters or use a more diversified range of status updates. In contrast to women, men are willing to engage in self-derision online; for example, by using free online software to create avatars for themselves or by creating short stories in which they make fun of a specific situation in their life.

Another example of the way dominant gendered norms are reproduced and reinforced on the more public spaces of social media comes from our south Indian site. Here gender emerges as an element of traditional family roles, such as the behaviour of the new bride or the established mother-in-law. Families collectively put effort into the Facebook profiles of the individual family members, so that the overall effect is an outward-facing expression of a respectable, idealised family. The intention is to avoid any appearance of family disputes or disharmony, and maintaining gendered familial roles online is important to this representation. Public-facing social media platforms such as Facebook, Instagram or QQ provide a space for the conscious construction of appearance, performing the self[12] or, as in the south Indian case, the family. While certain posts may have specific individuals or groups in mind as their audience, public-facing social media also creates a sense of a more general public or an imagined generic audience.

The field site in northern Chile again confirms this observation that public-facing social media has reinforced gendered norms; here both women and men behave according to social expectations, presenting a limited representation of gender models. Haynes writes that the differentiation between men's and women's work often reinforces gender norms: men primarily work in mining, construction and ports, while women manage the home or work in customer service or caring professions. Men's pride in work is very often expressed on social media, portraying their work as a sacrifice of time to provide financial support for the family. In contrast women frame their labour as caring for the family, a role that can appear as the naturalisation of gender differentiation. Such representation at times suppresses individual variation and gender categories appear far neater than they are in the offline world – where plenty of women tune up their own cars and many men are quite adept at baking cakes.

A generic public is also the imagined audience of the visual postings that often dominate social media. The advantage of studying gender norms through social media is perhaps most apparent in our other comparative volume, *Visualising Facebook*.[13] This is partly because that book consists largely of visual posting, enabling readers quite literally to see what gender norms look like for different populations within the English and Trinidadian field sites. Researchers in every field site have looked through thousands of photographic images that people have posted online. As a result the main conventions and genres used for the portrayal of normative forms such as gender become particularly clear after a while, and are supported by considerable evidence. The point is that, as academics, we can now literally perceive cultural norms as the constant repetition of images – so also can the people whose images we are looking at.

In particular we can now 'see' how the reproduction of gender identities works, often through a series of contrasting associations. For example, in the English material there is a very common association made between males and beer. One is likely to see this association hundreds of times when browsing online postings. By contrast large numbers of postings create an equally strong link between women and wine. There is never any suggestion that there are different kinds of wine, or that women have any interest or expertise in these differences. A single generic category called 'wine' emerges, becoming the basis for many funny memes about how women are supposed to be doing this domestic labour or showing an interest in that activity, while actually just wanting to sit back with a glass of wine. Memes may simply express the fondness for wine as in 'my book club only reads wine labels' or 'I am never drinking again.... Oh look... wine.' Wine has given women something to apply symmetrically to male use of beer. Offline we would associate clothing as the means by which gender is dressed to conform, but online where, as here, drink becomes a kind of dressing, there are wider arenas of potential gender distinctions that can be rendered consistent.

The corresponding differences in Trinidadian visual postings are usually based more on gender as a physical dimension; female images relate to glamour, sexuality and the flesh, though masculinity is just as closely associated with dressing and accessories. Many men appear with what is called 'metal' – i.e. heavy gold chains, rings or armbands that supposedly indicate wealth as much as strength. In Trinidad gendered norms also intersect with class and ethnicity. For example, young Afro-Trinidadian men tend to subscribe to or play the 'gangsta' image from US hip-hop, posting images of themselves in sunglasses, low-slung jeans, branded clothing and 'bling'; Indo-Trinidadian men, on the other hand, emphasise their professional or vocational image on Facebook. Middle-class women commonly post around areas of lifestyle and consumption, and people of all ages tend to emphasise attractiveness in images of themselves – or at least they would never post an image in which they did not look attractive. This again strongly contrasts with English usage. There is no suggestion of any change or transformation in either male or female uses of these associations. They simply make the wider associated material culture of being masculine and feminine much more visible. If there is an additional component, it is the ability to make fun of these associations through other visuals such as memes. It is very common for women to find fault with and disparage the way another woman has chosen to present herself online, but then this seems to be just as common offline.

To conclude this section, we have found that in several of our field sites there is an association between the visibility of the more public-facing social media platforms and a conservatism in the portrayal of gender norms that in several cases exceeds that of offline conservatism. From a gender perspective one could describe public-facing social media such as Facebook as almost hyper-conservative. This seems to be clearly a reflection of the sheer degree of surveillance to which images on public-facing social media are subject. These then have largely become spaces in which individuals want to demonstrate, and to have confirmed, their adherence to cultural norms.

Discontinuities

We now turn to the ways in which social media has led to a break with offline gendered practices and norms. Disruptions of existing gendered norms by social media are more diversified between field sites, and elements shared across different sites are few. In addition the focus shifts from acts largely directed to the crafting of self-presentation on semi-public or public online spaces to the implications of social media as sites in which people interact, sometimes in more secluded online settings.

In southeast Turkey the impact of social media in changing gender relations is perhaps even more significant than its impact upon conformity. Social media has greatly extended women's opportunities for social relationships where these are limited in the offline world. In Mardin the presence of women in public spaces has already increased in the last decade, with more female access to education and job opportunities outside the home. However, many young women express the desire to have more opportunities to extend their social networks; they complain about not only the lack of social events, but also about the control parents or husbands exert over them. As they often have limited access to public spaces such as cafes, restaurants and streets, young women use social media to maintain social relations and widen their social networks outside of family control. In the case of women from more conservative and religious backgrounds, effectively house-bound because their fathers or husbands do not allow them to study, work or meet friends, social media becomes a pivotal tool for keeping in touch with the external world. While physically within the home they can still remain in touch with friends – quite commonly through the use of fake accounts that maintain anonymity.

As well as creating new spaces for women's autonomy, however, new opportunities have also emerged for men to control their female relatives, to flirt with and harass other women and to cheat on their wives. This ease with which strangers and friends of the opposite sex can engage in dialogue has also led to social media becoming the main place where courtship occurs and romantic relationships are lived. While the offline possibilities remain highly restricted, it is now very common for unmarried youths to find romance through the private messaging systems provided by WhatsApp, Facebook, Viber, Tango or via SMS.

In south Italy too social media has expanded opportunities for communication for women. Despite being less visible online, women tend to use social media such as WhatsApp and comments on Facebook more intensively than men, especially within lower income families. Once again it is the women with more restricted opportunities offline, for similar reasons of respectability, who make fullest use of social media as an important tool for communicating with an extended network of others. Men have more opportunities to engage in conversations and social events offline, often meeting in bars, streets and the *piazza*. By contrast women rarely stop and talk in the streets for fear they would look lazy. As we saw in the previous section, this extensive communication is balanced by the way in which these women simultaneously develop strategies to preserve their respectability as mothers and wives.

In rural China, as in southeast Turkey, social media has opened up new opportunities for interactions between women and men. In Chinese culture there has been a long tradition of 'female interiority', with women being historically confined to the domestic sphere. Although recent decades have brought greatly increased freedoms as well as participation in labour for women, they nonetheless remain strongly associated with the domestic sphere; men are expected to be more mobile. To take an extreme example, women are typically restricted to their home during the period of 'sitting the month' immediately following the birth of a child. As a result many women now use social media to maintain regular contact with friends by sharing baby photographs online.

At the same time social media has also enlarged men's social networks: their easier access to cars, for example, means that they can travel with greater ease than women. Many men frequently visit urban places and some use location-based friend-finding services such as Momo or WeChat's 'People Close by' to talk to strangers, typically of the opposite sex. Some men told McDonald that they had organised affairs via this channel with women living in bigger urban areas; and though the numbers were likely to be small, it was enough to provoke widespread concern among townsfolk over social media's impact on marriage. Men's activities on social media were also partly legitimated by an expectation that men ought to be more 'expansively social' than women, and to cultivate social connections with other men. As such they tended to be heavier users of social media applications, which helped to provide 'cover' for taboo activities.

In south India the situation is similar in some respects. It is relatively common to find some young women from higher castes and young men using social media to flirt, despite significant differences in social class and caste. The main effect of social media has been in allowing people to meet others from beyond the boundaries of their traditional social networks, expanding their contacts beyond the workplace and educational institutions. Venkatraman shows how young men in his field site friend women from other Indian states, or even foreign countries such as Brazil or the United States.

The general understanding is that, when men use Facebook, they would be able to friend women from around the world, which could lead either to flirting online or at least potentially romantic relationships offline. To achieve this these men generally lied about their social status, stating that they attend a prestigious university or are employed by a reputed company in the belief that such claims enhance their appeal. In the Indian field site, in common with those in southeast Turkey and rural China, this desire to experience new intimate and friendship relations propels both women and men into a far wider network of people. In these three different field sites social media has opened new, private channels of communication, changing the notion of love and redefining local notions of masculinity and femininity. Women's social networks have expanded, and in some cases those of men have expanded more.

In our Brazilian site social media seems to have contributed to more gender equality in several domains of social life. As a consequence of the expansion of communication technology, growth of the tourism industry and expansion of Protestant churches, women now have increased access to job opportunities and more public visibility. Spyer suggests that social media has contributed to a general movement towards the visibility of new and alternative feminine and masculine identities that involve both the online and the offline world simultaneously. Facebook profiles, for instance, are used to share images displaying one's pride over the independence gained by having a formal job. Work has become an alternative to remaining subordinate to men, to a point that regional businesses prefer to hire women as they are seen as more productive and responsible. Young women as a whole do not see family as being the only or the main objectives in their lives; having a career and earning money is perceived as being equally important.

A significant break with normative models of femininity and masculinity occurred in industrial China. Whereas in rural China more public social media are used to reinforce normative notions of romance and family, in industrial China, among factory workers, both women and men often publicly perform unconventional gendered selves. Social media in industrial China is a place where people may experiment with what they cannot be in their offline lives, operating partly as a shelter from the constraints oppressing people offline. In the industrial Chinese site social constraints governing public behaviour are less powerful and rigid than elsewheere. Here social media allows people to perform a desired fantasy world. Men appear to display a greater variation between their online and offline lives than women do. In their daily life they must respect clear masculine norms that do not include romanticism, sweetness and sensitivity; they have to be emotionally tough and resolute, and in the offline places of sociality, such as the dinner table, they talk about politics and make dirty jokes. By contrast, on social media they feel free to express their romanticism. They share the same posts about romantic love that are shared also by women. They also portray themselves as young women, and express quite un-masculine ideals. In doing so they resist the expectations that society has over them, although they would be afraid to lose face if they expressed similar sentiments offline.

With respect to women Wang describes how '*sajiao*' ('acting like a spoilt child') is a common strategy employed by young women to win men's affection in offline situations. It is also socially acceptable for women deliberately to craft themselves as dependent and vulnerable, emphasising their weakness and helplessness in order to extract attention, care or favours from others. What has changed is that online the visual postings of *sajiao* are popular among both female and male migrant workers. Male Chinese factory workers tend to live in particularly harsh conditions; in this context social media becomes a very important space where they are able to carve out alternative lives in a more desirable world. By contrast, there is more consistency for women between their online and offline world – in much as being seen to be publicly moral and respectable remains a priority in both domains.

Non-heteronormative sexualities

Not surprisingly social media has also had an impact on LGBT populations. In more cosmopolitan urban areas digital media has been used by LGBT activists to engage in organised politics, leading to gay identities becoming more visible. In the Brazilian field site social media has contributed to a general process of increasing the visibility of LGBT people, part of a wider process facilitated by social media that has made individual and group peculiarity more visible. In the context of a town such as Mardin, however, social media has simply facilitated the ability to meet. In places such as southeast Turkey, where being openly gay is socially unacceptable, social media has created more opportunities for secret interactions among men. Gay identities have not become more visible and public, but homosexual encounters may now be secretly arranged more easily.

In north Chile, where non-normative sexual practices are somewhat more accepted, social media are sometimes used to proclaim such identities, for example on Instagram with selfies labelled as #instagay or #instalesbian. Grindr is also a popular app among men searching for same-sex partners (whether for romantic or purely sexual encounters), though primarily among more affluent men in the larger city of Iquique. Gay men and lesbians seem to have their presence on social media accepted as long as they perform in gender normative ways, for example remaining closely associated with their natal families and taking on work considered appropriate for their gender; in such cases they report experiencing little discrimination. However, those who act outside of gender norms experience disapproval. As a result individuals such as men who perform in drag create fake social media profiles for such pursuits – as one man put it, 'so as not to worry my mother'.

Of course, as the examples of southeast Turkey and north Chile make clear, the visibility of social media posts impacts on what types of information may be revealed. Similarly in the English field site a gay, middle-aged male constantly posts overtly sexual and sometimes deliberately outrageous images on his Facebook, while a young lesbian never explicitly refers to sexuality, although her relationships with women may be inferred from her pictures. Here men's ease with a more public representation of sexuality and women's relatively less explicit representations continue to follow gendered norms. Not only does this illustrate the range of visibility with which different people are comfortable, it also shows the ways in which more traditional gender roles continue to impact upon men and women's social media usage, even as they identify as LGBT.[14]

Conclusion

In this chapter we have explored when and where social media has reinforced, disrupted or simply shifted systems of gender relations and gender norms. The examples here demonstrate that the internet, and digital technologies more generally, are not inherently transformative or conservative. Instead they exist only through variable social practice. If, as this book argues, the world has changed social media, then one example is the way in which different gender relations, and different ideas of what it means to be a man or woman, have been inscribed upon social media. Cultural expectations for men and women in Turkey and Trinidad could hardly be more different from each other. There are occasions, such as the period leading up to Carnival, when women in Trinidad try to display as much flesh as possible within the context of a flamboyant sexuality, accompanied by the hyper-masculinity of Trinidadian men's 'gangsta' style. By contrast some religious women in southeast Turkey take huge precautions to prevent the visibility of flesh, or even a single visible body hair. In each case there is considerable internal variation. The same field sites included a wide range of different concerns over respectability, given that they both also include secular, ethnically diverse people and a wide spectrum of religiosity, for example, Pentecostalism in Trinidad. In other places, such as our south Italian or rural Chinese site, the main differences emerge through the course of life events, with women radically transforming their online portrayals following marriage or the birth of a child.

However, we did not limit our analysis to the observation of how social media reproduces gender relations. The unique opportunity of comparing nine different field sites allowed us to identify and highlight common patterns and to make anthropological generalisations. We found that the more public-facing social media in almost all our field sites (with the exception of industrial China and to a certain extent Brazil) have reinforced gendered normativity and are often more conservative than offline gendered sociality. By contrast in offline contexts women and men tend to perform more varied practices and roles, sometimes embodying both masculine and feminine aspects, on social media they tend to adhere more strictly to societal expectations on how they should behave. More public spaces of social media, such as Facebook or QZone, have created extraordinarily conservative spaces where women and men become especially concerned with meeting gendered ideals. In this regard the public-facing parts of social media emerge as the antithesis of the use of the internet prior to the development of these platforms, when it was welcomed as a liberating space by feminist theorists. Though 'online' may refer to both these previous internet and current social media spaces, their consequences for gender have been starkly different.

Yet, because social media are a configuration of different forms of scalable socialities, they also include smaller and more private groups where women and men are less concerned with following appropriate behaviours. These include platforms such as WhatsApp or private messaging on other platforms. Men and women also find ways to create the conditions for anonymised interactions. It is precisely these opportunities to create new and atypical social relations that have led to a disruption of existing gender relations and gender roles. One of the most significant consequences of social media may be that women living in the most restricted conditions can now, for the first time, find ways to create personal online relationships with people they would previously have not been able to encounter. This is why, in conclusion, it is important to understand social media as scalable sociality; this concept allows us to understand how social media can be simultaneously both more conservative and more liberating than life offline.

9
Inequality

As one might expect, there is a considerable interest in the capacity of the internet and social media to produce large-scale social change. Yet the question as to whether internet access and social media have improved the plight of the world's most disadvantaged populations or have rather exacerbated inequalities continues and is far from resolved. As previous chapters have pointed out, social media has had an important impact on education, work and gender relations, all of which are major components of this wider question. Several of our field sites represent low income and disadvantaged populations. Here we examine the ways in which social media may impact on people who do not have easy access to digital resources, and how their use may be a mode of change – or, conversely, how it may sustain their current social positions.

The number of people using digital communication has increased dramatically since the launch of commercial access to the internet in the mid-1990s. And it is not just the rich, cosmopolitan and educated; the current combination of mobile technology and social media has created a strong interest among various socially underprivileged populations, including illiterate or semi-literate people, low-wage manual migrant workers and migrants in places such as China, India and Brazil.[1]

As with all the chapters of this book the evidence will be presented from our long-term ethnographic engagement with nine different populations. We see that in each place inequality exists and is expressed in different ways, depending upon historical processes and current political and social structures. Drawing comparisons, therefore, is not always straightforward. In every site the disparities of income and wealth, as well as of social status, are associated with other forms of social difference including gender, age, education, religion and racial inequalities. Groups in every field site have a perception of their own social position that is largely relative to others in the same society, rather than set against some abstract scale.

What is inequality?

If we contend that inequality exists in a variety of forms, what exactly do we mean when we ask if social media affects inequality? Certainly one form of inequality is wealth distribution and poverty. We often think of the most disadvantaged people as living in slums, with no possibilities of work and without hope for a brighter future. Yet economic inequalities are often co-constituted with phenomena such as racism, lack of political representation and poor access both to physical resources, such as drinkable water or electricity, and more abstract resources such as education. In some of our field sites people are not necessarily impoverished, but lack political power. In others a cursory perusal of their belongings, which might include flat screen televisions and new Samsung[2] mobile phones, obscures the fact that they at times cannot pay their electricity bill. In other instances inequalities simply mean that certain parts of the population are discriminated against in terms of accessing resources, based on characteristics such as race or religion.[3]

Bourdieu outlined three different types of inequality corresponding to different types of 'capital'. Economic capital generally refers to access to money. Social capital describes the social relationships and institutionalised networks of which an individual is a part. Cultural capital includes knowledge or skills gained through education, cultural goods and qualifications. Each of these types of capital is influenced by the others, and Bourdieu's main concern is how they are used by elite groups to reproduce privilege.

Related to inequality is the concept of social mobility, which refers to the ability of an individual or group to improve their social position. Again this may take a number of forms, from better work opportunities to educational resources so that children will have better prospects in the future. Social mobility is not just about having more money, but about showing it in the right ways; in essence performing as part of a particular social class. This may mean buying the 'right' brands, owning the 'right' appliances, sending children to the 'right' schools or even dressing in a way that conforms to the norms of that social class. What is 'right' is upheld through discourses on taste and 'distinction',[4] which are often given a moral value.[5] This often requires either turning economic capital into social and cultural capital or indeed finding ways to acquire the latter in the absence of economic capital. Media technology has become one primary way in which some less privileged people may be able to access resources such as information previously only available to those with more privilege. It is thus no surprise that the internet may be posited as a tool for social mobility.

As a result facilitating access to new media is understood to have become basic to modern development and to helping people find a 'voice'.[6] People who do not have internet access miss out on possible resources that they could access online. Without the internet they may experience new and further barriers to improving their access to economic, social and cultural capital, while the rest of society is able to gain greater resources through its access to new technology. This lack of access therefore emerges as a force able to exacerbate and widen prior forms of inequality. Yet internet access does not automatically translate into greater access to information and resources.[7] In fact our field sites have shown that prior discourses of distinction and difference continue to influence, to a large extent, the particular ways people use the internet and social media, often reflective of social class. Furthermore it is entirely possible that the extraordinary spread of smartphones and social media does in and of itself represent a form of greater equality, but without that necessarily having any impact on inequality offline.

Approaches to social media and inequality: the positive, the negative and the grounded[8]

The relevant literature can largely be divided into two – almost entirely opposed – camps. The first argues that social media is bound to introduce greater inequality in society through concentrating educational and networking resources among those who are already privileged. Alternatively the 'techno-utopian' approach sees social media as a panacea for problems of inequality, giving disadvantaged people access to greater resources through the internet.

Literature falling within the category of 'digital divide' is often informed by notions that new ICTs exacerbate pre-existing inequalities in societies: poorer individuals are excluded, while wealthier persons are provided better access. Early studies, which focused on access to the internet itself rather than social media, were conducted largely in developed countries; they emphasised that, although the vast majority of people had internet access, an important minority either completely lacked or had sub-standard connections. Often the constraints that prevented people from benefiting from online communication were dictated by factors such as age, household income, educational achievement, English level, disability and rural/urban location.[9]

As internet access has improved and social media and other online resources have become increasingly available, scholars are suggesting that other kinds of divides are emerging. Much depends on the different forms of access, and the specifics of local context, which impacted upon how people used these technologies.[10] It has been proposed that the 'network divide' has a greater impact than the 'digital divide', and that the key distinction is now whether people are able to acquire the skills needed successfully to cultivate their social networks online.[11] This transformation has been informed by an increasing stress on 'digital literacies' by some scholars, emphasising that mastering the use of these networks has become as important as merely being able to access them (as discussed in Chapter 5).[12] Finally there are approaches that look more to systematic global inequalities. Even if individuals have both access and skills, there remain huge imbalances between the amount of content available in different languages or produced in areas of the world such as Latin America, Africa and India.[13]

Notwithstanding these issues of inequalities of access mentioned above, techno-utopian discourses claim the internet represents egalitarianism, freedom of speech and democracy.[14] These works portray social media as a tool that can be used to consolidate collective power against powerful institutions, often represented through the polarity of 'individual against government' or 'consumer against corporation'. These discourses therefore suggest that social networking acts as a kind of empowerment, promoting civil protagonism that challenges systems that produce inequalities.[15]

As demonstrated in the previous chapter on gender, early internet commentators wondered whether the online virtual communities that emerged during the 1990s would stimulate equality by allowing people free reign to create imaginative online identities that were independent from their own bodies. Such a concept equally has implications for inequalities based on other aspects of identity, for example age, race, wealth or class.[16] An associated question is whether, given the potential for online anonymity, social relations could exist apart from differences based in the body or other 'offline' circumstances, instead appreciating the online domain as a new, independent space in which the mind may be allowed to roam free of these prior constraints.[17] This question is a key component of the previous chapter on gender.

Less evident in both of these categories of literature, and of greater significance to our project, has been the way that inequality itself may mean different things to different people. A growing number of scholars have called for a move away from work that assumes social media must have either a good or bad effect on inequality, calling instead for approaches that consider the complex, nuanced and often contradictory range of effects that social media has on the 'messy reality' of people's lives.[18] More grounded, ethnographic approaches to internet use by teens in the US suggest that many of the problems young people face online remain rooted in long-running social and racial inequalities.[19] For instance, a study tracing the migration of educated, white, middle-class American teens from MySpace to Facebook compared the growing perception of Facebook as offering greater safety than MySpace to 'white flight' (a phenomenon in which affluent whites move to suburbs, away from the non-white population living in urban centres).[20] Another study conducted in the US looks at how social media use may exacerbate class differences, as under-privileged parents exercise greater control over their children's social media use to balance the risks that these young people face by living in less affluent neighbourhoods.[21] Our own project has endeavoured alongside others[22] to broaden the scope of these enquiries, and in particular to use comparison of the inequality found *within* each of our field sites with that found *between* these different field sites.

The diversity of difference

In our field sites in Brazil and rural China many individuals have high aspirations for social mobility connected to education. In our rural Chinese field site in particular, education is seen to be the key to future social mobility. Yet our work also acts as a caution in generalising this familiar observation about education in China, since evidence from our industrial Chinese site shows how the migration of similar rural workers into the factory sector has created a class of hundreds of millions who may now see education as of little value, recognising that they are destined to enter the factory work force at a young age. Social media is, however, used for sharing self-help tips on QQ, particularly tips related to financial success, which were very frequently shared. In general social media was seen as a place for enhanced cooperation, providing a place to share information related to work opportunities or non-traditional education.

In Brazil lowpaid manual workers have aspirations to use education as a foundation for social mobility, but the actual quality of local education available in the town was generally quite poor. These low income populations of young people use social media as a valuable alternative educational resource. Educational YouTube videos that taught job skills, such as Microsoft Word, were popular and often quite effective as a resource for young people hoping to find jobs that would allow them to achieve their desired social mobility. Although it is not the main object of our enquiry, we found in several of our sites that it would be hard to exaggerate the increasing importance of YouTube, in particular, as a mode for informal education.

In Brazil and in both our Chinese field sites the ability to access these resources also gave people a sense of self-esteem, as this technology evoked a feeling of moving from a 'backwards' lifestyle towards 'modernity'. In all three sites informants saw the digital domain as providing a degree of emancipation – not just allowing them to have the same smartphones as members of wealthier classes, but also giving them a degree of control over their self-presentations. Such control allowed them to craft an appearance more closely approximating to whom they now perceived themselves to be.

Yet opportunities for self-presentation are not always considered advantageous. In the Italian field site, where unemployment among all groups is high, we have seen in Chapter 6 how young people with degrees from prominent universities use social media to demonstrate skills that can help them obtain jobs. For young people from less affluent backgrounds, however, social media can often present unwelcome pressures to craft a public self-image. These young people often attend schools that focus on professional skills, for instance plumbing, mechanics or secretarial skills, and are encouraged to start working as soon as possible to contribute to the household income. For them being on social media can feel like a burden akin to a social obligation – for example going to a posh wedding where one has to dress up – thus making them more self-conscious of their lower social position. Here it is the parents who encourage their children to create Facebook accounts, since they worry that the lack of such a presence may expose their position of inequality. For these underprivileged Italians, therefore, being on social media is often an obligation they would prefer to avoid. Already, then, we can see quite profound differences among the basic relationships between social media and the aspiration for social mobility.

Making visible social mobility

The control over presentation that was important to Brazilians and Chinese factory workers reflects the sense that in modern life who one can be depends increasingly upon who one *appears* to be. For this one needs a good knowledge of the prevailing attitudes to good taste, reflecting back to the earlier comment upon how people try to turn economic capital into social and cultural capital. In Brazil attaining social visibility for newly enhanced material wealth and other signs of achievement allowed those from disadvantaged groups to claim entrée into new communities. The implication is that social media has shifted social status still further in the direction of visibility; today it is simply easier and more common actually to see people, at least online.

Sandra's wedding is an example of this process. Sandra, an Afro-descended Brazilian, was given up by her parents to work as a domestic servant when she was five years old. This practice of 'dar os filhos'[23] ('giving their children') was common among the poorer families in the region, particularly those of African descent.[24] In doing so the parents ensure that the child will be fed, dressed and sometimes sent to school while they acquire working practice and skills, such as domestic expertise for girls. Unfortunately, as was common in such circumstances, Sandra and her sisters were exposed to physical, emotional and sexual abuse.[25] However, Sandra regards one outcome of the experience as positive – her introduction to evangelical Christianity.

Christianity gave Sandra an incentive to learn to read, so that she could understand the Bible. Later through church connections she found a job as a part-time salesperson at the local Christian bookstore in the village. This informal job pays only half the minimum wage and does not include benefits, but she is able to use the store's computer during quieter hours to play online games and watch Christian movies on YouTube. Sandra's primary concern at this point, considering she feels she has done her share of hard work in life, is not for greater economic capital; rather she desires a form of cultural capital that has value within her specific church community.

When Sandra was planning her wedding, she saw it as an important way to gain full membership in the evangelical community. Evangelical Christians in the Brazilian field site are often among the most prosperous local families. With the financial help of friends and family, her ceremony included decorations equal to those seen on wedding programmes on television: flowers, fruits, colourful cloth and fancy illumination, a proper wedding dress and party food for over 300 guests. With such fanfare she successfully portrayed herself as a socially mobile individual and part of the evangelical community.

In addition her family asserted their own form of social mobility by selecting many of the official photographs of the wedding to be displayed on her sister's Facebook account. This provided a week-long opportunity for all guests to find themselves on the images and comment eloquently on how wonderful the event was. In essence both Sandra and her wedding guests were able to access a form of cultural capital through planning, attending and then reminiscing and representing the event through photographs on social media. Just as young people in the Brazilian field site would rather take a selfie at the gym or swimming pool than against a plain brick wall, Sandra and her guests knew that *portraying* themselves as socially mobile was just as important as actually being able to afford fancy wedding decorations or a gym membership. This is because of the way different forms of capital, such as economic resources, taste and social connections, work in conjunction, giving a natural appearance to the fact that some people have more privileges than others.

A key lesson from the example of Sandra is that we cannot assume the emphasis on visibility is to be interpreted as a new form of superficiality that comes with social media and its focus upon appearance. In this case the key driving force is the fundamental principles of Protestant Christianity, which centuries before social media argued that it was only through outward appearance that an individual could establish whether they were among the 'saved', which is the primary aspiration for this branch of Christianity.[26] Such principles were also behind the drive for upward social mobility through hard work and wealth. Zuckerberg may have provided the means, but Calvin devised the cause.

The limits to social media's impact on social mobility

While visually portraying upward mobility in the Brazilian field site is important, the mere photographic evidence of goods considered to be in good taste does not grant access to elite class membership in all contexts. Anthropologists encounter many strategies for social mobility that fail, while class differences are reproduced through everyday actions, often unknowingly.[27] These same everyday discourses of taste are used to maintain inequality among groups with similar levels of wealth: certain tastes are denigrated as vulgar, kitsch or unsophisticated[28] in strictures often associated with race, religion, region, urban/rural divides or even a sense of 'old' versus 'new' class identities (i.e. the new middle class vs. the old middle class). As much as people in Trinidad make more use of Facebook's visibility to make claims to wealth others find creative and humorous ways to ridicule their attempts as simply vulgar and unsophisticated. Denigration of taste when going through other people's Facebook accounts is a substantial part of Trinidadian entertainment today.

We can see these limits by returning to the case of Sandra. Her ability to use social media to create a new visual identity making clear what she has now achieved worked with respect to the main part of this field site that comprised the lower income population. However, there is also a new, gentrified part of the village, a touristic ocean front resort area, only about one kilometre away from the core of the village where low-paid manual workers such as Sandra live. Despite this proximity the daily contact between these two worlds happens almost exclusively as a consequence of labour relations: one group works for the other. Wealthier employers, both online and offline, tend to stay in contact only with those who share the same class background and thus sense of taste. They see their values as contrasting with those of the employed villagers, whom they describe as loud, uncultured and either overly sexualised or overly religious.

These social distances, which developed from centuries of slave-based work in that region, remain naturalised and unquestioned. Only recently have these wealthier residents even recognised that social media is equally popular among the low-paid families in the region, but they have no desire to friend the domestic workers they employ. Online these affluent locals may share among themselves progressive political and social views, but this rarely results in transcending the social boundaries between them and their less well-off neighbours. Instead they voice concerns about ecology, often complaining that problematic low income settlements negatively affect the environment or require heightened policing to prevent crime. Social media may therefore have changed the social position of Sandra relative to her peers, but it will have made no impact upon this wider social chasm between her part of the village and where the employers reside.

Similarly in Italy many elite social media users become involved in progressive political activism through Twitter or Facebook, demonstrating their sympathy for left-wing positions. As in Brazil, however, this rarely connects to any practical actions that would reduce inequality in their own village. In Italy 'caring about the poor' is a culture in and of itself that is easy to express on social media, but which may have very little to do with actual impoverished people in the local area. Their welfare is left to state organisations and the church.

In the same manner that 'caring about the poor' signals a certain class position in Italy and Brazil, portraying oneself as cosmopolitan or international achieves a similar goal in other field sites. In the south

Indian field site traditional social divisions were rigidly retained and policed online, particularly through the content that people shared. On Facebook wealthier locals share articles, often in English and produced by international media outlets such as *The Guardian* or *The New York Times*. Both the college-educated IT executives and the traditional villagers from lower castes have a keen interest in local cinema, politics and cricket. However, only the content related to cricket is equally likely to be found on the timelines of the more and less affluent. News about politics and cinema are differentiated according to caste and class, so that the affluent post about international art films and Hollywood while lower income people post clips of Tamil movies. The main impact of social media is the extended use of claims to cosmopolitanism which exacerbate prior social differences.

In the Trinidadian field site young female professionals in their early 20s with university degrees also share images on social media that display global influences. These images include fancy cuisine served in high-class restaurants and photographs of international holidays.[29] Other references include the content of fashion bloggers and YouTube 'vloggers'[30] based in the US, UK and Singapore. These online resources help them to forge a sense of cosmopolitanism based on exchanging references to global trends in beauty, consumption and lifestyle. Social media posts make still more visible the differential access that these individuals have to such international experiences. This same higher class tries to avoid online forums that discuss sexual relationships and romance, a key interest and practice for lower income Trinidadians. Instead they post material about being close to one's family, sustaining a long-lasting marriage and the companionship that can be gained from a partner. Social boundaries are also made explicit by the online use of derogatory expressions, for example 'ghetto' refers to people who display attributes such as loudness, lack of taste and limited formal education, all associated with lower income Afro-Trinidadians. In the case of Trinidad, however, we also find considerable evidence for how lower income groups contest these attempts to maintain separation through the manipulation of taste. Many humorous and ironic phrases and gestures on social media are explicitly aimed at puncturing the pretentions and claims made by those who think they are more sophisticated.

Trinidad has always had a powerful undercurrent of egalitarian pressure, which has its own weapons in this fight. If social media favours a visibility that allows the wealthier to portray their sophistication, it has also become a key site for humour, memes and entertainment. One of the most common versions of these is a vast array of fun material aimed at disparaging the pretentions of these same cosmopolitans and mocking the 'arrogance' of those who appear to 'think they are better than everyone else'. This is the flip side to the previously mentioned entertainment that the elite gain from disparaging the vulgarity of their social inferiors.

The Chilean field site, situated in the north of the country, is characterised by a certain kind of inequality. The region is quite rich in mineral resources, which are translated into a great deal of wealth for elite classes in the country as a whole. However, most people in the specific city of the field site are low-paid manual labourers, who do not receive a great deal of financial benefits from the mines that extract the minerals. While steady work is readily available in the mines, and pays more than other work options, local people still regard themselves as marginalised and exploited by the international companies and the national government who extract most of the benefits.

This was another site where some people would display pictures on social media of luxury goods, brand name clothing or vacations in order to make visible their new wealth. Yet this disrupts the wider solidarity of the local region[31] that is defined in relation to the country as a whole. As a result such people were portrayed as selfish for not sharing their wealth and foolish for spending their money unwisely – or even gossiped about for having possible connections to the drug trade. It was suggested that people who are too quick to display wealth would really be better off in a larger city, where those around them valued material goods over community mindedness. They could thereby become excluded through social boundaries constructed around an ideology of mutual benefit and solidarity.

A more successful use of social media than flaunting individual wealth is as a method of connecting with others through humour. From disenfranchisement in politics to frustrations with not being able to pay one's phone bill or buy a special meal such as sushi, memes, photographs and text on Facebook often fall into the genre of 'it's funny how poor I am'. Even the relatively well-off residents of Alto Hospicio post this genre of comic memes and texts about how funny it is to be poor, recognising this wider solidarity based on the idea that no one is privileged in the grand scheme of things. This in turn means cultivating a certain type of pride in their collective marginality.

Though these complaints are usually aimed simply at making the local audience laugh, in April 2014 an earthquake of 8.2 Richter magnitude struck the region and the intended audience changed.

During the weeks and even months that followed the earthquake, social media – primarily Facebook and Instagram – became spaces to draw attention to the plight of those affected and highlight the lack of assistance offered by the national government. In particular more than 4000 families were left without homes; they lived in tents for almost two months before the governmental natural disaster relief agency provided them with temporary housing. During this time social media posts turned outward from the usual in-community form of sociality in order to draw attention to the victims' plight, and thus pressure the national government to provide resources.

Conclusion

As shown in our review of the literature, we have to be careful about what we mean by inequality and how it is generalised. We also have to differentiate two potential consequences of access to social media: the equality that this represents in its own right and its potential subsequent impact on wider forms of inequality. In one sense our evidence is that social media has created a form of equality. The possession of a smartphone and access to social media by a vast population of low income people in places such as Brazil, China and India does represent a profound change in their lives. They now have devices of extraordinary sophistication, often identical to those used by the wealthy. There are many examples described throughout this book which show how they are thereby enabled to do much that was not previously possible. So it would be quite wrong to deny or ignore this form of equality. Yet the main concern of this chapter has been a more difficult question: what is the consequence of this online equality for offline inequality? What most of the examples have shown is that possession of a smartphone and access or even skill with social media is absolutely no guarantee of any change at all in inequality offline; it may lessen, but equally may increase.

This is one of the chapters that most clearly justifies our choice of title for this volume. Instead of just considering the way in which social media changes the world, our emphasis has been on the way the world has diversified social media. As it has become increasingly embedded in our lives, it comes to reflect the cultural diversity of our world. More specifically we see that the relationship between social media and social mobility is extremely different when viewed across all nine field sites.

This more fully reflects the prior literature on this topic, which was also found to contain a huge variety of positions from extremely optimistic to highly pessimistic. So in a way our conclusion is to support this broad range within the literature, but to then suggest that rather than encountering it as a fight between global generalisations as to an assumed overall impact, it would be better to recognise that most of these stances on the impact of social media on equality may be appropriate, but to different regions and populations.

One of the simplest examples of how the world changed social media occurs in the case of south India. Here highly rigid and hierarchical social structures that have developed over many centuries in turn colonised these new media and made them reflect such distinctions. Social media has an impact mainly though laying greater emphasis on differential claims to cosmopolitanism, which can be supported by acts of sharing international materials found online. This increased emphasis upon cosmopolitanism is found in most of our field sites, where it generally exacerbates prior inequalities. A similar problem develops in our Italian field site. Here social media is perceived as an oppressive obligation to take part in something that is bound to make one still more conscious of one's lower position in society. In all of these cases social media makes inequality more visible and entrenched.

However, when we turned to the relations between social media, education and social mobility we found some extremely different cases. As noted in Chapter 5, the attention to the role of social media with respect to a high commitment to formal education in rural China is very different from the use of social media in informal education. This may be because people do not care much about formal education, which is the case in industrial China, or because they cannot get access to a decent quality of formal education, as in the Brazilian site. The use of social media as a resource within informal education is probably the most important additional component noted in the first section, which helps people to struggle against inequality.

Over much of the chapter we saw a tension between two of the most commonly observed properties of social media. The first of these is the increase in visibility that it accords, but the second, arguably equally important, is the use of social media as a site for humour and ironic disparagement. In the case of Sandra and Brazil we found that visibility can change one's social position by demonstrating one's respectability, and thus be an instrument of social mobility. Yet equally we discovered the limits to this process, since neither of these goals are achieved with respect to a larger social distinction that includes employers as well as employees. Indeed the use of social media to express concern about the poor is found to be one of the key boundaries that separate the wealthy from the poor.

In both Trinidad and Chile we saw people's use of visibility to try and portray cosmopolitanism and wealth countered by the use of humour to prick these bubbles of pretentiousness and advance a more egalitarian agenda. However, in the final case of Chile we also saw that, as previously in our Brazilian case, much depends on whether one's focus zooms into, or takes a wide-angle perspective on, the larger landscape. When the people of this locality consider themselves in respect to the larger country, as they were forced to do by an earthquake, internal divisions become less important than their bigger relationship to the nation or to the international contexts in which they all live.

To conclude, this chapter has shown the difficulty in making claims respecting the impact of social media on inequality. We clearly do not wish to add to such inequality by failing to respect the different ways in which people in each site understand and experience social difference. At the same time there is another equally important sensitivity that consists of not conflating equality of access with any assumed consequences, since one of our most general observations is that the vast increase in access to social media is no guarantee in and of itself of any change in other forms of social inequality.

10
Politics

In academic discussion there is an entirely reasonable concern with the degree to which social media is transforming politics – understood as institutions of governance and debates and conflicts over those institutions. In an ethnographic study, however, we do not privilege this as a focus of research. Instead we try and demote politics merely to that which actually emerges from observations of the social media used by our informants. If you look for political debate you will find it, but that does not allow you to assess it fairly as an element of ordinary people's lives in particular locations. Indeed our opening case study reveals that in the field site most dominated by political conflict politics may, for that very reason, not dominate social media.

Mardin, in southeast Turkey, has had a long history of political conflict and violence. Close to the Syrian border, the various ethnic, linguistic and religious groups who live in the town have clashed on many occasions. For Costa, who had a particular interest in political engagement in the region, Mardin was an obvious choice of field site. However, she found that the people of Mardin refrained from discussing politics and other sensitive topics openly or in public spaces. They mainly spoke about politics in their private homes, with family and close friends who shared their opinions and values. On social media, and Facebook in particular, there were few references to politics, especially local politics. During the heated campaigns leading up to local elections in March 2014 some supporters did break their silence and joined public gatherings in solidarity with their political party. But even then on Facebook very few people shared posts on their own timelines. At the most a few followed the pages of local politicians and 'liked' some of their posts.

Facebook is primarily used for maintaining good relationships with friends and relatives, so public silence on local political issues is important for peaceful coexistence both online and offline. Such political activity as there is on social media is usually at a national level and is conducted mainly by supporters of the current government, since people are aware of state surveillance online. These government supporters may express solidarity towards the ruling AKP and the prime minister, Recep Tayyip Erdoğan. During the Gezi Park protests in the spring and summer of 2013 AKP supporters shared memes, videos and news that reproduced state propaganda and discredited activists, facilitated by the government's active engagement with social media. In September 2013 the AKP was allegedly able to recruit over 6000 social media users to influence public opinion.[1]

Outside of local politics, the Kurdish population of Mardin do use Facebook to express solidarity towards Kurds in Syria and Iraq, especially in their struggles against the so-called Islamic State (IS). As long as the political issue was outside of Turkey they felt free to be extremely active on social media in support of Kurdish people living in these neighbouring countries. Many changed their profile image to the word *Rojava* ('West'), referring to the free Kurdish region in north Syria. When Islamic State (IS) occupied Sinjar in Kurdish Iraq, the Kurdish population in Mardin used Facebook to show support and organise a collection of funds, clothes and goods to distribute to the Yezidi refugees who had arrived in the town. Similarly when IS occupied Kobane in Rojava many Kurds in Mardin posted memes, images and news stories in solidarity with the population under siege. Although they found the Turkish state complicit in these advances, they again refrained from posting material directly condemning the state's role. In general, therefore, social media reinforces the prior conditions of politics in the town, including the absence of debate over local politics and the suppression of opposition views, but facilitates the expression of Kurdish solidarity with Kurds in other countries.

The immense literature available on the internet and politics, and more specifically on politics and social media, has changed over time. It began with a focus upon the role of the internet in new social movements in the 1990s,[2] and was followed by the problem of digital divides and e-governance,[3] the role of Web 2.0 platforms and user-generated content.[4] Most recent studies have considered the consequences of the affordances of WiFi and mobile media such as smartphones, particularly regarding their role in organising collective political activity.[5] Chadwick and Howard present an excellent volume on the critical debates about the relationship between the internet, state politics and citizenship, while Postill concisely summarises key research in digital politics and the ways in which ethnographic inquiry contributes to understanding the ecologies of protest movements.[6] In the early 2000s there was a distinct sense of optimism around e-governance and e-government, and the potential they offered for bridging the digital divide.[7] The internet and social networking sites were seen to be transforming 'the public sphere', a concept associated with social theorist Jurgen Habermas.[8] More recently attention has been turned to the role of social media in organising political action, particularly in the various regional experiences of the Arab Spring.[9] This was in a sense the turning point in such studies, prompted by Morozov's work on the use of digital technologies for political repression during these events. Since then there has been a growing body of research critical of assumptions that the main role of digital technologies is to increase meaningful democratic participation.[10] However, there is also considerable interest in the use of new media as the basis for alternative forms of collective action, for example research by the anthropologist Coleman on Anonymous and other online political activists.[11]

As an anthropological study this chapter views politics as that which is regarded as 'political' by our informants across the nine sites, rather than applying any given definition in relation to the democratic process, civil society or governance.[12] The same would be true of political participation. Most researchers with an interest in politics are drawn to situations seen to be significant in political terms or with a high degree of political activity, especially that which may have resulted from the use of social media.[13] By contrast, with the exception of Costa's selection of Mardin, all of our field sites were chosen precisely because they were 'ordinary'. As a result we could judge the degree of actual political activity outside of the bias created by the selection of sites for the express purpose of political study.

Our main finding has been the wide diversity in the way the various meanings of 'politics' are interwoven with social media across the nine sites, though in general our research shows social media as having less of an impact than would be inferred from the prior literature.[14] However, we would argue that this is a highly significant finding, since it is just as important to ascertain the degree to which social media is involved in politics for ordinary people in more typical circumstances as it is to study the role of social media in more politically charged moments and places.

As we have noted in places such as Mardin, social media generally reflects the strategies of political debate and silence that were developed in the offline world. Commonly we worked in sites where most people's engagement with politics is limited and often indirect. There are a variety of reasons why offline political debate may not be reproduced online. These include feelings of indifference, disillusionment or apathy, or not wanting to be seen by others as 'being political'. In addition people in our south Italian field site mainly expressed disenchantment towards the corruption of national politicians. In the English field site they mainly engaged with politics as a source of humour, while in the Trinidadian field site people were attracted to political issues mainly when they involved spectacle and scandal.

Notwithstanding this diversity in how people engage with politics over social media, our research did lead to a generalised conclusion that seems to apply across all of our nine sites. Political participation over social media in small, medium-sized and semi-urban towns is hugely influenced by social relations in these relatively small places. Informants were concerned with maintaining or strengthening relations with their social media contacts, and did not want to risk damaging friendships or relationships with extended family or work colleagues. Even in countries such as Turkey and China, where the state more explicitly and more systematically controls social media uses, it is not only this control *per se* that mainly influences political expression. Rather it is the way in which the state's power is manifested through social norms that govern the relationships between individuals.[15] As such this chapter identifies three issues: how social relationships impose norms that play out over social media; how state surveillance and national politics permeate discussion and in different ways come to include the way people express themselves on social media; and how, as a consequence of these two forces, political participation generally takes different forms on social media.

The concern with social relations makes social media a conservative place

In common with the arguments made in the previous chapter with respect to gender, personal political views in public (or semi-public) spaces such as Facebook are expressed in a manner that protects people's social relationships and their personal reputations. The exceptions would be small minorities who identify with being political activists, for example militant university students or members of local political parties, but these represent a small minority in our sites. Otherwise social media is largely used in an attempt to increase one's social status or popularity, affiliate with groups who are viewed as prestigious or simply maintain good relations with others. The same observation could be made about offline daily interactions, as people tend to be wary of discussing politics with those who have radically different points of view, and of challenging those in their social circles with different political positions. Noelle-Neumann coined the term the 'spiral of silence' to describe this phenomenon, and people's fear that politics might lead to them becoming isolated or ostracised.[16] This is especially clear on social media because of its enhanced visibility. Instead social media becomes a space for expressing shared ideas and values.

For example, in our field site in south Italy, although it is common to be friends with politicians from different political groups, individuals are extremely cautious about engaging with politics on such a visible space as Facebook. It would be highly unusual to 'like', comment on or share any political post regarding a local politician. It is the local politicians themselves who readily share any kind of positive publicity in the local media and construct long status updates to describe any achievements in the local council. Instead of engaging with these, other people use social media to direct criticism towards public figures that represent 'Europe', the 'state' and the 'region', or to refer to general issues upon which everybody they know agrees, such as unemployment, government inefficiency and corruption.

The situation is similar in the south Indian field site. Social media users rarely post serious content relating to local politics which would be viewed by their peers, and might in fact provoke a negative reaction from these same local politicians. Instead criticism about the state of local politics and governance takes place within private conversations. The only people who are politically active on social media are those who work for local political parties; their posts are clearly intended to gain support through highlighting some positive event or action. Such posts attract 'likes' and comments only from close friends and other party workers. Most of these activists belong to a lower socio-economic class or live in rural areas, and their posts would rarely be seen by the new middle and upper-middle classes in urban areas. Otherwise there was very little engagement with local politics on Facebook. Posts around politics at the national or state level, which were seen as expressing a more general political opinion, were more common.

In both the south Indian and the Brazilian field sites there is a genuine fear of direct negative consequences for oneself and one's family should members of rival parties feel antagonised. Along with this exists a commensurate concern to maintain good relationships with local political leaders and parties. Another factor might be situations where relatives were working for different politicians and parties, making people concerned that posting about local political issues might have repercussions for those relatives. In August 2014, during the Brazilian electoral campaigns, publicity vehicles travelled through several villages, airing slogans and jingles of each politician over loudspeakers. Groups of people reacted to their presence with brief conversation, but there was no online political commentary other than to express support for or criticism of parties at the state or national level.

In rural China this trend takes a different form. The acceptable topic of politics is corruption, also the most pressing issue for residents in the area. Rather than expressing their opinions openly online, however, those affected attempt to remedy their own situations by discreetly approaching individuals who they believe may have more power and influence. If this avenue is unsuccessful, people might consider petitioning at a higher level, but they almost never air their grievances or express their frustrations on social media platforms. When the issue of corruption does appear online, it is about corruption in other towns or in other parts of the country.

All of this means that public-facing social media has generally become a highly conservative place, reflecting prevailing values and social norms that rule relations between people at the local level. If anything, politics online is exploited as a source of comedy for increasing popularity among friends or to create new, useful social connections. This is particularly evident in the English field site, where political discussion on social media largely takes the form of online banter between friends. Serious memes and comments are mainly found either among the highest income groups who favour green issues or among the lowest income groups who live in social housing and promote nationalist causes such as supporting the army or banning immigrants. Apart from these the predominant mode is humour at the expense of politicians. Politics on social media is mainly useful for the purposes of entertainment and bonding with friends.

Finally the field site in industrial China provides a variation on this theme of personal relationships. There are examples here of social media being used with the intention of strategically strengthening 'guanxi' ('instrumental relationships'). Factory owners' WeChat profiles show that people choose not to post anything about politics to avoid placing themselves in potentially difficult situations. Instead they sometimes use social media to cultivate relationships with local government officials, in the hope that these friendships will help them to maintain good connections with the government for the potential benefit of their businesses.

State surveillance and national politics

Concern for social relations has prevented those living in most of our field sites from disagreeing over, discussing or expressing political opinions, especially with regard to local politics. This section considers another force that shapes political participation on social media, making these online spaces radically different from the Habermasian model of the 'public sphere' – a place where people can freely discuss common matters and interests with the aim of reaching common agreement.[17] In China and Turkey the state exercises control over the uses of social media and the content that can be accessed over the internet. State surveillance is a powerful force that has influenced how the semi-public spaces of social media are used.

In the two Chinese field sites there was no evidence of an overall concern with state censorship of social media. The central government's control over the internet has been not only far-reaching but also remarkably precise and subtle, compared to the direct coercion of, and constraints placed upon, citizens. As a result of the history of local media and its position in respect to other parts of life, residents in the sites simply do not conceive of social media as an appropriate or potential place for discussing politics and criticising the central government. Instead they view social media platforms such as QQ and WeChat as places of entertainment for having fun, creating new relationships and strengthening old ones. These perceptions are common to both our industrial and rural Chinese sites.

This lack of critique towards the government or any other kind of political engagement online appears more significant when compared with people's strong interest in discussing political issues offline: intense debate often takes place over dinner or tea. The power of the Chinese state is also expressed in the usage of social media for propaganda purposes, through the delivery of news stories that often follow or reproduce the official party line on different issues. Both QQ and WeChat deliver three news reports a day, produced by the social media companies themselves. There is a general perception that this news is useful, although there is also a critical awareness of the news stories' bias towards the state. State propaganda also becomes embodied and reproduced by social media users, as seen in the abundance of nationalist postings such as those displaying anti-Japanese sentiment or admiration towards central party leaders.

As a result there is no need for specific acts of coercion. The researchers in China did not come across any instances of repression or constraint in the uses of social media in their respective sites. There were a few cases of individual criticism towards the central government in the industrial China field site, but these did not result in any repercussions such as a direct ban on the account or other punitive measures. These examples thus support the findings of previous studies, which argue that censorship in China is mainly directed at preventing any collective action rather than supressing individual criticism.[18]

Outside the more overtly political sphere, McDonald observed other cases of everyday resistance through the circumvention of government-imposed restrictions. For example, throughout China, a ban prohibits youth under the age of 18 from using internet cafés, with users required to show a national ID card before logging on. However, at the only internet café in the field site the manager kept a supply of spare ID cards (borrowed from friends and extended family) for underage users to borrow in order to log on. These underage users were typically accommodated in two 'secret' rooms in the back of the café, away from the street and as such out of view of other townsfolk and inspectors. Despite only two per cent of middle school children surveyed identifying the internet café as their main place of internet use, these schoolchildren still seemed to be the most common type of customer in the café.

In southeast Turkey Kurds and left-leaning dissidents have suffered the consequences of state-sanctioned violence on several recent occasions. During the 1980s and 1990s imprisonment and torture, disappearance and murders were experienced by political activists, and other forms of suppression, for example the prohibition of speaking in Kurdish, were part of daily life. Today sympathisers with the Kurdish movement[19] are reluctant openly and publically to criticise a state that is clearly willing to use violence against them. In this context internet censorship is another expression of the state's power and violence, and so shapes the uses of social media.

Unlike the Chinese examples the inhabitants of Mardin have also often been the direct target of bans and blocks: pages on Facebook supporting what at that time was the Kurdish Peace and Democracy Party (BDP) have in some cases been closed; in addition some people have been charged with defamation for their criticism of powerful figures. Government opponents generally feel the pressure of being watched and being under surveillance. As we have seen this has led to a suppression of open political discussion online, even as it has previously been repressed offline. Social media leads to an interweaving of the social and political fabric, to the extent that state surveillance overlaps with – and is reinforced by – the social surveillance of friends, acquaintances or family members.

Local issues in political participation

This chapter began with the discussion of Mardin. There we saw that in places that have the most political tensions, actual posting on social media is highly constrained and careful. This section describes other forms of political engagement over social media. As with so much of this study, we will see how it is local factors that are paramount. Yet these examples also conform to our broader generalisation that the use of social media is carefully controlled, so as not to damage individual social relations and personal reputations.

We have seen how in the English field site humour about politics is really mostly designed to entertain friends and show how clever or funny the individual is. Similarly in the south Indian field site the most popular way to engage with politics over social media is through humour and sarcasm. As noted at the start of this chapter, direct political comment is rare. However, trolling (derogatory or insulting postings aimed at an individual) Tamil political personalities is common from those between the ages of 20 and 45, appearing on Facebook timelines and WhatsApp conversations. Such posts are directed with care, mostly at Tamil politicians who are not too powerful, and most onlookers would find these trolls funny because of their sarcastic tone. Yet the same people who might circulate these types of posts also distance themselves from trolls that are especially hurtful or use foul language to make a point – such users are perceived as taking the joke too far.

Only anonymity allows people to express themselves more directly on particularly sensitive issues. Several anonymous trolls on You Tube use offensive language and show little respect towards politicians. Some IT workers from the Indian field site comment on very sensitive issues, for instance Christian conversion of Hindus, Islamic terrorism or criticism of Pakistan, but mostly under fake user names to avoid being identified by other people. For example Sandeep, a 24-year-old employee of a small IT app development company, does not miss a chance to leave a sarcastic comment about Pakistan and its link with Islamic terrorism using one of his six fake accounts. However, he is very serious about taking care not to disclose his real identity.

The Trinidadian field site provides another example of how a political event played out online. Sinanan describes a hunger strike by the activist Dr Wayne Kublalsingh, a lecturer at the University of the West Indies, St Augustine, Trinidad. Kublalsingh was the leader of an activist group, the Highway Re-route Movement (HRM), protesting about the construction of a section of a highway in the south of the country. Beginning in 2006, a group of residents in the area had tried and failed in requesting information and consultation from the state government over what they perceived to be their unfair relocation. When construction commenced in the disputed area, Kublalsingh embarked on a hunger strike in front of the prime minister's office. It lasted for 21 days. His aim was to force the government to reconsider its decision to build this section of the highway. Although construction has continued, Kublalsingh's actions were successful to the degree that an independent inquiry was conducted and subsequently published.

The HRM, the activist group behind Kublalsingh, had an active Facebook page that received hundreds of comments during the hunger strike. Some were funny and others contained serious discussion, but most were by people who did not otherwise identify themselves as being 'activists'. Kublalsingh's own strategy was to draw attention to the issue through the spectacular act of the hunger strike. His concern was to promote public discussion, regardless of whether people agreed with him or not. The hunger strike was also a media event, where posts and photographs of Kublalsingh's deteriorating body were displayed on both social and mainstream media. People thereby became not only embroiled in the unfolding drama, but also more exposed to the issues of development and governance surrounding the implementation of the highway as a large-scale state project. After the prime minister agreed to reassess the decision to construct this section of the highway and Kublalsingh ended his hunger strike, these conversations largely died down among the general public – although activists circles continued to post updates on Facebook, blogs and independent online platforms.

If, however, we examine this event through the local lens of our Trinidadian field site, people barely engaged with the issue on social media other than through a few jokes and memes, even though they were happy to express their views in everyday conversations. This case illustrates two points about political participation and social media in Trinidad. Firstly, although conversations around the important issues of governance and development were raised, they were largely overshadowed by the spectacle of the hunger strike itself. It is characteristic of politics in Trinidad that what resonated with people was the display of the body following from Kublalsingh's decision to mount a hunger strike and the performance of people associated with this event, rather than any engagement with the deeper issues being contested.[20] Secondly the case showed that for people in a small town activism and visible political participation is something with which most people would rather not associate themselves. Conversations and banter about politics are fine, but 'being political', as reflected in a serious comment on social media, is not. People from the town are concerned to avoid being considered a political activist, a role that they perceive as belonging to urban elites, university students or artistic circles. The point is similar to that made about humour in England. Issues of scandal, gossip or things that make for visible spectacles are enjoyed and resonate, so these are the aspects of the political event that actually find their way into local social media. The contrast is with domains such as morality and religion, where people do commonly share serious memes.

To understand the situation in our field site in Chile we need again to consider what we mean by politics. So far we have talked about whether people engage with or avoid issues of local politics or national politics, but in this instance the core political issue was the construction of something that could be regarded as the local, as distinct from the national. As previously noted, residents in the area feel that the region (which only became part of Chile in the nineteenth century) is exploited for its natural resources, which sustain the entire country's economy, and yet they are neglected by the government. Most people feel alienated from expressions of the nation as a political entity. Yet Haynes notes that these northerners are intensely proud of being 'culturally Chilean' when it comes to cheering for the national football team, preparing traditional Chilean food and drink, or even when discussing economic or social rivalries with neighbouring countries. Even the slang used online is uniquely Chilean, and hard to decipher by other Spanish speakers. Social media in particular becomes a place to claim Chileanness through cultural and linguistic references while simultaneously criticising the national government and asserting a regionalism founded in marginality, using funny memes. This field site represents our clearest instance of social media as an instrument for bringing together the inhabitants of a town that has struggled to achieve more visibility within the nation.

Another common trait of political participation on social media is what can be called 'passive participation', referring to the tendency to criticise things in a more resigned way. In industrial China local middle-class men, for example the owners of small shops, used social media to make fun of politics and to make innocent jokes about politicians, in an attempt to appear funny and smart in front of their peers. In a similar way to 'older' media, social media was mainly used by ordinary people to 'watch' politics, even as spectators watch a football match, rather than to 'do' politics. As in the English and Trinidadian examples, the key to social media's relationship with politics is that it is seen as a source of entertainment. Politics, like sport, is something that provides a common spectacle that people can exploit where and when they choose.

The same principle can apply to serious as well as humorous usage. In south Italy social media became the place where people expressed frustration and anger about politics generally, issues upon which most people agree. It is not that Facebook is being used to protest or initiate change in the current situation, despite many sharing hard feelings about the state of contemporary politics. Instead people use social media to criticise a well-known issue that many feel they are unable to change. As with humour, therefore, being engaged with politics does not amount to 'doing' politics, but rather to *using* politics for local purposes as a source of common discourse and often to express frustrations ('*stogare*'). The advantage of politics is that, as with sport or celebrities, it offers a shared common culture.

Conclusion

The purpose of this chapter has been to explore how and why social media may be engaged with politics in field sites chosen primarily for reasons that have nothing to do with politics. We hoped this would balance the majority of discussions on this subject based on research in places where politics was of particular significance. In general we have found that, if one turns to ordinary field sites, politics on social media has a much lower profile than we might otherwise have expected. In some cases this may be because it is suppressed, leading to a highly conservative representation of people's lives and opinions online. In other cases, however, it is because social media is more associated with entertainment and social bonding than with serious issues such as politics.

These observations can be summarised as three main findings which equate to the three sections of this chapter. Firstly personal relationships are the key influence that shapes online political engagement and action. People's primary concern is how their postings will impact upon their family and friendships. In several of our field sites people felt that expressing political views and opinions could result in antagonism or conflict; as a result politics remains invisible and discussion is reserved for private spaces among one's closest friends and family. It is only in places where people use fake and anonymised profiles that direct political comment is common. We do, however, have many instances of indirect political comment, for instance in south India and China comments are on national rather than local issues.

Secondly social norms, media genres and boundaries of acceptability are also influential in determining whether individuals enter political discussion or not. For example, we found that in our Chinese sites direct repression of individual politics was absent and perhaps not even required. More important was the historical development of social media that meant these sites were seen as naturally places for entertainment and friendship; political engagement would seem inappropriate to such media.

In our third section the emphasis was more on local factors: the way in which politics tends to be seen within the context of spectacle in Trinidad or as a means for creating local identity in opposition to national politics in our Chilean site. In another instance, for example the English site, people simply feel it is more useful to employ politics as a source of humour than to become seriously involved. This brings us back to our initial and most general point, which is that social media is most often a mode of small-scale group interaction and sociality. For most people, therefore, it makes more sense to exploit politics to enhance social media rather than to use social media to 'do' politics.

11
Visual images

Angela is 23 years old and lives in the Trinidadian field site. Her father owns an office supplies shop where she works most days. During quiet times she scrolls through her Facebook timeline on her BlackBerry. She also posts two to three times a day, starting with a greeting such as 'Good morning peeps!' Sometimes she gives an insight into what is happening in her life: 'Even thou still smile, ppl do not no how much they hurt u.' The posts that attract the most 'likes' and comments, however – around 20 'likes' – are when she posts a genre of memes that Sinanan terms 'inspirational': religious verses or motivational sayings with a scenic or animated background. When Angela is bored and experiments with hair and make-up and posts a selfie, she can attract more than a hundred 'likes'. From the perspective of her friends, Angela's visual postings are by far the most communicative.

In many of our field sites, posting on social media is overwhelmingly visual. The growing popularity of platforms such as Instagram and Snapchat has shown that social media can work effectively where the core content is photographic and text is relatively peripheral or – as in Snapchat (the clue is in the name) – what we have previously thought of as conversation can be almost entirely visual.[1] It is also possible to populate WhatsApp with baby photographs and Facebook with selfies and memes.

The visual aspects of social media have been a constant theme throughout the previous chapters. In the chapters on gender and on politics they helped to explain why public-facing social media is generally highly conservative. We have also seen the use of social media photographic images in relation to class position and social aspiration. In our Brazilian and Trinidadian field sites categories of social class are commonly claimed visually through association with branded goods. A young man may post images of himself together with bottles of expensive liqueurs and designer sunglasses. However, his audience would not necessarily accept this as a demonstration of actual wealth or status. Research participants generally assumed that people seek to show the best or idealised versions of themselves to their peers, at least on the most public platforms.

There are several stages to our analysis. We may start by exploring how a person tries to use visual associations to influence others in deciding who – and specifically how socially 'upmarket' – they might be. We then need to consider how others respond to that, however, and above all how such actions relate to norms in that society regarding what are or are not appropriate ways to present oneself – what we call normative behaviour. Since this is a comparative study the analysis will in turn reveal how what is taken as normative in one society compares with that in others. All of this would be true for visual analysis prior to social media, but there may also be shifts and unprecedented elements in the latter. For example, we shall see how memes in particular now provide clear insights not only into what is regarded as normative, but also how people strive to control the normative in online worlds.

In some respects, however, the situation we encountered in this project was profoundly different from the domain of traditional visual anthropology. While in the past anthropologists might even have given cameras to populations in order to study how they would employ them, camera phones have been common within most of our field sites for about a decade. People are now very used to photographing and displaying what is important to them, as well as things that might have previously been too unimportant to merit a photograph. Social media is also about much more than simply posting one's photographs. People are now much more used to reworking them, using filters on Instagram, adding their own text overlays and sharing, recirculating and reconstructing the images that constitute memes as well.

Social media has given photography an unprecedented ubiquity as part of daily life. Where having a photograph taken was once a kind of mini event, dozens of images can now flow within a few minutes as an ongoing conversation. Furthermore, with the spread of smartphones a vast population of low income households all around the world have now become daily photographers. We start with two essential claims. The first is that the vast majority of all photography today now is social media photography. The second is that our relationship to visual images has reached a level of ubiquity that is historically unprecedented. While our emphasis is on photography, most recently we are witnessing another rapid expansion in short video clips, including both postings on WhatsApp and also shares from YouTube.

A variety of different approaches to visual images and photography have arisen within anthropology. Several of these consider the relationships between the image as a form of representation and the peoples who have produced them. Examples of the way anthropologists have studied photography include Ginsburg, MacDougall, Sprague and, for overviews, Edwards and Pinney.[2] Visual anthropology has also long been concerned with the visual systems of particular societies.[3]

Other approaches highlight the role of the ethnographer as representing the society they work in through film or photography.[4] In a project based on nine field sites we have to be just as concerned with issues of cultural difference as with how images relate to social relations in general – but our primary aim is to determine the role of the visual component of social media. This chapter begins with a brief discussion of the treatment of visual material generally within anthropology before focusing upon the more specific question of visual social media. Themes include self-presentation, increasingly accessible communication and the role of the visual in creating scalable sociality. These issues are also explored in Chapter 3 of our respective monographs and the volume dedicated to the comparison of visual postings in England and Trinidad.[5] One of the questions posed by that comparative volume is what kind of ethnography would emerge if the focus was almost entirely on what we learn from these visual postings – compared to what we know from more conventional offline ethnography. The point is that our ability now to view thousands of images of everyday life makes visual analysis a hugely significant part of ethnographic enquiry.

Self-presentation

While it is a popular perception that the rise of online self-presentation has created a more artificial or overly constructed relationship to self-expression, as Sherry Turkle[6] points out in her earlier writings, humans have in fact always lived within roles and frames. We may think of online postings as curated or even performed for an audience, but it is also important to note that, at least since the time of Erving Goffman, academics have understood that individuals are always constructing, performing and presenting themselves consciously in particular ways. This would be very obvious in studies of clothing, for example. Indeed it is entirely possible that some people will feel they can appear more natural online, where they are engaged within their own peer groups, independent from some offline interactions that made them more self-conscious (for example, meeting an anthropologist).

The selfie is often criticised as merely a form of narcissism.[7] In fact selfies may also be viewed as an important genre for better understanding issues of identity, aspiration and social expectations. Certainly in taking selfies individuals actively craft the impressions they hope to give, making such images a significant form of self-expression.[8] The term narcissism, however, suggests an orientation towards the self, whereas selfies are mostly used in relation to specific audiences and to maintain social relationships.[9] For example, in our English field site young people posted on Facebook five times as many selfies featuring groups than they did images of individuals. Furthermore, as an element within social media, selfies, alongside other photographs, are more engaged in acts of sharing and circulation. Both in terms of content and of what happens to them, selfies may represent a more socialised and less individually focused activity than traditional photography – almost the opposite of what is commonly claimed.[10] This circulation of images reinforces sharing current experiences, as well as sharing memory.[11]

In comparing the material presented in the respective third chapters of each of our monographs, we found that, while it is a common observation that people may want to create 'idealised' versions of themselves through the images they post, these all relate to particular social and historical contexts.[12] In particular it seems that both the terms 'aspiration' and 'idealised selves' mean quite different things across the field sites. In industrial China posts of future aspirations around consumption dominate – hardly surprising, given a population of migrant factory workers who see this work as a stage towards obtaining wealth. Creating fantasies of consumption, young men post images of cars, beautiful women and branded clothing, while young women post princess-style bedrooms. For youth in particular posting these images shows a fantastic world that contrasts with lives mostly spent in factory work. Visual images also allow them to convey emotions, when they might not feel especially confident or articulate either in textual posting or speaking.

By contrast in our rural Chinese field site economic aspirations intersect with conservative traditions. Posts of babies at significant milestones are a dominant genre, including a tradition in which parents spend a substantial amount of money on studio photographs. These photographs, especially those taken after the baby's first hundred days, also reference a child's debt to their parents and the obligation that children are expected to have towards their parents later in life. Along with posts

(a)

(b)

Fig. 11.1 Images of fantasies of consumption posted on QQ

(c)

Fig. 11.1 *Continued*

concerning babies, posts about love and marriage emphasise the importance of enduring relationships as the foundation of family life, while others express affection and gratitude, ostensibly towards parents. Although the primary focus is on traditional values, social media photography is also starting to express individual aspirations – for romance expressed in the relationships of couples, for instance, or for young people's autonomy from their parents.

In the cases of Brazil and Trinidad achieving greater social visibility is an aspiration in itself and appears predominantly on Facebook. In the Brazilian field site social media parallels the church as a space that gives visibility to new wealth or the aspiration to it. The story of Sandra in Chapter 9 is relevant here. Evangelical Christians believe that wealth achieved through hard work represents one of the public virtues of a person; they consequently embrace a visible materialism as a sign of religiosity, not of superficiality. In Trinidad people see the cultivation of external appearance as a testimony of the truth of that person reflecting their actual labour, rather than viewing this as a distortion of a natural, authentic self. People therefore take considerable effort to create images showing their commitment to this craft of beautification, again reflecting the idea that appearance is profound.

In southern Italy the visibility of a person on public social media is heavily intertwined with social position. People perceived to be higher in the local social hierarchy post more photographs of themselves than

(a)

(b)

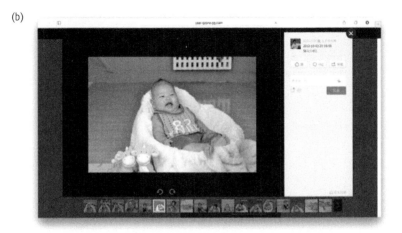

Fig. 11.2 Images of babies taken at professional studios and posted by parents on QQ

those at lower levels. Nicolescu argues that this phenomenon is related to older traditions of visibility for those in the upper levels of Italian society. Yet this tradition is challenged by the new tendency for teenagers and young people to post selfies on Facebook. Young women spend hours staging a 'good' selfie. They select from multiple photographs they have taken, edit them online and finally upload one as a profile picture. This passion for self-expression online decreases with marriage. After this Italian women post less about themselves and more about their family, including children's accomplishments and scenes of different family gatherings.

Fig. 11.3 Selfies posted on Facebook by young Trinidadian women

(c)

Fig. 11.3 *Continued*

Curating how one appears on Facebook was also important in our south Indian field site. Here it was viewed in terms of building a personal identity, often as part of a claim to status associated with one's work. Several people posted images of themselves in work outfits or in apparently professional settings, even though their actual work was something entirely different from what these visual images implied. In all of these cases, therefore, we can say that people use visual images to express aspirations, but we can now see that the nature of those aspirations is quite local and specific.

In some cases the normative rules of self-presentation are not about looking your best, but simply about presenting the self in line with social expectations. This emerged very clearly in the contexts of northern Chile and the English village field sites; here it is the prevalence of a simple ordinariness that is most striking in the posting of images. Typical selfies in northern Chile, even for young people, are usually taken in their home or a friend's, at work or during a brief outing; they do not give the sense of much glamour. Teens and young adults often post several pictures a day, usually of mundane items such as new gym shoes, breakfast, their freshly washed car, selfies taken at school or work and photo collages made with another app, all giving a sense of the everyday monotony of life and often including hashtags such as #bored #aburrido or #fome.[13] A few photographs even express the ultimate boredom: waiting in line while running errands.

One common version of the selfie is the foot photo, or 'footie', almost always taken in a lounging position while watching television or playing a video game. Not only does this give the viewer a sense of the mundane life that they wished to capture; it also demonstrates the fact that it is simply not necessary to pose. The 'footie' is so casual that the photographer does not even have to move from their resting position.

(a)
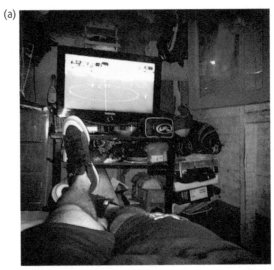

(b)
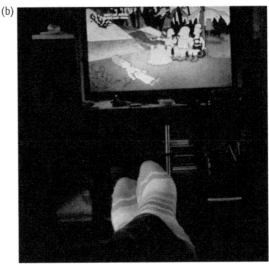

Fig. 11.4 'Footies' posted by young Chileans

In southern Italy the same genre appears, but is almost always taken on the coast or with the feet directed towards the sea. Here the 'footie' symbolises the presence of the individual within the spectacle and beauty of nature. The vast majority of postings by adults in the English village seem to display no attempt to have dressed or prepared oneself for the image. Social media photography seems to be associated with the decline of make-up and the ubiquity of clothes such as jeans and T-shirts as a landscape of unpretentious modesty. Indeed adults in the village usually only started posting selfies when an apparently charitable cause based on posting 'no make-up selfies' helped them to create a distance from the prevalent association between the selfie and narcissism.

There are elements of both continuity and change here compared to prior uses of analogue photography. In Bourdieu's study of peasant photography in France in the 1960s he noted that the most common photographs captured are from weddings and social festivities – yet these images were mainly kept in boxes, with only a few formal wedding photographs on display in the home.[14] He argues that these types of photographs are 'sociograms', providing visual records of social roles and relations. Such ceremonies are deemed to be worth photographing because they lie outside everyday routine. They also solemnise and materialise these 'climactic moments of social life' wherein the group reasserts its unity.[15]

By contrast most social media photography is now mundane, and on sites such as WhatsApp is related more to transience than to memory. However, we can also find examples of continuity, for example when Facebook is used today as the place to record occasions that are either special in some way or celebrations. The photograph has also now been associated with the greeting card. People acknowledge relationships through sending and sharing photographs, but also send greeting-style memes on special occasions, especially in Trinidad and south India. Diwali, Christmas and New Year holidays, birthdays and a graduation are all events where traditionally one might have sent a card in Trinidad; such occasions are now often marked by circulating images on Facebook.

In our south Indian field site, in addition to special occasions, everyday greetings are posted – almost ritualistically, as the common belief, based on the Hindu concept of karma, is that positivity must be shared with a person's social networks to balance the negativity that

Fig. 11.5 Holiday greetings shared by Trinidadians on Facebook

also exists around them. These posts are usually words on a plain background or with a scenic image, accompanied by a status that reads 'Good morning', 'Have a grt…dy' or 'Have a good day'.

Social media does not just represent a shift towards ubiquitous visual images. In some cases this results in people today posting up to hundreds of photographs of themselves that were previously kept strictly outside of the public gaze. This may represent a major shift not only in personal photography, but also in how people understand their social relations. We see this in our field site in southeast Turkey. Here, prior to social media, photographs were intended to be private, with the exception of formal portraits or wedding photography displayed in the home or carefully stored in albums. Images kept in boxes were more informal and featured family members dressed more casually, as images

(a) Gud afternoon friends — with

Share

1 share

(b) Gud even.

காதல்
சொல்ல முடியாத ககம்
விழுங்க முடியாத அமுதம்
மறக்க முடியாத கனவு

கனவு மெய்பட வேண்டும்...

👍 Like   💬 Comment

20 people like this.

Write a comment...

Press Enter to post.

Fig. 11.6 Afternoon and evening greetings circulated on Facebook in Tamil Nadu

were only circulated among those within the house – effectively in limited and controlled situations. With Facebook, however, ordinary family events such as lunches and dinners have become much more important as visible events. Yet because of the limits and local conventions around making photographs of people public, many Facebook users started to find ways that allow them still to express their attachment to other people and the quality of time spent together, but without focusing too much on people's faces. As a result at family reunions they prefer to photograph different dishes served throughout the evening and tables set up beforehand. In this way they have responded to the new possibilities of circulation, but, mindful of traditional concerns with privacy, they have taken the precaution of lowering the gaze from the face to the food.

(a)

Fig. 11.7 Images of food taken at family gatherings in southeast Turkey

Fig. 11.7 *Continued*

Increasingly accessible and moral communication

One relatively clear-cut result of online communication becoming more visual is that communication is also more accessible to those with lower levels of literacy. Just as comic books invited those with poor literacy to read more, visual aspects of social media encourage similar groups to become more digitally active.[16] In the Brazilian field site adults wanted to be active on social media just as much as the younger population. This was not so much because they wanted to keep up with the trends of young people. It was rather because being on social media was a way of showing themselves as more outward-looking and worldly, possessing enough income to afford a smartphone and competent and confident with new technologies – all things that connote 'being modern'. The level of literacy has changed rapidly among poorer Brazilians in the last two decades. Around one-third of the population over the age of 50 is illiterate, compared to only two per cent of teenagers.[17] While younger people may see social media as space where they can craft their own image away from the gaze of adults, increasingly adults too want simply to socialise in the same space, among their own peers.

Adults with a lower level of literacy still use Facebook, more for circulating content rather than posting their own. 'Liking' was the most common activity, although people still made shorter, abbreviated comments, such as 'kkkkk', the equivalent of 'lol'. Although this group did not post as many personal statuses, through sharing memes, images and videos they can still express their opinions, values and taste. Memes therefore become more important as a mode of expression for those less articulate or who have less confidence in putting their own words out into a public space.

In the south Indian field site the symbols within Facebook, for example the thumbs up for 'liking' and the arrow for sharing, also allowed young men with lower levels of literacy to participate. As in our Brazilian field site the shares were mostly images, memes and video clips. Simply being able to 'like' the posts of others gave these users more confidence to be socially present online. Although literacy levels in the industrial Chinese field site were higher, several low-educated groups also used visuals on social media as a form of expression. For the rural migrant population in the factory town, young people in particular shared images edited by others with motivational or sentimental wording and picturesque imagery. Some accompanied their shared images with a few words of their own, such

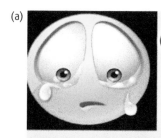

(a)

Quantas vezes eu fui para o culto assim...

Lá DEUS falou comigo, e eu saí assim!!!

Pastora Patrícia

(b)

SE EU QUISESSE AGRADAR TODO MUNDO EU NÃO FARIA UM PERFIL NO FACEBOOK. FARIA UM CHURRASCO.

Fig. 11.8 Memes circulated on Facebook in northeast Brazil: 'I went to church many times like this . . . there God spoke to me and I left like this!!!' and 'If I wanted to please everybody I wouldn't make a Facebook profile, I'd make a barbeque'

as 'wo' (I), implying that the image is expressing what the person thinks or is experiencing.

For more educated populations images are used in expanding the range of subjects and experiences communicated. The most popular genre of memes in southern Italy relates to more abstract ideas and ideals that people would not necessarily want to articulate through text,

我

暖男 枣：

爱的人，把眼泪留给，最疼我的人，把微笑，留给伤过我的人。

评论(2)　　转发　　赞　　收藏　　...

Fig. 11.9   This post on QQ reads: 'I will leave my tears for those who really love me, and leave a smile for those who once hurt me.' The person who has shared it has commented 'wo' – 'I' in Mandarin – at the top of the post

for example when criticising the state of politics. More generally memes create an indirect way of reflecting upon society that does not transgress any social norm, in contrast to a verbal post in which people are constrained by social positioning.

Memes circulate as a mode of both moralising and humour; as such they are a way of reinforcing social norms. In northern Chile memes often portrayed acceptance of, or even pride in, ordinary life. Key examples included a Kermit the Frog genre ('*la Rana Rene*' in Spanish) expressing sentiments such as 'Sometimes I'd like to have a really big house. Then I remember I don't like to sweep and I get over it'. Others contrasted the 'expected' – pictures of fit, tanned bodies, shiny new cars or gourmet meals – with the 'reality' of overweight bodies, rusted-out trucks and a burned dinner.

Joking provides a safe and popular way for people to express their preferences for the style of life they feel comfortable with, as well as a critique of those who would look down on them.[18] Trinidad provided its own appropriation of the Kermit meme, taken from a television advertisement for Lipton tea.[19] In the advertisement Kermit is sitting in a café watching the chaos of a New York City street from inside. He sips calmly on his cup of tea and says the catch phrase 'But that's none of my business'. In the memes that appeared in the Trinidad field site the catchphrase was used to point out what another person or group was doing. Quite serious critical comments might circulate under the guise of this humour. Given the common usage of memes in this manner across our various field sites, there seems to be a case for regarding memes more generally as a kind of 'internet police', attempting to assert moral control through social media.

Fig. 11.10 Kermit memes posted to Facebook in the Chilean site: 'Sometimes I'd like to go far away, but then I remember I don't even have enough to cover a ticket and I get over it' and 'Sometimes I'd like to quit working. Then I remember I don't have anybody to support me and I get over it'

(a) You Be Lurking On My Page
Cause You Miss Me But Thats
None Of My Business...

(b) dudes be like "these hoes ain't
loyal" but have a wifey, 4 side
chicks and 2 "friends"... but
that's none of my business

Fig. 11.11 Kermit memes circulated on Facebook in Trinidad

Scalable sociality

There are precedents to the way in which social media circulates images, building on the prior spread of camera phones and digital images more generally. These have been widely studied in other disciplines such as HCI (Human Computer Interaction) and STS (Science and Technology Studies). Ito, who conducted an ethnographic study on the uses of camera phones in Japan, describes this pervasive photo-sharing as 'intimate visual co-presence': a new form of social awareness and exchange of perceptions and perspectives.[20] Similar suggestions have been made regarding the spread of camera phones and photo-sharing platforms more generally,[21] also returning to the earlier theme of how these are used in the maintenance of social relations.[22]

Lindtner et al. and others have noted that visual images are shared with a variety of different kinds of 'public'.[23] For example, when friends see what the friends of their friends have posted then the sense that 'this is aimed for me to see' goes beyond the prior relationship between these people. Many people now have several networks that might previously have been separated out, for example friends, family and work colleagues, all now congregating on the open-plan space of Facebook. One way in which people deal with the condition of 'context collapse'[24] is through posting images with references comprehensible to some of the viewers but not others. As noted in Chapter 1, scalable sociality can be constructed within a given platform in this manner, and not just by mapping different social groups across different platforms.

Although the intention is to confirm an in-group within the audience, this still leaves the remaining presence on the platform of what might be termed the 'overhearers' – those who do not interact with the person posting, and are not the intended audience, but who take meaning from what they see nonetheless.[25] When people are participating in multiple publics simultaneously it should come as no surprise that, as a result, there is always a problem of images being seen as appropriate by some and not others. We have seen that in each context people find ways to deal with this. In some cases this involves scalable sociality, as for example in Trinidad, by using content unintelligible to some. Or, as in our south Italian field site, many people choose to post anything that could be considered inappropriate on more intimate platforms, for example WhatsApp. Instead of scalable sociality we found that in southeast Turkey people increasingly tend to post photographs of food instead of people at events so that no one is excluded. Sometimes, however, these strategies for keeping postings within intended audiences fail and the context collapse simply exposes inappropriate images to inappropriate audiences. The most obvious example of unintended exposure is the circulation of sexualised images, originally taken and shared as private messages in the context of intimate relationships. In south India there is a phenomenon around leaked photographs of women from their mobile phones. Women do not post these images themselves; rather the men to whom they were sent betray this trust by uploading them online. As a result women are becoming increasingly vigilant in ensuring that their phones are locked and always within close proximity; they also make sure that their partners take similar precautions in securing their phones. Finally women rarely post photographs of themselves alone, but instead pose for and upload group pictures. They also post images with symbolic value, such as the heroine from a movie or another pop culture icon, here employed as a representation of themselves.

The phenomenon known as 'revenge porn' was noticed in Trinidad some time before this term was invented to describe the widespread development of the deliberate leaking of intimate material after a relationship has ended. In English schools and elsewhere there was a short phase in the development of Snapchat during which users did not realise images could easily be screen-captured. As a result some young girls shared images that they later came to regret.

This inadvertent leakage of images is not confined to sexual content and nudity. For example, similar problems arise when a post intended for peers complaining about a friend is then seen by work colleagues. The mere presence of an image featuring a member of the opposite sex may exacerbate fear and jealousy within a marriage. Another scenario is when posted photographs are taken out of context. They may portray parties and celebrations where people tend to drink and behave differently to how they would at work or family occasions; in such circumstances it is difficult to control the new audience's perception of the image.

Nor should we assume leakage is always inadvertent. There is a blurred boundary between this issue and the rise of 'indirects'. For example, an English schoolchild may post a photo of a pig on a beach hinting that this represents someone in the class, but without saying who. In Trinidad the population tends to see itself as particularly given to both gossip and scandal (the local term is 'bacchanal'). For this reason there is considerable interest in the way visuals provide 'evidence' for the juxtaposition between people that lends itself to endless reinterpretations.[26] Ambiguous visual postings are sometimes encouraged as a form of popular entertainment and the visual equivalent of innuendo. On the other hand the fact that one now never knows who may be taking images and posting them on social media has reputedly made infidelity less common in Trinidad and reduced corruption in China. There are unexpected consequences to such changes. A firm selling premium spirits in China claimed that their sales had collapsed since officials were now afraid that a photograph of them drinking these expensive brands might appear on social media.

Conclusion

Underlying many of the discussions in this chapter is a more general point. Social media represents a significant acceleration in the possibility that communication itself can become more visual, in the sense that it is now possible to hold something very close to a conversation that is almost entirely without voice or text. Snapchat is the dominant social media platform for many teenagers in the English field site, and is typically employed in this conversational mode. People take photographs of their own face that are clearly reminiscent of the development of the emoji as a simple means for conveying how one is feeling at that time. The fact that some 750 million photographs are circulated daily through this platform means it has now become a significant contribution to the use of visual images in communication.

This is merely one example of a wider development in which users of social media, and those developing these technologies, seek to devise new ways by which more can be said through images. Other examples include the expanded potential for people with low levels of literacy now to participate in social media. Another is the ability of people with limited self-confidence to find new ways of expressing sentiments indirectly through memes. A third was the development of the meme as a powerful but indirect way of patrolling internet 'morality'.

None of this necessarily means that what is being communicated is new. As we have argued in other chapters, for instance that on gender, the increase in visibility created by social media has often led to a greater conservatism. This was especially true of our site in southeast

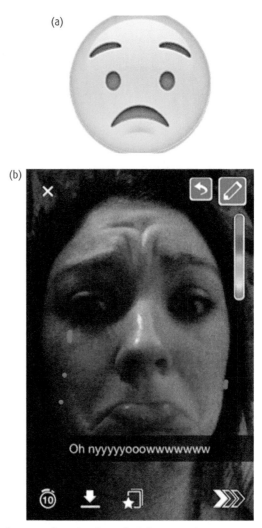

(a)

(b)

Fig. 11.12 Images showing how facial expressions can emulate those of emojis in Snapchat

Turkey. We also saw how photography is used to reinforce traditional family values in rural China. Yet at the same time we find entirely different consequences for this spread of visual forms in our industrial China site, where the orientation is to fantasy and the future rather than to tradition and the present.[27] Visual postings show that people use social media to reinvent their own understanding of tradition, conformity and normativity, which is why understanding the precise context is essential to appreciating what people choose to post.

(c)

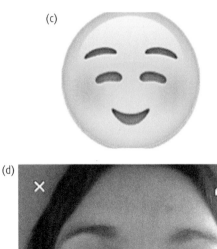

(d)

Fig. 11.12 *Continued*

This chapter has also shown that scalable sociality includes dealing with multiple audiences within the same platform, not just across platforms. The combination means that navigating these several audiences within one's social networks is an increasing concern. The same social media may be used to create small, discrete groups with particular interests, but equally to claim and create a wide consensus around core moral issues – or simply everyday practices such as the expression of daily greetings in south India or the repudiation of glamour in our

English adult selfie and the Chilean 'footie' selfie. All of these can be used to help create a mundane 'ordinary aesthetics' of ubiquitous social media photography.[28] Today, as in the past, the issues of representation and communication are made more complex because of the way a photograph is regarded as a form of evidence, bringing with it further issues of reliability and truth. [29]

This may be the final point of interest for anthropology. Through our ethnographies we seek to follow the dynamics of cultural norms for the populations we study. We can literally see if the degree to which gender is understood by consistently portraying men as manual workers and women as care workers is increasing or declining. This huge increase in visual images, including vast numbers of photographs and the now quite explicit morality of memes, should assist us in this enterprise. In trying to understand people's values we have benefited hugely from being able to scan thousands of visual images posted as part of daily communication. We are at a very nascent stage, but it is likely that if visual images are becoming increasingly important as the complement to textual and oral communication, then these will also form an increasingly important component of anthropology.[30]

12
Individualism[1]

Individualism and networks

A concern with the nature of individualism, balanced between a fear
that it might be growing at the expense of our social engagement and the
desire for its cultivation as a project in life, has been central to Western
thought at least since the age of romanticism.[2] Almost all the founding figures of social science ascribed to a grand narrative which took
for granted a general movement towards individualism in the Western
world.[3] In different ways this would include Mauss, Marx, Simmel,
Tonnies and Weber. This grand narrative is a story about how, once
upon a time, people lived in systems of intense social relations within
communities usually underpinned by some system of kinship. Over the
last two centuries a combination of forces that might include capitalism,
industrialisation and urbanisation caused a decline in the fabric of these
social forces. This decline led to a commensurate development of new
forms of personal autonomy and individualism on the one hand, but to
loneliness, isolation and social fragmentation on the other.

Each social theorist gave this a different inflection. For example,
de Tocqueville[4] wrote on the ambivalence of individualism as a form
of political and social thinking. Durkheim contrasted holism with individualism, while Marx saw a progressive potential in this retreat from
conservative forces. More recently sociologists such as Giddens discuss
in some detail the particular nature of this modern individualism – for
example, where people are moving towards a self based upon a more
self-conscious narrative about themselves.[5]

This academic presumption is fully supported by the dominant
concerns of modern popular journalism. The idea that social media

is contributing to the continued decline in community and social values, and to a corresponding rise of narcissistic self-centred individuals, is probably the single most common theme of newspaper articles clearly designed to respond to, and indeed to create, popular anxiety.[6] Furthermore the ideas that social media is either a further movement towards individualised self-expression or a withdrawal from social life were very common assertions among our informants in several of our field sites. This was perhaps particularly true in England, although there it was often mixed with an even greater fear over the loss of privacy.

In Chapter 2 we discussed the main schools of sociology that seemed relevant to the rise of social media. Neither fit easily into this trajectory. Castells is more concerned with quite other topics related to the rise of a new era of 'information capitalism'.[7] More relevant is the work of Rainie and Wellman. They have argued for a succession of three revolutions driven by spectacular advancements in technology and communication – namely the Social Network Revolution, the Internet Revolution and the Mobile Revolution. Rainie and Wellman have done important work in contesting the simplistic story portrayed in newspapers and do not regard a rise of individualised networking as a withdrawal from social life. It is rather to be seen as an enhancement, often associated with an increase in offline sociality.

At the same time they do argue that there has been a decline in traditional associations around groups, replaced by a phenomenon they describe as 'networked individualism'.[8] The authors see the social world as a succession of ego-centred networks[9] in which 'new media is the new neighbourhood';[10] here 'people think they are individuals, but they are in networks'.[11] However, they suggest that this does not mark a shift towards social isolation, but rather towards flexible autonomy.[12] Both Castells and Wellman try in different ways to transcend the more simplistic rendering of this dualism of the individual and the social through a focus upon networks.

To summarise the evidence described in this chapter, we will present some instances that seem to accord well with the arguments of Rainie and Wellman. Yet our more common findings and generalisations are in strong contrast with their position. Rather than viewing social media as a continuation of the trends that had developed around the growth of the internet, we see many instances where these seem to go into reverse. Our main general definition of social media around scalable sociality suggests that social media may represent an increased, though more flexible, orientation to groups – rather than, as appeared in the earlier internet, a continued rise of ego-centred networks. These groups may be traditional, as in the Indian caste and family, or new, as for factory workers in China. However, a key property of social media is its ability to repair the rupture that modern life has caused to traditional groups such as the family, and to facilitate a return to an orientation to the group. The question is why and when trends seem to favour the trajectory Rainie and Wellman describe, and why and when trends seem to go in the opposite direction. Along with them we contest the idea that either necessarily means that social media makes us *more* or *less* social, though sometimes it does.[13] Instead we examine the more specific effects of social media on the way we socialise, and the ways in which individuals and groups relate to each other through this medium.

It is also worth noting that the concept of group is not in itself opposed to that of an individually-based network. Indeed the traditional antithesis to the idea of the fragmented individualism of contemporary society was the anthropological focus upon kinship as the primary form of social organisation for tribal and other small-scale societies.[14] Yet all societies are formed from individuals, and one of the most common ways of portraying kinship was as an ego-based individual's network of relationships. One definition of anthropology, as opposed to psychology or economics, is that we do not treat people as individuals: instead we treat the individual as a social networking site. Traditional sociality as organised through the alignment to groups, such as the tribe, was thus always also a form of individual-based social networking. The difference was the degree to which that in turn defined the position and identity of that individual, and the degree to which this was culturally prescribed. In traditional kinship systems a person's social obligations arise from the fact that they are a mother's brother's child, rather than coming from an individually chosen network of friends who determine their own level of reciprocal obligation.

What difference does social media make?

Turning to our evidence, in our Italian field site, generally speaking, as long as people's offline lives were largely satisfactory they made little use of social media. It is only when they experienced difficulties or discontent in their life that social media might become an important way to address these. For instance, single mothers tend to be far more active on Facebook than their peers, receiving ongoing and dependable support from their online friends. Separated families often use a combination of

Facebook, Skype and WhatsApp to recreate domestic spaces. So in this Italian field site social media mainly made sense as a complement, or indeed often a repair to, offline social life.

Repair is a common theme, since most people in most places do feel that the intensity of social connections they associated with an ideal of past community has been lost in modern life. This is perceived to be the result of growing individuality, which in turn reflects changes in the modern political economy including a rise in migration, longer commuting to work and many other instances of social separation. As a result there exists a widespread fear in some societies that sociality itself is something we are losing, or indeed have lost, and that modern individualism is less generous and less concerned with institutions such as the family or the nation, representing a shift towards individual self-interest. It is not surprising then that social media is seen as having the potential for re-asserting social connectivity.

In our English field site, one of the main reasons adults adopted social media such as Facebook, and before that platforms such as Friends Reunited, was to compensate for this perceived decline in sociality. Social media also has an important role for new mothers; they use it to create new social networks with other mothers at a time when they need support and would otherwise be isolated at home. Young people in our Brazilian site are also comforted by the idea that social media will allow them to retain their links with their peers while venturing forth to new opportunities in the world of education, work or elsewhere. A similar theme of repair is central to Trinidadian transnational families' use of social media.

The situation is more complex in our southeast Turkish field site where social media is having a much more profound impact upon the way in which people socialise. For instance, where families tradition-ally limited young women's movement and social networks, social media has become the main way they are able to develop new social but also individual relationships outside the family. Some female high-school students may have hundreds of Facebook friends; in some cases they use fake accounts in order not to be recognised by their relatives or family friends. As noted in Chapter 8, in Muslim societies honour and value for men has traditionally depended upon the control of women's social networks and movements; now social media is giving women the opportunity to slip away from such controls. The ability to engage in continuous online communication between young women and men, including falling in love, was previously highly restricted for pre-marital partners.

So this evidence would support a rise in the use of individualised networking on the lines described by Rainie and Wellman, but even here this may not be at the expense of group allegiance. Especially in the case of the Kurdish population, the primary effect is to reproduce forms of traditional kinship organisation. Kurds use Facebook and WhatsApp extensively to keep in touch with distant relatives living in other towns in Turkey and abroad. Young Kurdish people often have several hundred relatives connected on Facebook. Usually these are same-sex peers who, together with their siblings of the other sex and their older relatives who are not connected to the internet, compose a whole lineage. Several of these lineages then form a tribe, historically the primary social unit for Kurdish society. Some of these relatives have never actually met face to face. Social media has become an online space where men and women can feel part of the extended family, lineage or tribe by simply spending time looking at images and pictures and information about their relatives. Social media has thereby shaped new, modern forms of tribal allegiances. Partly this is in compensation for the migration and forced migration that means people are no longer living close to each other, so there is still an element of repair.

Similarly in our south Indian field site society is strictly organised according to a series of social categorisations including kinship, age, gender, class and caste. Most of these traditional categories are in turn found on social media, to a degree that – at least for the lower classes and castes – social media could arguably be called 'kinship media'. The highly socialised usage of social media extends to using the platforms for the further monitoring of other members within the same family and caste. As such, it is hard for people to use social media to develop themselves as autonomous individuals online unless they use fake profiles, which some do, but this represents the exception, not the norm. Social media acts to curb prior trends towards individualism and away from the group. Sometimes this sense of social custom and tradition is quite explicit. It is particularly so in our rural Chinese field site, since this lies near the birthplace of Confucius and local people still feel a strong affinity – informed by this and other factors – with a philosophy centred on the ideal of social conformity and the values of devotion to parents and elders.

What all three cases have in common is that the ways in which social media fosters sociality is relative to the condition of prior offline sociality. In Italy people often simply do not need to use online means to create this sociality. In southeast Turkey, on the other hand, young people in particular have seized upon the new possibilities offered by social media – both for repairing the rupture of separation and also for creating new forms of individualised networking, which have profoundly altered their lives as a result.

The problem is that we cannot ignore the primary backdrop to this discussion which puts us in the position of needing to resist claims for some general trend to individualism, simply because this narrative dominates journalism and popular perception of the impact of social media. A new genre on social media such as the selfie is thus automatically viewed as yet another example of rampant individualism. In academic work too there is a suggestion that the selfie must imply growing self-expression, if not narcissism.[15] As we found in Chapter 11, however, by studying the selfie within our ethnographies we again see more continuity with traditional associations among groups rather than merely self-portraits. In a broader compass there is no evidence to suggest that selfies are particularly associated with more individualistic societies. Selfies are often a means of showing one's association to family or church (as in the Philippines).[16] It is clearly also the case that the selfie is involved in teenage self-expression and absorption in how they look, but this does not necessarily mean the selfie has created or even accentuated that concern.

In north Chile the increased visibility afforded by public social media functioned as a means by which community members recognised each other as similar to themselves, trustworthy and a legitimate part of the community. In making relationships visible, people highlighted family and friendship, in effect solidifying and expanding these connections. Everyday selfies were regarded as an integral part of this sociality, together with self-derision, mocking friends and commenting intensively. Such evidence merely reinforces the semantics of social media as almost always 'social'.

Conformity and collectivity: 'because everybody else does it'

Our collective project has gathered considerable evidence that social media tends to make things more visible – and as a result becomes a powerful means for creating and maintaining social conformity. Parents in the Italian field site encourage their children to join social media in order to be more like their peers. People in both Chinese field sites share idealistic thoughts on WeChat and QQ because everybody else is doing the same thing. Almost everywhere people show constant reciprocal support through 'likes' and comments because they want to associate with people similar to themselves, or to make them more similar to themselves.

This becomes especially clear in the Chilean field site. People there often engage in a semi-public dialogue on their social media profile that is visible to the friends of friends who join in the most popular joking exchanges. While this includes mockery and playful insults, it also binds the wider audience into a shared cultural knowledge. These humorous exchanges almost always make extensive use of Chilean language conventions such as slang, which gives people a way of marking their authenticity as a member of the shared language community. As a result, individuals who do not know each other become acquaintances and sometimes later friends through these exchanges. In turn, becoming Facebook friends leads people to engage in face to face leisure activities, for example sharing meals, playing sports and going out. Having more local acquaintances also helps in finding new jobs, buying and selling used items online and in searching for potential romantic partners.

Arguments in previous chapters around the conservative impact of public-facing social media with respect to gender and politics are equally examples of this use of social media to ensure conformity. Such a sense of conformity is evident in the south Italian site, where people have largely rejected platforms they regard as individualistic such as Twitter and Instagram. What people want to express is not individual differentiation but collective differentiation, such as a social meaning of beauty,[17] which may be found in the local landscape but also in the collective adoption of styles and accessories promoted by the local and national experts, such as designers, fashionistas and hairstylists.

For example, Roberta is a married women and mother of two in her early 40s. Like most women of her age she puts considerable effort in to being well dressed and styled personally and in keeping her house extremely tidy. She goes at least once a month to a hairstylist who she has known for many years and who will recommend a hairstyle that is popular for the season. Likewise Roberta always buys sunglasses and reading glasses recommended by her optician, who similarly knows what is fashionable. Keeping up with fashion is an attempt not to stand out as an individual, but rather to conform to the styles of other women in the town who have the same social position. Being married, these women may refrain from posting photographs of themselves on Facebook. Instead they use WhatsApp to share images of clothes, haircuts or accessories, together with family and female peers.

While these modes of consumption are stable in our Italian site, they become more dynamic forms of aspiration in a field site within Brazil characterised by an emergent class. In Brazil barbecues, cars, branded clothes and expensive music players have always been associated with affluence and power, and posts depicting these are often attempts to claim upward mobility, a theme discussed in Chapter 12. However, the evidence from Trinidad shows this has to be tempered. While looking good is important in Trinidad, Facebook posts that suggest that an individual is trying to look better than anyone else or to stand out too much attract insults and sarcasm, which again limits any tendency to individualism. What this section suggests is that social media may be employed for differentiation and mobility, but this may not imply *individualism* since it is all performed with the moral censure of social conformity. The common point is that social media makes the creation and maintenance of conformity that much easier.

Privacy and sociability

Of all the debates around the impact of social media, deliberations about privacy and social media seem to best highlight how people of different regions have very different ideas about what we otherwise take to be a common concept. The very heated debate over privacy covers several different dimensions.[18] One is a concern that all of our personal data is being extracted by companies and used for commercial purposes, or alternatively for state surveillance. In practice this anxiety was much less apparent in our actual field sites than anticipated. People in our southeast Turkey field site certainly did talk about a general potential loss of privacy; they were also concerned with what might happen to their personal information in a situation of highly charged political conflict. In Chapter 5 we showed how people in our English field site are concerned with the commercial use of their data for targeted advertising. However, taking our project as a whole, such concerns were muted.

Central to this discussion are the assumptions behind the primary debates in Europe and North America: the belief that privacy is a kind of natural condition now threatened by online visibility.[19] In the English field site there was constantly reiterated concern about who might use social media to know more about one's private life. In China the situation is very different. Historically the local understanding of such issues would have differed from the western concept of 'privacy' within traditional social life.[20] Even today, while people in urban China may have become familiar with the concept of 'yinsi' (privacy), for those in rural areas 'privacy' is regarded as a fashionable or Western word. The traditional rural family was a more collective unit, in which there was no expectation that people would want or need private space. They did not have this 'frame' of expected privacy.

Even in the industrial Chinese field site factory workers live either together in collective factory dormitories, where six or eight persons share one room, or with a whole family in rental rooms. People cook in public space and visit each other's rooms without knocking. Daily life is still highly collective. It is widely believed that the only thing a person would try to hide from the public gaze would be a bad secret. In such a context the use of social media, especially given that most such usage in China is based on anonymity, has become one of the first times that privacy itself has gained some legitimacy and that people have an experience of privacy. On social media migrant factory workers are able to record their thoughts and secrets in a relatively private environment,[21] without worrying about the immediate judgments of people who live in the shared offline space. Clearly in this case the rise of digital technology has had a significant impact on Chinese factory workers' daily lives – but in a manner that is the direct opposite of debates that assume social media represents the destruction of privacy.

A rather different dimension of these debates on privacy derives from an argument common in the early days of the internet – that going online was in some respects an anti-social development.[22] The point was effectively critiqued by Hampton and Wellman, who found that online sociality could just as well increase offline sociality.[23] This opens up a broader question: how does this online sociality reflect upon prior offline sociality? To take one example, in the south Italian site people with lower education generally do not use social media to be more social, while those with higher education, and who have spent time in different metropolitan places such as Milan, Rome and Bologna, actually do. The reason is that the first group have no claim to becoming more cosmopolitan. For them it makes more sense to emphasise their offline social relations far more than their online ones. However, their more cosmopolitan neighbours want to use social media in order to retain their wider connections with people from other urban spaces – if anything such users want to reduce their association with what they perceive as the oppressing connectivity of local society. What they have in common is that both want to use social media and new digital technologies to make their social relations more meaningful, both in online and offline contexts.

There was always an inherent contradiction to the common claim that our increased devotion to screens has made us anti-social. It made more sense in the days when, for example, computer gaming was largely practiced by autonomous individuals. However, when people now mainly use devices with screens precisely in order to socialise with other people through social media (or indeed through group gaming), the criticism looks far more suspect. The fact that people in our Turkish, Trinidadian and Brazilian field sites spend lots of time looking at other people's social media profiles does not mean that they actually talk less in face to face interactions. On the contrary: onscreen they find more issues that they have in common and can address in direct conversations. Furthermore with webcams the distinction between online and offline conversation has itself become blurred, especially when people use what we call 'always-on' webcam that remains in the background without anyone needing to converse through it. This is one of the clearest examples of where it makes more sense to think of people actually living together, but online.[24]

Correspondingly the fact that in our Italian field site most people do not often directly check each other's Facebook profiles does not mean they are not interested in their peers or do not try to expand their understanding of their peers. The high levels of unemployment and long siesta time in south Italy has not generated more usage of social media. In other places time away from work might be considered appropriate for networking online. Yet this is not how the siesta is understood. Rather people associate online socialisation with their traditions of offline sociality which were always linked to particular periods of time and settings, such as when at work, when taking a cup of coffee or during the evening in the city squares. So the people who do spend more time looking up other people's Facebook profiles are mainly shop assistants or public servants who do this during their idle times at work, just as they also use these periods for chatting.

So far we have argued that the use of social media reflects the way people see sociality and social relations in their respective and local contexts – for example through the prism of different concepts of privacy or, in some cases, as a mode for promoting social conformity. We will now explore one of our main findings, which is the way people use social media to adjust their actual relations, for instance by making them either more or less visible, with the prime intention of creating a sense of balance in their sociality.

Finding a balance: using social media to adjust relationships

Instead of seeing social media as a mode for becoming either more social or more individual, people in our English village field site use social media platforms, such as Facebook, primarily for keeping people at the 'right' distance.[25] They can calibrate their relationships as a form of scalable sociality in many different ways. This might range from constant commenting to just occasional 'liking' another person's posts; from incorporating them into a small WhatsApp group merely to acknowledging them as a follower on Twitter. From there they could move either towards more personal relations through private messaging and phone calls or towards essentially professional ones through LinkedIn and email. This exemplifies the more general concept of scalable sociality.

Affordances of social media such as asynchronicity can be exploited for such purposes, as when people choose to respond quickly to close friends and slowly to people they do not particularly want to encourage to communicate too often. As significant delays between messages are acceptable on social media, people have enough time to manage their self-presentations more strategically.[26] In places such as industrial China migrants tend to restrict the topics of daily long-distance phone calls with families and friends in their home towns mainly to concerns about money, resolving financial issues and gossip. Thoughts about personal aspirations and life in general are considered 'unspeakable' within phone conversations, and are therefore pushed onto QQ where they seem more appropriate.

People may also use social media to negotiate a balance between people they know and the potential role of strangers.[27] Given the considerable emphasis on respect for tradition in our rural Chinese field site, people were often at pains to claim that they used their social media pages for communicating only with people they knew from the town or other networks such as family, work or school. However, McDonald found that this was contradicted by their use of functions built into the most popular social media platforms, which allowed them to connect with complete strangers. By this means they were engaging in a completely new kind of sociality that had previously been unthinkable. Often this is exactly what makes people curious about such encounters. As they can also provide a degree of anonymity previously unavailable, this becomes another instance of the way Chinese people use social media to experience what for them is a largely unprecedented idea of privacy. In addition to scalable sociality, people also have a sense of a scale from the most traditional to most modern forms of sociality. Again they may look for a balance here, using social media both for entirely innovative but also highly traditional forms of socialising. Another example is the previously described use of social media in southeast Turkey both for new kinds of individualised flirting and chatting, but also for re-alignment with traditional groups such as the tribe.

This concept of balance also refers back to our earlier point as evident in the study of youth subcultures: becoming individual is generally a social project.[28] As punks or goths young people see themselves as asserting individuality against the dominant established society, but the outsider sees them as now conforming to the aesthetics of their chosen sub-culture. They may be interested in fashion and change, but want to adapt to these dynamics as part of a group. Social media helps them accomplish this to an extent that was simply not possible before because increased visibility means that it is now clearer what other people are doing and how they look. It is even easier to become an individualised punk or goth who looks just the same as other punks and goths. Many of the observations within this chapter come together here. If we see the expression of many versions of individualism as in fact demonstrating the way in which social media can be used to develop social conformity, we have come a long way from our original simple opposition between the individual and the social.

There are therefore three primary conclusions to this chapter. We have seen how the visibility of social media assists the project of social conformity, even when people see themselves as using it to express individuality. We have also seen how social media as scalable sociality provides a series of mechanisms by which people can find a balance between, for example, keeping other people close or at a distance, or between using media for new and for traditional forms of sociality. There is, however, a third generalisation that emerges from comparative analysis. In conditions where people sense a decline in communal sociality, then the group component of social media may be seen as a way of retaining or reinforcing that group sociality such as family, caste or tribe. In many cases this is a quite deliberate attempt to stem what is seen as a decline in traditional orientations to society and to groups such as the family. By contrast where people find social conformity or community to be oppressive, as, for example, with the constraints on women's behaviour in several societies, then social media does allow some movement towards individualised networking.

13
Does social media make people happier?

For anthropologists, considering whether something makes people happy is a complicated if not impossible task. Individuals conceive of happiness in widely varying ways, often aligned with broader cultural ideals and value systems associated with class, religion, gender, age, philosophical perspective, educational level and any number of collective characteristics. Beyond these cultural orientations to 'happiness', individuals have varying senses of what makes them happy, and even these almost certainly change over time. It is also not at all clear how far we should regard people's claims to happiness as evidence of how happy they actually are. To frame a question about happiness and social media from an anthropological perspective, therefore, we must consider not only what cultural factors shape happiness, but also how individuals interpret questions about happiness and what discourses of happiness are publically acceptable. For example, we must consider for each cultural context whether happiness refers to instantaneous gratification or life-long satisfaction, to a slight improvement in mood or a deeper sense of self-actualisation. Do people consider happiness to be something that comes from a metaphysical concept such as religion or nature, human relationships or even material goods? Would it be rude to claim to be happy, or would it be rude or ungrateful to claim to be anything other than happy? All of these will profoundly affect individual responses to any question about happiness.

The cultural relativism implicit in the term happiness may explain why anthropologists have historically been reluctant to undertake what could be called 'happiness research'.[1] This is one of the chapters we have included because we felt a duty to respond to the questions people commonly ask us, as well as to the ones we would like to answer. Yet even from our perspective some value remains in approaching this subject, particularly in the context of technological change.

Debates about whether modernity might bring more or less happiness date back at least to Rousseau,[2] who argued that civilisation had ushered in a loss of authentic happiness. The notion of happiness is also prominent in the works of Durkheim,[3] James,[4] Weber,[5] Locke[6] and Comte,[7] all of whom contemplated the various ways in which modernity affects notions of happiness and individuality. Yet as Thin[8] argues, the anthropology of the twentieth (and now twenty-first) centuries has been largely silent on the issue, in part because cultural relativism has deterred cross-cultural comparisons.[9]

Instead cross-cultural evaluations of happiness have been the domain of economists such as Sen,[10] who suggest measures of welfare based on Gross Domestic Product[11] should be supplemented with indications such as the Gross National Happiness index[12] or the World Happiness Report.[13] These assessments stress factors such as health, educational attainment and other 'human development' indicators, as defined by the United Nations.[14] Such indices follow Maslow[15] in recognising that happiness depends on far more than physiological and safety needs; it encompasses positive and negative emotions, as well as feelings of purpose or meaning in life.[16] Certainly including 'happiness' in welfare assessment is preferable to a simple economic measure, but these broad quantitative measures tell us little about local and individual differences in defining happiness.

As anthropologists, studying happiness comparatively through ethnography gives such a question more depth, but also poses the problem of comparing a concept that is defined differently in different contexts. As a starting point we take Thin's[17] broad definition of happiness which outlines three general senses: motive, evaluation and emotion. In his formulation, motive is related to ambition and perceived purpose of life. Evaluation is related to individuals' perceptions of their own quality of life as related to cultural values and morality. Emotion is associated with temporary pleasures and more enduring emotional states of well-being. Happiness then includes feelings, expressions and reports of emotions, as well as the important stories that people tell, the relationships that they build and their aesthetic preferences.[18]

Thin's definition allows not only for cultural variation in concepts of happiness, but also for individual emotion and variation within those concepts. Moral living may be closely associated with religion in one place, while more humanistic goals of education or environmental awareness dominate in another. The ways in which people seek pleasure may involve aesthetics, sexuality, social relationships, food, festivals and parties, drugs, religious transformation, consumption, adventure or differing combinations of these.

Studies on social media and happiness

While anthropology may shy away from such a topic, public debates about the relationship between social media and personal happiness (or more often, unhappiness) are ample, increasingly appearing in high-profile publications. In the last five years, several popular news outlets (including *Time, Forbes, The Huffington Post, The New Yorker* and *The Daily Mirror*) have cited psychological studies suggesting that social media may increase depression,[19] dissatisfaction,[20] jealousy,[21] negative body image[22] and loneliness.[23] These studies attribute negative feelings to a variety of causes. At times users may feel that their contacts ignore them on social media.[24] In different studies users compare their own lives to the images they see of their acquaintances' lives online.[25] In still other cases people feel depressed because they consider their time on Facebook to be unproductive.[26] Yet other studies critique and contradict these results.[27] Some find that using social networks to chat or make plans increases satisfaction;[28] they may discover a positive correlation between the use of Facebook and increased social capital, trust and civic engagement, and therefore a feeling of gratification in life.[29] Even Facebook conducted its own controversial study,[30] which found that when users were shown posts with more positive words, their posts contained more; when shown posts with fewer of these words, their own posts also contained fewer. Researchers confirmed that the 'emotional contagion' of Facebook posts worked just as emotional contagion does offline, where the presence of happy people in one's life makes an individual happier, while negative people make her or him less content.

The fact that some studies highlight negative emotional consequences of social media while others see potential for positive emotional support may simply reflect the fact that people do very different things on it. In fact a user may have different experiences of social media day to day or even minute by minute. Social media platforms such as Facebook or QQ are not one single thing, but take on different forms depending on the individual user. They may be used for keeping in touch with family, showing off holiday photographs or developing new friendships with banter or emotional support. Obviously, when social media plays symbolically different roles at different times, it does not affect emotions in a singular and straightforward way.[31] Our problem is that we can continue to assert that asking if social media makes people happier is far too simplistic a question, but we cannot deny that the question's popularity reveals an overwhelming interest in social media's impact on people's emotions. This is true not just of journalism. These questions as to whether social media makes us happy or unhappy, or more generally is good or bad for us, are now entirely standard conversations for people all around the world.

Taking this public interest into account, each of our study's nine researchers included a question about happiness in their surveys[32] of social media users. The purpose was not to bolster or disprove these other studies' results, but rather to give a sense of how widely responses differ across multiple geographic locations. Indeed, as Fig. 4.26 demonstrates, answers to the question 'Does social media make you happier?'[33] varied significantly depending on location.

Of course, these results should not be over-interpreted. It is possible that people in China feel that positive association with new media is what they are *supposed* to think, reflecting the Chinese government's promotion of new media as the vanguard of modernity; as a result they answer overwhelmingly that social media makes them happier. Similarly some individuals in our south India and southeast Turkey field sites may feel that attributing happiness to social media detracts from their position in more traditional value systems associated with the family, caste or tribe, resulting in a relatively higher percentage of people who claim social media makes them less happy. In most of the field sites, the majority of people say that social media has made no difference in their happiness. Relatively few follow the more common reports in the media suggesting various ways in which they have been made unhappy. By putting these statistics into context and examining concepts of happiness within the individuals' cultural milieus, we may at least learn something about what is at stake when people make claims regarding happiness – even if ultimately we cannot determine whether social media makes people happy or not.

Capacity and aspiration

Internet access and social media often provide people with increased capacities, whether for learning skills, connecting with new people and ideas or simply attaining a public voice. Yet the connection between new capacities, increased aspirations and increased happiness based on what Thin calls 'motive' is not always clear-cut.

New technology often allows individuals to imagine different kinds of lives, or the 'capacity to aspire', which Appadurai[34] argues is a key element in empowerment of the poor. One might therefore assume that if social media provides a gateway to new aspirations, and at times gives greater access to that to which people aspire, it would thereby increase happiness. This correlation is crucial to Wang's[35] study of Chinese factory workers, most of whom are the type of poor to whom Appadurai refers. These rural migrants turned factory workers often use QQ to represent their fantasies of 'cool and modern' lifestyles. As illustrated in Fig. 11.1, female factory workers post photographs of wedding dresses and 'princess' fantasies, while males prefer pictures of rock stars, sexy women and fancy sports cars. In each case the images serve as an escape from the drudgery of factory work.

Yet this type of aspiration is not inevitable. In Haynes's[36] field site in northern Chile, also populated by economic migrants who often think of their city as a marginal, boring and ugly place, Facebook and Instagram are not spaces of fantasy; they rather serve to represent their lives much as they are. In Figs 11.4 and 11.10 we saw the photographs and memes that present their lives within the confines of simple ambitions, closely adhering to the types of normativity displayed by their neighbours. They banish their boredom by posting Instagram photographs of the line to pay their phone bill or of their computer at work, accompanied by hashtags such as #instabored. Even the funny memes of which they are so fond often represent their ambitions as minimal, with pictures of a grave stone marking 'my desire to study' or the Kermit the Frog memes of Fig. 11.10.

At first glance the contexts of these two sites seem quite similar, with large populations migrating for new work opportunities. Yet while in industrial China individuals migrate toward the relatively developed and more cosmopolitan areas such as Shanghai, northern Chile is often thought by residents to be 'only partially incorporated into the nation', implying that they have moved both physically and symbolically away from the cosmopolitan centre to the periphery.[37] Instead of ambitions related to greater wealth, higher education or wider social networks, the ambitions of northern Chileans revolve around comfort and support for their families. The Chinese have migrated towards the centre and the Chileans have migrated towards the margins, which may explain something of the difference in their aspirations. To return to Appadurai, these two examples suggest that social media's role in happiness may have less to do with the capacity for new aspirations than with showing how aspirations reflect the wider social and economic context in which people live.

An example from Spyer's[38] Brazilian field site makes this even more evident. Spyer uses the term 'emergent class' to describe the residents of his field site who have also moved for work opportunities. We have seen how social media is important for representing social mobility. The images of consumption taken at exclusive sites such as the gym or swimming pool, or featuring prestigious brand clothing, reflect in material form individuals' imagination about their futures and who they dream of becoming. By contrast sharing a photograph near something associated with backwardness, for example an unfinished brick wall, is taboo. Heightened aspirations at times lead to increased pressure to fulfil them, and some individuals fear being seen as those who fall behind in their neighbourhoods as everyone else moves up. Social mobility brings considerable competition among neighbours, colleagues at work or school and even between friends. While residents see these new capacities as advantageous, therefore, they also reminisce about the past as a time of greater fulfilment – an age when everyone knew each other, young people were more respectful, crime and violence were minimal and money was not a daily concern. Although new capacities and new aspirations associated with social media may in some cases lead to the imagination of greater happiness, they may also serve as a catalyst for the new pressures and failures that complicate this narrative.

Enduring social values

In each of these cases people associate change with the destruction of values, with alienation and diminished societal ideals. They may then look to social media to strengthen what they perceive as their traditional values and ways of life – vital to the preserving of what they see as the conditions for happiness. In such instances social media may be used not to increase capacities, but to reiterate conventional ideals. For example, in McDonald's[39] field site in rural China moral cultivation and righteousness is highly valued; it is seen as stemming in part from the area's Confucian, Taoist and Buddhist history, in addition to its relationships with the modern Chinese state.

Individuals often use social media to propagate a moral life, responding to both their own and the Chinese government's worries that new 'foreign' technologies such as the internet may be incompatible with moral and right ways of acting, and may have a negative effect on Chinese social values.[40] These rural Chinese people develop online dispositions related not to fantasy but to filial piety, duty, sincerity, wisdom, honesty, correct behaviour and courage,[41] hoping in turn that these will positively influence government and society. The family is central to Confucian morality, and so presenting the self as embedded in family life is important in using social media. The most popular posts are memes glorifying love and marriage, photographs of new-born babies and status messages thanking one's parents for their devotion and support. Even when messages of filial piety on QZone remain unseen by parents, they are expressions of the idealised version of parental devotion that is performed for others in order to represent the self as a moral person. These popular postings and genres reveal a set of ideals that emphasise the Chinese idiom *bao xi, bu bao you* ('share happiness, do not share worries'), thus appropriating social media to reproduce and strengthen existing moral frameworks.

McDonald's example reflects Miller's findings in his earlier study in Trinidad,[42] in which he concluded that Facebook was best understood not as a radical space of social change but as a conservative space that strives to effect a return to traditional values of community. This is quite an abstract ideal. A more original use of social media concerns the way in which people actually find ways in practice to deal with the traditional demands of community. While social media may act as an instrument of nostalgia for the sense of community, it may also act as a funnelling mechanism when the demands of actual community are overwhelming. In Sinanan's[43] ethnography of a Trinidadian town, she notes that people often feel burdened by endless social demands made by their extended family and friends. People often worry that in spending time with one person they may offend six others whose invitations were turned down. Sometimes socialising through social media can complement socialising in person, allowing one's time to accommodate more social relationships.

In our English field site many individuals discovered that, after reconnecting with past school friends through social media, they were simply reminded why they had not bothered to remain in contact in the first place. Instead they found that social media provided a way to keep these people, who fell somewhere between close friend and distant acquaintance, in a position that was neither too 'hot' nor too 'cold': the 'Goldilocks Strategy'. By remaining connected on social media, users were able to give the appearance of being in touch without having to spend significant time and energy meeting them in person. In such cases social media might be quite successful in reinforcing conventional ideals, whether by providing a space for reiterating traditional values or by providing new mechanisms to alleviate longstanding social conundrums.

In summary, a major factor for most people in their sense of happiness is their relationships with other people. If social media can assist people to manage degrees of scalable sociality through the platforms they use, this may help to keep these balanced and under control. So we have moved from the idea that what matters to people is an abstract relationship with the values of the past to an observation that social media may actually have become an important component in how they deal with these traditional obligations in the present.

Temporary pleasure

While individuals' aspirations and social values are usually long-lasting structures that affect the details of day-to-day life, people may also experience happiness more fluidly as a temporary form of pleasure. One of the most common discourses about social media in several of our field sites, particularly among young people, is that social media does bring happiness, but only of a fleeting kind. Even as individuals find excitement and pleasure in technologies such as electronic games, music, television and film, so does social media provide a source of entertainment that makes people happy, for a while.

For instance, a young man from our rural China field site described online games to McDonald: 'When I go up a level I feel incredibly happy. As my points increase more and more, and I gradually move to the top of this level, I will be very happy...but there are no [direct] benefits, only your skill has improved, it doesn't really mean anything, it's just an entertainment.' It is common for young people in China to try to extend their prestige on QQ by adding golden bars and gadgets to their profiles. These prestige icons can be bought using digital money gained simply by remaining logged in and active. In our industrial Chinese field site it was found that some factory workers spend the equivalent of a month's rent on purchasing digital luxury cars or a 'noble title on a social media platform such as YY'.[44] Clearly spending such time and money might indicate these individuals are happy in their hours spent online. When one of McDonald's informants comments, 'it doesn't really mean anything', however, this hedging suggests he enjoys the pleasure that comes with gaming and social media as an individual, but must also defer to the larger and more collective cultural discourses which insist that 'true happiness' is more enduring; the transient pleasure of gaming cannot 'count' in this larger game of happiness.

Romantic involvement is another source of (sometimes fleeting) happiness often associated with social media use. In our Brazilian field site new opportunities for flirting are among the most important advantages of social media. This is positive both for shy people, who are able to hide their insecurities behind the screen, and for the outgoing, who are able to access more people and establish less visible channels of communication with the potential for affairs. Spyer writes that Facebook is seen as a sort of Disneyland for flirting, but most individuals in his field site depict flirting on social media as a temporary form of pleasure rather than an attempt to discover lifelong love. These attitudes reflect the common critique of applications such as Tinder or Grindr as tools for superficial relationships, dominated by users seeking casual sexual encounters and one-night stands rather than long-term relationships. Just as with gaming, individuals may find pleasure in online flirting, but they almost always describe these activities as superficial and inferior to more lasting forms of happiness.

At the same time, while there does not yet seem to be any quantitative research on the subject, people in many of our field sites suggested that dating applications often do actually lead to long-term relationships and help individuals overcome all sorts of constraints, anxieties and barriers to forming relationships offline. Yet dominant discourses continue to condemn them as tools only for casual and carnal encounters. This brings us to one of the most important conclusions of this chapter. We may not learn much about whether social media brings people happiness. Yet as we examine the details, we are learning a good deal about *conceptions* of happiness and the ways in which people adhere to these discourses, for instance the denigration of transient happiness, even while pursuing happiness in ways that are contrary to popular rhetoric.

Social media and added stress

Even if our survey material lends little credence to the journalistic emphasis on social media as a source of unhappiness (the numbers stating social media made them unhappier in Fig. 4.26 are remarkably small), it is still an important element to this question. While our last section entirely refutes Tolstoy's presumption that 'All happy families are alike; each unhappy family is unhappy in its own way', we do see as much variation in unhappiness as in happiness.

Social media at times presents a beautified view of life, and this may add pressure for others to keep up. In industrial China, especially among middle-class local residents, 'knowing each other's daily life' may lead to comparisons that make individuals feel inferior. Some people report feeing lonely or depressed while others report increased anxiety, worrying about what others looking at their social media profile will think.[45] In some extreme cases isolation on social media and online bullying may have significant impacts. A factory official, Da Fei, in south China describes being thrown out of a WeChat group by his colleagues as the final straw that led him to quit his job and leave the town. These effects are echoed in some of the bullying found among school peers in the English village site. People have always had the capacity to be spiteful or mean, but social media may well have increased both the capacity and the range of ways in which people can be horrible to each other.

Often people who claim that social media makes them less happy tend to have had some specific bad experience online, for example stalking, harassment or an unfaithful partner. Nicolescu[46] writes that lawyers in his field site in south Italy agree that an increase in divorce is caused by Facebook and mobile phones because partners often discover their significant other cheating through those media. The visibility of Facebook threatens both the romantic couple and the family. As a result many people in the area starting a committed relationship prefer either to close their Facebook accounts or to open a shared account, which is considered the ultimate proof of commitment to the relationship.

McDonald adds that in rural China some women inspect their husband's phones, looking for evidence of infidelity and blaming social media as a threat to marriage. In Trinidad the only difference is that such checking of phones works both ways. Being too visible on social media, or visible in the wrong ways, can carry a risk of others misinterpreting one's intention and aspersions being cast over one's morality. Costa[47] reports that women in southeast Turkey also see social media as contributing to an increase in cheating husbands. One of Costa's first encounters in the field site was with a woman who was crying because her ex-husband had left her to live with a younger woman he met on Facebook. He had taken their children and would not allow his previous partner to see them. For women in Turkey and China, just as for the Italian lawyers, social media is often seen as the root of infidelity – and thus unhappiness – rather than the medium through which it is manifest. While mobile phones and social media make organising private encounters more discreet, the possibility of photographic evidence of those encounters surfacing makes them more risky. Increased policing of partners was also evident in Brazil and Trinidad, where suspicions of affairs were common, adding to stress for both partners. In all these cases we are reporting a *perception* of cause rather than any systematic comparison with marital relationships prior to social media, since we were not present at that time. There may actually be no increase in either infidelity or divorce.

What we can say is that the visibility associated with social media has added stress around fears of infidelity, but also contributes to surveillance in other ways. While women in southeast Turkey have gained greater capacities for social relationships as a result of social media, these are also the media through which men increasingly harass them. We also saw in previous chapters the stress that comes from the use of social media for surveillance, both by the state and by society. There is more political control and censorship of Kurdish activities, as well as more social control on an intimate scale carried out by family, acquaintances and friends.

Even in contexts where honour is less of a concern, social media may contribute to stress about how individuals present themselves to others. For example, in Nicolescu's study in Italy, he found that individuals (in particular adult women) experience a burden to create a certain kind of positive image in public. This lies at the core of local social values and precedes the development of social media, but social media becomes a new space in which this pressure is felt. Women have long considered it necessary to dress well when leaving the house, even if only to run errands, and they now feel pressure to craft their self-presentation carefully when uploading photographs or even writing status updates. Just as these women feel a responsibility to represent an Italian ideal of beauty and elegance through their Facebook posts, the educated elite feel they must display their intellectual or artistic credentials online in order to sustain their social prestige.

In each of these cases social media creates a space for both displaying and reconstituting cultural capital in a setting in which people feel that they should have a public presence that corresponds to their social position. However, this is often felt to be an obligation rather than an opportunity. A general increase in visibility provides not only opportunity, however, but also anxiety and a burden – at least comparable to worrying about what to wear in public.

Discussion: does social media make people *look* happier?

One result of this pressure to look appropriate online was noted by Venkatraman in his south Indian field site.[48] He observes that people always seem happy on Facebook, just as they report pressure to appear happy whenever in public. With happy pictures, positive messages and even frustrations expressed as jokes, happiness is not in this instance the by-product of other aspirations: it is the very object of aspiration itself. Given a context in which multiple media provide options for different kinds of communication, private conversations through Facebook messenger, WhatsApp or other forms of dyadic messages may carry more information about 'authentic' emotional states, while more public Tweets and Facebook status updates are places in which individuals are more likely to 'perform' happiness in order to craft a particular view of their lives for their presumed audience.[49] In India happiness *is* the social value, and as public forms of social media proliferate they simply become new spaces to express an appearance of happiness.

Social media may be a place to reconnect or to feel overly connected. It may be a place to express true happiness or to put on a deceptively smiling face for the public. Perhaps this duality is why so many people responded that social media makes no difference to their happiness[50] (an average of 56.68 per cent across all nine field sites). So even if we acknowledge problems in defining happiness, there is some benefit to the question posed by this chapter because social media has created a huge additional space within which people present and represent happiness and emotions. We have also seen how this space regulates the balance between visual display, increased access to information, the associated development of aspiration and in some cases, for instance in industrial China, the possibilities of fulfilment of those aspirations. So the value of asking whether social media has an impact on happiness may not be learning whether people are happier because of social media. Rather it is in learning how we can use social media to understand more about what happiness means to its users, and how and where they express this.

14
The future

Perhaps the main reason anthropologists are wary of being involved in making predictions is that in studying the present we also see the fate of past predictions. More than that: we understand why they are so rarely of value. Daily life as observed in ethnography with its holistic contextualisation is so much more complex than a laboratory, in which one is able to control the variables. We also appreciate that prediction is often highly motivated. Given the nature of modern share markets, there are many people who make money out of getting the future right.

Yet fear of adding to such frenzy should not prevent us from exploring other concerns with the future. We may still write policy documents for a hospice suggesting how they might use social media in the future,[1] or plan to refine our methods of study in anthropology to take the impact of new media into account. We quite reasonably take responsibility for helping people to consider the consequences of social media in ways that might in the future enhance rather than detract from their welfare, for example making advance provisions for what will happen to their online materials at death. So there are many good reasons for at least trying to use the evidence of the present for envisaging what might happen next.

The 'theory of attainment'[2] that was developed prior to this project in order to theorise the impact of new media technologies on our understanding of humanity argues that typically new media are first used conservatively, to attain something already desired but more easily achieved with the help of this new media. For example, social media is used to repair the rupture sustained by separated transnational families or for overcoming previously frustrated desires to share photographs more easily. Soon, however, things move on to new realms. By 2016 the emphasis in using social media is no longer on repairing lost connections (as in Friends Reunited) or a fantasy of entirely new connections. Instead what we see today reveals something closer to refinement. Considered in the light of our theory of scalable sociality, the small groups of WhatsApp are now being used to balance the larger groups of Facebook. The intimacy of Snapchat balances the contact with strangers on Twitter and Instagram. Online gaming consoles such as Xbox and Playstation, along with social media games that followed from Farmville, now balance the previous isolation of single-person gaming with more social possibilities. Scalable sociality is not only an observation of a pattern developing across social media, but also a prediction that new platforms will colonise other spaces along these scales.

New media constantly attains new possibilities. With respect to time, there are greater opportunities for both simultaneity in communication and also various versions of asynchronous conversation. With respect to space, we see the 'death of distance' enriched by the new possibilities of a 'sort of' co-presence, for example couples living in different countries who 'sort of' live together online; such possibilities are explored more fully in the study of webcam.[3] Digital devices also change our sense of collective memory,[4] creating a new form or combination of internal and external faculties for retaining information. We do not just make jokes about online being a second brain.[5] We see a radical expansion not only in photography and visual communication,[6] but also, perhaps more dramatically, in our capacity to share. Scalable sociality is therefore just one of many ways in which our project recognises that social media expands our capacity but, we insist, does not change our essential humanity. The point of the theory of attainment is that none of this should be seen either as a loss of humanity or as evidence that we are becoming 'post-human'.[7]

Four trends

Within the vast field of consequences of new social media, as anthropologists our research selectively focuses upon their implications for sociality. Within this narrower remit, this section will examine four trends. The first is already evident as scalable sociality, in which an increasing number of social media platforms can be aligned with the diversity of the social groups to which we might want to relate. There seems to be an acceleration in the development of new platforms – probably because, as seems to have been the case with WhatsApp, the costs of developing new start-up platforms has fallen, while the time it takes for them to become established has shrunk. As a result there is even less impediment to new devices and platforms taking up any little niche that still waits to be exploited. Fine-tuning this balance between private and public communications is becoming crucial to the way people in our Brazilian and our Italian field sites, for instance, experience social media.

In Chapter 1 it was suggested that scalable sociality should also include prior media, for example dyadic telephone calls and public broadcasting. It is possible that as this spectrum is more fully covered, it will be harder to designate any particular group along this spectrum which could be isolated as the 'social media'. In short, one consequence of this prediction is that the very idea of 'social media' might gradually disappear; instead we simply have an increasingly diverse set of media and increasingly sophisticated exploitation of the possibilities these media have created, including other trends such as obtaining information, sharing information or making communication more visual. All media was always social, and the separation of a group called social media within the overall spectrum may become less useful over time.

The prediction that social media's successful conclusion may result in its demise as a separate sphere also points to another important technological development: the smartphone. However powerful and important the advent of social media in some of our field sites has become, it would be hard to place this ahead of the impact and significance of smartphones, within which social media platforms may often be seen as just another kind of *app*[8]. Furthermore it is smartphones that facilitate social media's importance as a mix of polymedia, making clear the range of media possibilities as they lie side by side within one easily accessible device. People can not only choose the scale of the group they want to communicate with, but also the mix of textual, visual and auditory components as appropriate to the situation. As we can see with Snapchat or the use of Facebook by illiterate populations in south India, it is possible that a 'conversation' can now be almost entirely visual. As smartphones become smarter, they may well accelerate the dissolving of social media into this wider array of communicative possibilities. This fluid mix of communicative forms suits the way users flow between activities such as talking, gaming, texting, masturbating, learning and purchasing.

With an increased emphasis on the smartphone it is not just social media that may become more integrated, but also the individual platforms themselves. At the moment we typically discuss social media in terms of QQ or Facebook, Twitter or Instagram. Yet until recently instant messaging would also have been understood in terms of platforms such as AIM, MSN or BBM. Today, however, a text message may equally come through WhatsApp, WeChat, the smartphone's own messaging facility, a private Facebook message or an app such as Viber. People are becoming increasingly unconcerned as to which this is. The trend is therefore towards content transcending the platform by which it is communicated, and this may well continue. Moreover the evidence from this project suggests that these platforms are not just technical facilities: we also have a relationship to them as a 'kind-of' friend. QQ has been around for a longer time than most other social media platforms; where once it was regarded as new and exciting, many now feel it to be a bit like a comforting but older relative. Judging by its loss of cool among young people in England, Facebook may have started going the same way. Young people looking for new experiences and spaces may create a dynamic in social media that has nothing to do with functionality and everything to do with fashion and their own peer relationships. Perhaps we may continue to use platforms as trade names to stand for that facility, just as British people did with *Hoover* (vacuum cleaners), *Biro* (ballpoint pens) or *Sellotape* (sticky tape). We might still talk about tweeting even when Twitter no longer exists. One clear conclusion of this project is that platforms matter much less than we once thought.

Both of these trends are closely linked to a third, very straightforward prediction – the movement towards ubiquity. An excellent book on the rise of new media is entitled *The Great Indian Phone Book*.[9] Although not particularly concerned with social media it gives a well-researched overview of what seems to be happening as the vast population of India are becoming phone owners. Carla Wallis has a comparable book with respect to China.[10] Between them these regions represent half the world's population. These books demonstrate that we will not have to wait until the elimination of poverty in order to see the possible ubiquity of phone-based social media. This is partly because the prices of such devices continue to fall as a result of the Chinese mass production of high-quality, domestically produced smartphones. But equally it is due to the prioritisation of these devices by the relatively poor. Of the informants in the Chinese factory town, 91 per cent now access the internet through such smartphones.[11]

The fastest growing global population is in Africa. Here Kenya and South Africa already lead the way, while experts predict extremely rapid growth in smartphone possession more generally.[12] Overall *The Economist*[13] predicts that 80 per cent of the world's adult population will have decently connected smartphones by 2020, noting that already the ten biggest messaging apps represent three billion users. Nor is this just a case of possession; people spend several hours of each day on these devices. This could be represented as the end of the *digital divide*. Yet, while most people in the world will have access to some relevant technology, our chapter on inequality suggests that equality of access to devices may have very little impact on wider inequality in society. Also, as Mark Graham who works on African media argues, the presence of considerable African usage of the internet does not necessarily mean African concerns are suddenly going to be more present on Wikipedia or Google.[14]

One of the driving forces behind our project is that previous academic study has largely failed to follow the global expansion of social media. While in the future devices may be more ubiquitous in all corners of the globe, inequality will therefore remain in terms of the services available in certain locations and the lack of attention paid to the needs and desires of certain populations. At the same time, recognising that this may not necessarily impact on any other aspect of inequality should not prevent us from recognising that there is in one aspect an increasing and significant *equality*: merely having a smartphone provides a significant change with respect to the capacities of its owner.

In a similar movement to ubiquity, social media are not only becoming indispensable to geographically dispersed populations, but also to a more dispersed age range. Conservatism with regard to social media has until recently been mostly associated with age. When our project began, long ago in the mists of 2012, many people assumed that social media possessed some kind of natural affinity with the young, mainly because reaching the young had been the priority of virtually all the commercial forces which created social media platforms. In some ways, however, there is an inverse relationship between these commercial forces and what anthropologists have previously observed in many countries—the fact that social communication as an activity is most commonly associated with older women, not with young males. It is most often older women who do the collective work of maintaining community and social norms through what may disparagingly be considered 'gossip'. In most of our field sites there remains something of a generational divide, with as yet very limited use by older people in the major populations of rural Brazil, China and India. This is eroding, however, and seems much less true of the spread of smartphones than of social media platforms. As noted, the increasing ubiquity of the smartphone is the catalyst for more general usage of social media. Older people in some of our field sites seemed to take easily to visual media such as Skype or Facetime and to tablets such as iPads. To the degree that social media remains associated with core genres of social communication such as gossip, the future of social media may well rest more with older women than younger men – think landlines.

Juxtaposing these three separate trends within the context of our field results lead to a fourth prediction which is much less intuitively obvious, but which emerges from our ethnographic evidence. As this volume's chapters concerning gender, politics and inequality suggest, social media has its most profound impacts upon populations that were traditionally the most constrained. While social media is neither wholly good nor bad for any population, it does seem to have emancipatory effects for many marginalised populations. Perhaps the single best example of radical transformation is Costa's work among women in Mardin who use social media to overcome severe constraints in their freedom to communicate with others; such practice also echoes findings elsewhere in the Middle East on the impact of social media in countries such as Saudi Arabia.[15] The point is really rather simple. The more individuals live within culturally imposed constraints on communication, the more a new technology may mean that what was previously forbidden now becomes possible. Costa's study shows that the impact radically changes the social relations between women and men – and, potentially, women's overall position within the society. None of this is gainsaid by the evidence that social media is equally and in the same society far more conservative than we had previously appreciated.

Both – simultaneously

While some of these trends may rest upon current and future technical developments, as all of the field sites of this project reveal, the precise selection of social media within an environment of polymedia is based less upon technological affordances and more on local genres of social interaction or cultural significance. Older people in England would be very well served by the technological affordances offered by the spread of Facebook. However, if young people stop posting on Facebook and older people remain keen on keeping connected to the young they may then be forced to follow the young onto a less suitable platform: the social connection is more important than how well a platform meets their needs.

Similarly in China the pattern of differential usage of platforms tends to reflect emerging class consciousness and the pre-existing urban–rural divide, rather than simply show what a platform is good at doing. When the Chinese factory workers become competent in one platform such as QQ, they may look to newer sites that help them remain modern in comparison with others. In the rural China site McDonald notes how migration to urban areas for short periods of work and study often resulted in people starting to use WeChat to communicate with new contacts in these places.

The desire to emulate more metropolitan regions is strong in some areas which regard themselves as peripheral, for example in our south Italian site where people of lower cultural and educational capital try and emulate those with more. As always in our project there are exceptions, however, where people do not use social media to express social distinctions in this way. Central to Haynes's analysis of her Chile site is her considerable evidence that the town creates its identity precisely through *refusing* to emulate, or even to respect, the metropolitan region represented by Chile's capital Santiago. People in Alto Hospicio often refer to the area as '*Santi-asco*' – 'asco' being the Spanish word for 'disgust'.

So while we can generalise about the continued importance of social status and emulation in determining which media people use, as opposed to merely technical affordances, we cannot simply predict any particular outcome of this. While some might expect that there will be a long-term movement towards greater or more efficient alignment though social media between affordances and needs, this is actually unlikely if factors such as fashion and emulation continue to prove more powerful than functionality.

After all not everything moves over time to become more functional or efficient. We would not say that most clothing or food is more efficient today than several centuries ago: rather they have increased in diversity for reasons related to fashion and social differentiation. Indeed functional clothing, as also healthy eating, are both mostly encountered as examples of lifestyle. We are thus merely suggesting that social media may be more like clothing and food than we had realised. What our studies find to be relatively robust and enduring are *not* the social media platforms that people use, but rather the culturally informed genres of behaviour enacted on and through these sites. The way Chinese people socialise around food, English people around the pub, Trinidadians around partying, Indians around the extended family or Italians around public space are almost always reproduced on social media. Here, as in so many areas, social media represents a change in the place where things happen rather than a change in what is happening.

For these reasons anthropologists would expect that future developments on these platforms would also include an increasing accommodation to, and affinity with, local cultural genres. As noted in the discussion of work and commerce in Chapter 5, financial matters are seen as opposed to intimate and personal life in Europe, but as an expression of intimacy in China. As a result Amazon represents a further de-socialising of commerce as compared to offline shopping – we have even less connection with real people in making transactions.[16] However Taobao, the Chinese shopping equivalent, represents a re-socialising of economic life as a place where people make personal connections. McDonald notes that in his rural Chinese town, at least, using social media for commercial purposes is viewed as an integral part of family life; it is a moral activity *in and of itself.* While in the North Atlantic regions it is mainly companies such as Facebook that further commerce, in our Chilean field site an increasing amount of commerce is conducted through individuals on Facebook. They create groups such as 'Buy and Sell Everything', which work as an online forum both for posting items for sale and for requesting those desired. It would be misleading just to regard this as a form of commerce, however. In such groups, as in our Italian site, commerce is used to expand a window onto public life as much as to earn money.

The study of technical affordances has perhaps greater potential to assist prediction when seen as potential alignments with cultural preferences. Brazil was dominated by Orkut, for example, which connected individuals not only to everyone they already knew, but also to those with whom they already had much in common, but who were not previously part of their social networks. This aligned with a Brazilian sensibility that social media should be a place where 'everyone is'. While similar to Facebook in many ways, Orkut was separated from any messenger service. Given this expansion to include new friends who had been strangers, however, people wanted to have the security of private conversation. This led first to a shift to Facebook and then in turn to WhatsApp, which seemed more Brazilian, because they incorporate such features. In a way, therefore, social media helps Brazilians to become even more Brazilian than they were able to be in the past. As in our theory of attainment, a study of prior social life would reveal a latent desire to be connected to others in this complex manner which includes both a private and public dimension. Such a desire is attained more fully thanks to social media. Similarly social media allows these Brazilians to feel more modern, repudiating their sense that they were merely backward and rural, but achieving this without having to break their contacts with their families and places of origin. We are thus not arguing here for some general movements towards more effective functionality, but rather an exploitation of those potentials in social media which fit a local, culturally attuned pattern of socialising.

These predictions also explain why a common answer to many of the questions tackled by this volume is 'neither "X" nor "Y" but both simultaneously'. Theories of culture, as opposed to popular discussion, tend not to emphasise trends in any one direction, but rather to acknowledge contradictions.[17] We have shown that social media makes the world both more globally homogeneous and more locally heterogeneous, more individual and more social, more equal and more unequal, more liberal and more conservative, increasing both commodification and decommodification. The future is usually more of both. For example, in Trinidad the rise of individual mobile phones may well have facilitated secret sexual relationships, since direct contact was much easier than previously – but being tagged on Facebook photographs with the wrong partner made hiding an affair much more difficult. WhatsApp provides more scope for privacy, but most people would be shocked to see their daily wanderings faithfully recorded on Google locational history. We see more threats to privacy, as highlighted by Edward Snowden and WikiLeaks, but also more capacity for privacy and anonymity – as in Costa's account of intimate relations in Mardin and some people's first experiences of personal privacy in China. So the best response to most questions about the future impact of social media on social behaviour is 'both simultaneously', where this corresponds to the expansion of contradictory trends[18].

Imagining the future

One of the things that may have changed during the course of our field work between 2013 and 2014 is the relationship between social media and the conceptualisation of the future. New technology does not just change the manner in which people go about their everyday lives: it also facilitates our imagination of the future. There is often an implicit connection between discourses of the future and notions of technology, so that if we see a television programme with a title such as *Tomorrow's World* we expect that the topic will be technology.

While not part of our study, we recognise that the development of social media as new technology is dependent upon people who spend a great deal of time thinking and wondering about the future, and how they can devise technology to help bring it about. Malaby has surveyed the various forms of often utopian techno-liberationist ideals[19] important in the development of some digital platforms such as Second Life. These include the more anarchistic ideals found by

Coleman in her study of hacker communities,[20] or the study by Kelty of idealists who take as their model for the future public domain the development of Open Source coding.[21] While these groups are relatively small and specific, larger populations also take part indirectly through activities such Crowdsourcing and Kickstarter campaigns or the spread of Open Access publishing. These all speak to a new, imagined future that strives towards idealism. While none of these impinged upon our study, this book has many examples of how social media has stood as a sign of aspiration and modernity, explaining the shift from QQ to WeChat in China or the decline in the status of Facebook for young people.

For populations in the West over many years an apparently authentic vision of an ever-extending future was manifested by the incremental development of hardware such as the PC and software such as Windows Office. For more than a decade, every year seemed to bring new models and improvements. Yet it turned out that this was not an infinite process; once a certain level was achieved, having a still better PC or version of Office shifted from something of intense excitement to a subject creating almost no interest at all. Windows has just announced that its operating system is not going to advance beyond the number ten. Instead attention shifts to something else, such as the latest tablet. For people in lower income countries the equivalent to this has been the annual release of new smartphones, as well as their anticipation of, and encounter with, social media itself. It may have briefly seemed as if social media had completed its evolution with the ubiquity of Facebook and QQ. However, the last two years have shown a new movement towards polymedia and platforms such as Tinder or Snapchat or WeChat have grown in popularity, all of which helps us to retain this link between new social media and the anticipation of future developments.

Yet just as the idea that the latest computer expressed the future has now diminished, it is likely that the role of social media as symbolic of the future may already be in decline. Instead, as with all new digital technologies and as argued by Miller and Horst,[22] the single most astonishing point about these technologies is that they can move from being emblematic of an almost unreachable future to becoming so taken for granted that it feels like a personal slight when they do not work. This process can take only a matter of months or even weeks. Perhaps the primary examples of this during the period of field work were WhatsApp and WeChat. One of our very first blogposts for this project was a note that in Trinidad people were taking up WhatsApp at a time when it was barely known in England.[23] Fifteen months later, when our fieldwork had ended, WhatsApp had clearly become established as another of those globally ubiquitous platforms; now entirely taken for granted, we can hardly imagine they did not previously exist.

The way technology in and of itself becomes a symbol of being modern is one of the reasons it becomes expressive of, rather than distinct from, cultural values.[24] However, this too depends on the specific sense of becoming modern pertinent to each of our sites. As argued in the volume on industrial China,[25] a 'humiliating' history – representing a comparative lack of technological development in modern China during much of the twentieth century – is what led the entire country, from elites to rural peasants, coming to view new technology as a symbol of national revival. This led to considerable government investment, and actually much of the population shares the government's focus upon this endeavour. As a result one is less likely to find in China the kind of digital resistance noted by Sinanan for her site in Trinidad, where refusal to take up new media technology can be a kind of affectation,[26] though there are some equivalents in the rural China site. This also led to a leapfrog effect. In China, for example, people were already storing all their digital content online[27] before the development of cloud computing in the West; they had not been part of the previous stage of development and so had none of the conservatism that comes from previous attachments.

Conclusion

It is obviously going to be hard to predict the future for something as dynamic as social media. The only confident prediction is that much of our future forecasting will turn out to be wrong. More important to this volume, however, is the recognition that in some ways just as difficult as forecasting the future is knowing the present. The purpose of this study has been, above all, an argument about how many of our assumptions about what we think we already know are in fact suspect. Once we appreciate that knowing social media is not an exercise in delineating the properties of a set of platforms, but rather of acknowledging what the world has already turned these into, by way of content, the immensity of the problem is revealed. How can we know what social media has already become for oil workers in Alaska, tribal people in Amazonia and the *nouveau riche* of Moscow?

Of course we cannot know what social media actually is, set against this ideal of comprehensive knowledge, but we can at least face up to our ignorance. By giving equal weight to nine sites around the world, we hope that in this volume we have also helped to clarify what forms of understanding are still possible. We can give a sense of the creativity of wider populations as well as of geeks in producing the social media we actually use. We can show how the task of understanding social media has in turn gifted us intimate portraits of our contemporaries' lives. We have shown how anthropology complements the many other disciplines that study social media, each of which adds its own perspective. Finally we have tried to show how comparative anthropology creates particular varieties of knowledge of both breadth and depth. What makes these essential within the context of our complex modern world, however, is that these are forms of understanding based on empathy.

Appendix – The nine ethnographies

Below we briefly describe the settings for each of the nine field sites where we carried out this research.

Costa, E. *Social Media in Southeast Turkey*

This book is set in Mardin, a medium-sized town in southeast Turkey. Mardin is a multi-ethnic and multi-religious city located 30 km away from the border with Syria, in the middle of Turkey's Kurdistan. It is inhabited mainly by Muslim Kurds and Arabs, and Christian Syriacs. The town has significantly changed in the last 10 to 15 years; expansion of the modern area called *Yenişehir* ('New City') has attracted people from the nearby towns and from the Old City of Mardin, in search of a modern lifestyle. The ethnography has mainly focused on this part of the city, and on the new generation of young Kurds and Arabs who inhabit it. This context raises many issues concerned with the impact of social media on gender and on politics.

Haynes, N. *Social Media in Northern Chile*

Alto Hospicio is a city of 100,000 people in the north of Chile. The city is an outgrowth of nearby Iquique, an important port city for western South America, and links the port with mines in the nearby highlands of the country, which produce almost one-third of the world's copper. These industries have attracted a large number of immigrants from other regions of Chile as well as nearby countries such as Peru and Bolivia. Though the region is rich in resources it is politically marginalised, and most residents of Alto Hospicio are marginalised citizens within the region. The city was only incorporated in 2004, and thus combines the precariousness of unofficial growth with a spirit of community development. Ethnographic research in Alto Hospicio included mining families and those working in the port and tax-free import zone sales, as well as small business owners. It also included work with cultural and neighbourhood groups such as folkloric dance societies, neighbour advocate committees and community organisations dedicated to improving the education and lives of the city's children. The overall emphasis is on the role of social media in creating this new locality.

McDonald, T. *Social Media in Rural China*

This book is set in a small rural town and its surrounding villages in China's northern Shandong province. The township has a population of 31000 persons, while the town 'proper' has a population of just 6000. Agriculture remains a major occupation in the town, although several small factories also provide the town with a major economic boost; for those families who have a member working in these factories, this has often become their main source of income. The population is almost entirely comprised of local people, with relatively few outside migrants. Despite having growing and increasingly convenient links with nearby urban centres, this field site remains distinctively rural, and local people identify strongly with the area's Confucian, Taoist and Buddhist cultural heritage. As such this ethnography charts the complex interactions between traditional Chinese ethical values and new social media platforms.

Miller, D. *Social Media in an English Village*

This ethnography took place in two linked villages, called here The Glades, comprising Leeglade with a population of around 11000 and Highglade with a population of around 6500. They are rural but can be reached within one hour by train from central London; they also have good motorway links. Unusually for modern England they are homogeneously white, with hardly any ethnic minorities, and are largely middle-class within a relatively affluent area with low unemployment. In addition to the overall ethnography the research included four local secondary schools and long-term work with a hospice from another area, working with patients with terminal diagnoses. The primary theme is the impact of social media on an Englishness which historically has been determined by a separation of the public from the private domain.

Nicolescu, N. *Social Media in Southeast Italy*

This book is set in a small town in the Apulia region of south Italy. This is an area that underwent dramatic economic changes over the last century, but is currently experiencing a high rate of unemployment. There are historical reasons which perhaps explain why people are very concerned with the way in which social visibility reflects their social status. The book focuses on the essential difference that people in a middle-sized town in the region constantly make between on the one hand crafting a public image that assures conformity and on the other hand managing their more intimate and personal relationships. In this context the book shows how social media and new communication technology actually help people to navigate between these two primary modes of socialisation while respecting the strong social normativity that they imply.

Sinanan, J. *Social Media in Trinidad*

This book is set in a semi-urban town I have called 'El Mirador', situated in one of the least developed areas of Trinidad. The population is around 18000 and is fairly reflective of Trinidad's wider population, which is 40 per cent Afro-Trinidadian, 40 per cent Indo-Trinidadian and 20 per cent made up of Syrian-Lebanese, Chinese, Anglo-European and other mixed heritages. Although El Mirador is perceived as being far from urban centres and a place of special interest, it is also a town where the residents pride themselves on their quiet country lifestyle and family and community orientation. The study of social media also reveals particular attitudes towards visibility and appearance which need to be understood within this local context.

Spyer, J. *Social Media in Emergent Brazil*

This ethnography took place in Balduíno (fictional name) in Bahia, the region of Brazil with the highest level of social inequality but also where recently more poor people have been experiencing upward social mobility. The village has about 15000 people, most of whom migrated as the region's coast became an international tourist destination. Formal and informal employment has allowed families for the first time to buy smartphones, computers and motorcycles, and to send their children to college. Traditionally a fishing village, Balduíno's population is now dealing with growing criminality and the influence of Pentecostal Christianity, a duality which helps us to understand the local appropriation of social media.

Venkatraman, S. *Social Media in South India*

This ethnography was conducted in a peri-urban field site called 'Panchagrami' (a pseudonym) near the metropolis of Chennai in the south Indian state of Tamil Nadu. Originally a group of five villages, it is now the site of a government initiative to establish a major IT park. On a working day this field site not only hosts approximately 30,000 permanent settlers of this area, but also caters to over 200,000 IT workers commuting to work there. As a result this area has undergone transformations both in infrastructure and population, and is in the midst of changing its identity from an agriculture-based economy to a knowledge-based one. These new opportunities have also attracted other businesses and services such as education and housing. Panchagrami provides a particularly complex and contrasting environment for the reception of new social media.

Wang, X. *Social Media in Industrial China*

This book is set in a factory town in southeast China, a few hours from Shanghai by train. More than two-thirds of the residents (total inhabitants: 60000) are a part of the biggest migration in human history, in which over 200 million Chinese peasants left their homes in rural areas to work in factories and cities. The migrant workers who labour in more than 60 local factories are the human faces behind 'Made in China'. The daily life of this town gives a concrete form to numerous abstract forces that have constituted China's rapid development over the last three decades – globalisation, industrialisation, migration and the rise of information and communication technologies. We see the significant consequences of social media use for people who, after a day's hard labour, view this as their main form of socialisation and entertainment, as well as the place where they develop their aspirations towards modernity.

In addition there is an eleventh volume in this series of publications.

Miller, D. and Sinanan, J. *Visualising Facebook*

This book provides a direct comparison between the photographs and memes placed on Facebook in our English and our Trinidadian field sites, and shows how much we can learn from this extensive and unprecedented visual expression of peoples' values and concerns. It also complements the present volume in visibly demonstrating the evidence for cultural difference in social media posting.

A summary of our research findings may also be found on the Why We Post website,[1] which is also linked to approximately eight to ten short videos for each of the field sites, available on YouTube.[2] We strongly recommend that you watch some of these videos alongside reading this book. That way you can meet, through film, some of the people that this text is about. Finally we have also produced a free online university course with the title *The Anthropology of Social Media*.[3] Both the website and the MOOC are available in the following languages: Chinese, English, Italian, Portuguese, Spanish, Tamil and Turkish.[4]

Notes

Chapter 1

1   In this book the singular is used to refer to social media in general and the plural if the reference is specifically to social media as a range of platforms.

2   Including one of our team – Miller, D. 2011. *Tales From Facebook*. Cambridge: Polity Press.

3   Though in some regions WhatsApp is often used to send voice-based messages.

4   The study of sociality has a long history. Its key founder was perhaps the sociologist Georg Simmel, who at the start of the twentieth century tried to work out the different properties of the dyad of two, the triad of three and the larger qualities of what we call society or community. See Simmel, G. and Wolff, K. H. 1950. *The Sociology of Georg Simmel*. Glencoe, IL: Free Press.

5   Madianou, M. and Miller, D. 2012. *Migration and New Media*. London: Routledge.

6   See also Marwick, A. and boyd, d. 2014. 'Networked privacy: How teenagers negotiate context in social media.' *New Media & Society* 16(7): 1051–67.

7   The material upon which those comparisons are based is available in more detail in the respective nine monographs, as well as in another volume in this series called *Visualising Facebook* that systematically compares visual postings on Facebook from England and Trinidad.

8   Miller, D. and Sinanan, J. 2014. *Webcam*. Cambridge: Polity Press. Chapter one.

9   Goffman, E. 1959. *The Presentation of the Self in Everyday Life*. Garden City, NY: Anchor Books.

Chapter 2

1   She prefers to de-capitalise her name.

2   This is not to ignore decades of prior work on computer mediated communication, but simply to acknowledge the moment at which such work really seemed to take off as the specific study of social networking sites.

3   boyd, d. and Ellison, N. B. 2007. 'Social Network Sites: Definition, History and Scholarship.' *Journal of Computer-Mediated Communication* 13(1): 210–30.

4   boyd, d. 2014. *It's Complicated: The Social Lives of Networked Teens*. New Haven, CT; London: Yale University Press. 6–14.

5   When the term 'social networking sites' was more prevalent there was perhaps also a greater focus on approaches concerned with networking e.g. Papacharissi, Z., ed. 2011. *A Networked Self*. London: Routledge.

6   boyd, d. and Ellison, N. B. 2007. Social Network Sites: Definition, History and Scholarship. *Journal of Computer-Mediated Communication* 13(1): 210–30.

7   Weller, K. et al., eds. 2013. *Twitter and Society*. New York: Peter Lang. See especially the papers by Rodgers, R., Schmidt, J.-H., Bruns, A. and Moe, H. and by Halavais, A.

8   We are not tempted to call these 'networked privates'.

9   Van Dijck, J. 2013a. *The Culture of Connectivity*. Oxford: Oxford University Press.

10 e.g. Graham, M. and Dutton, W., eds. 2014. *Society and the Internet*. Oxford: Oxford University Press. The introduction provides a succinct guide to lessons learnt from the history of internet studies and a summary of key domains of importance.

11 See, for example, Miller, D. and Slater, D. 2000. *The Internet: An Ethnographic Approach*. Oxford: Berg.

12 Miller, D. and Slater, D. 2000. *The Internet: An Ethnographic Approach*. Oxford: Berg.

13 http://www.danah.org/researchBibs/sns.php

14 We have not cited sources for these figures as we simply do not know if there are any authoritative sources that can be trusted. Instead we have tended to browse the internet looking for what might be called 'typical' figures based on several sites. Our figures therefore reflect a generalised 'internet' picture as viewed during May/June 2015.

15 There is one reference to the Chinese site of Renren: Qiu, L., Lin, H. and Leung, A. K.-y. 2013. 'Cultural Differences and Switching of In-Group Sharing Behavior Between an American (Facebook) and a Chinese (Renren) Social Networking Site.' *Journal of Cross-Cultural Psychology* 44(1): 106–21.

16 We do not know of a comparable bibliography of work in the Chinese language.

17 boyd, d. and Ellison, N. B. 2007. 'Social Network Sites: Definition, History and Scholarship.' *Journal of Computer-Mediated Communication* 13(1): 210–30.

18 Hjorth, L. 2009. 'Gifts of Presence: A Case Study of a South Korean Virtual Community, Cyworld's Mini-Hompy.' *Internationalising the Internet* anthology. Goggin, G. and McLelland, M., eds. 237–51. London: Routledge. Hjorth, L. 2010. 'The Game of Being Social: Web 2.0, Social Media, and Online Games.' *Iowa Journal of Communication* 42(1): 73–92.

19 Chambers, D. 2013. *Social Media and Personal Relationships: Online Intimacies and Networked Friendship*. Basingstoke: Palgrave Macmillan. Mehdizadeh, S. 2010. 'Self-Presentation 2.0: Narcissism and Self-Esteem on Facebook.' *Cyberpsychology, Behaviour and Social Networking* 13(4): 357–64. Rainie, L. and Wellman, B. 2012. *Networked*. Cambridge, MA: The MIT Press.

20 For example Fuchs, C. 2013. *Social Media: A Critical Introduction*. London: Sage.

21 As may anthropologists, for example Gershon, I. 2011. 'Un-Friend My Heart: Facebook, Promiscuity and Heartbreak in a Neoliberal Age.' *Anthropological Quarterly* 84(4): 865–94.

22 De Tocqueville, A. 1994 (1840). *Democracy in America*. London: David Campbell.

23 Xiong, C. and Lv, Y. 2013. 'Social Network Service and Social Development in China.' *Studies in Communication Sciences* 13(2): 133–8.

24 As of November 2014 Renren has 45 million monthly active users according to http://www.chinainternetwatch.com/10928/renren-q3-2014/, and in 2015 WeChat has 600 million and QQ 843 million according to http://www.chinainternetwatch.com/14304/wechat-maus-reached-600-million-in-q2-2015/

25 In this book an app on a smartphone can be a social media platform which does not need to be present as a website.

26 There are many books on the development of the net, the web and Silicon Valley, for example Naughton, J. 2012. *From Guttenberg to Zuckerberg*. London: Quercus.

27 As previously noted these are based on 'typical' online figures from several sites from the period May/June 2015.

28 A book such as *Twitter and Society* (Weller, K. et al., eds. 2013. New York: Peter Lang) shows through the variety of its chapters the tension between the desire to study a platform in its own right and a recognition both that such a platform is now diversified into many different uses and consequences and that it is increasingly the product of its users.

29 Miller, D. 2011. *Tales from Facebook*. Cambridge: Polity Press.

30 For one of the few attempts to look systematically at these processes and the impact of the media see Rantanen, T. 2005. *The Media and Globalization*. New York: Sage.

31 This review is certainly deficient in that it only covered publications in English, while recognising that many significant local studies exist which tend to be in the language appropriate to that place.

32 We have no qualifications for appraising such work.

33 For example Ellison, N. B., Steinfield, C. and Lampe, C. 2007. 'The Benefits of Facebook "Friends": Exploring the Relationship between College Students' Use of Online Social Networks and Social Capital.' *Journal of Computer-Mediated Communication* 12(3), 1143–68.

34 boyd, d. and Ellison, N. B. 2007. 'Social Network Sites: Definition, History and Scholarship.' *Journal of Computer-Mediated Communication* 13(1): 211.

35 boyd, d. 2008. 'Facebook's Privacy Trainwreck: Exposure, Invasion, and Social Convergence.' *Convergence* 14(1): 13–20. Livingstone, S. 2008. 'Taking Risky Opportunities in Youthful Content Creation: Teenagers' Use of Social Networking Sites for Intimacy, Privacy and Self-expression.' *New Media & Society* 10(3): 393–411.

36 boyd, d. 2008. 'Facebook's Privacy Trainwreck: Exposure, Invasion, and Social Convergence.' *Convergence* 14(1): 13–20. Livingstone, S. 2008. 'Taking Risky Opportunities in Youthful Content Creation: Teenagers' Use of Social Networking Sites for Intimacy, Privacy and Self-Expression.' *New Media & Society* 10(3): 393–411.

37 A guide to many of these can be found in Wilson, R., Gosling, S. and Graham, L. 2012. 'A Review of Facebook Research in the Social Sciences.' *Perspectives on Psychological Science* 7.

38 Baym, N. 2010. *Personal Connections in the Digital Age*. Cambridge: Polity Press.

39 Chambers, D. 2013. *Social Media and Personal Relationships: Online Intimacies and Networked Friendship*. Basingstoke: Palgrave Macmillan.

40 Noor Al-Deen, H. and Hendricks, J., eds. 2012. *Social Media: Usage and Impact*. Lanham, MD: Lexington Books.

41 For a recent example see Lenhart, A. 2015. 'Teens, Social Media & Technology Overview.' http://www.pewinternet.org/2015/04/09/teens-social-media-technology-2015/

42 For example Adorno, T. W., with Horkheimer, M. 2002. *Dialectic of Enlightenment*. Stanford, CA: Stanford University Press.

43 Fuchs, C. 2013. *Social Media: A Critical Introduction*. London: Sage.

44 For example Hunsiger, J. and Senft, T., eds. 2014. *The Social Media Handbook*. New York: Routledge.

45 For example Hanna, R., Rohm, A. and Crittenden, V. L. 2010. 'We're All Connected: The Power of the Social Media Ecosystem.' *Business Horizons* 54(3): 265–73. Jussila, J., Kärkkäinen, H. and Leino, M. 2011. 'Benefits of Social Media in Business-to-Business Customer Interface in Innovation.' *Proceedings of the 15th International Academic MindTrek Conference: Envisioning Future Media Environments*. 167–74. Mangold, W. G. and Faulds, D. J. 2009. 'Social Media: The New Hybrid Element of the Promotion Mix.' *Business Horizons* 52(4): 357–65. Culnan, M. J., McHugh, P. J. and Zubillaga, J. I. 2010. 'How Large US Companies Can Use Twitter and Other Social Media to Gain Business Value.' *MIS Quarterly Executive* 9(4): 243–59.

46 Lomborg, S. 2014. *Social Media, Social Genres: Making Sense of the Ordinary*. New York: Routledge. See also Jones, G., Schiefllin, B. and Smith, R. 2011. 'When Friends Who Talk Together Stalk Together: Online Gossip as Meta Communication.' Thurlow, C. and Mroczek, K., eds. *Digital Discourse: Language in the New Media*. Oxford: Oxford University Press. 26–47.

47 McLaughlin, C. and Vitak, J. 2012. 'Norm Evolution and Violation on Facebook.' *New Media & Society* 14(2): 299–315.

48 Edited collections often provide the juxtaposition of cases from different parts of the world, for example Alev Degim, I., Johnson, J. and Fu, T., eds. 2015. *Interpersonal Interactions Across Borders*. Amsterdam: Institute of Network Cultures.

49 boyd, d. 2014. *It's Complicated: The Social Lives of Networked Teens*. New Haven; London: Yale University Press. 6–14. Clark, L. S. 2013. *The Parent App*. Oxford: Oxford University Press. Ito, M. et al. 2010. *Hanging Out, Messing Around, and Geeking Out*. Cambridge, MA: The MIT Press. Livingstone, S. 2009. *Children and the Internet*. Cambridge: Polity Press. Livingstone, S. and Sefton-Green, J. Forthcoming. *The Class: Connections and Disconnections in the Digital Age*. New York: New York University Press.

50 Levine, G., ed. 1971. *Georg Simmel on Individuality and Social Forms*. Chicago: Chicago University Press.

51 Castells, M. 1996. *The Rise of the Network Society, The Information Age: Economy, Society and Culture Vol. I*. Oxford: Blackwell. Castells, M. 2000. *The Information Age: Economy, Society and Culture*, updated edition, 3 vols. Oxford: Blackwell.

52 Castells, M. 1996. *The Rise of the Network Society. The Information Age: Economy, Society and Culture Vol. I*. Oxford: Blackwell. 370.

53 Miller, D. and Slater, D. 2000. *The Internet: An Ethnographic Approach*. Oxford: Berg. Askew, K. and Wilk, R. 2002. *Anthropology of Media: A Reader*. Oxford: Blackwell. Postill,

J. 2008. 'Localizing the Internet Beyond Communities and Networks.' *New Media & Society* 10(3): 413.

54 Rainie, L. and Wellman, B. 2012. *Networked*. Cambridge, MA: The MIT Press.

55 See Chapter 12.

56 See Chapter 7.

57 Boase, J. and Wellman, B. 2006. 'Personal Relationships: On and Off the Internet.' In Perlman, D. and Vangelisti, A., eds. *Handbook of Personal Relations*. Cambridge: Cambridge University Press.

58 Godelier, M. 2012. *The Metamorphosis of Kinship*. London: Verso.

59 Mauss, M. 1966. *The Gift*. London: Cohen and West.

60 A focus on the normative is of course recognised in other disciplines, for example media studies. Couldry, N. 2015. 'Social Media: Human Life.' *Social Media + Society* 1(2).

61 Bourdieu, P. 1972. *Outline to a Theory of Practice*. Cambridge: Cambridge University Press.

62 Askew, K. and Wilk, R. 2002. *Anthropology of Media: A Reader*. Oxford: Blackwell. Ginsburg, F., Abu-Lughod, L. and Larkin, B., eds. 2002. *Media Worlds*. Berkeley, CA: University of California Press.

63 For example http://www.media-anthropology.net/

64 Coleman, G. 2010. 'Ethnographic Approaches to Digital Media.' *Annual Review of Anthropology* 39: 487–505. Horst, H. and Miller, D., eds. *Digital Anthropology*. Oxford: Berg.

65 Landzelius, K., ed. 2006. *Native on the Net*. London: Routledge.

66 Bernal, V. 2014. *Nation as Network*. Chicago: University of Chicago Press.

67 Greschke, H. 2012. *Is There a Home in Cyberspace?: The Internet in Migrants' Everyday Life and the Emergence of Global Communities*. London: Routledge.

68 Oosterbaan, M. 2010. Virtual Migration. Brazilian Diasporic Media and the Reconfigurations of Place and Space. *Revue Européenne des Migrations Internationales* 26(1): 81–102.Oosterbaan, M. 2010. 'Virtual Re-evangelization: Brazilian Churches, Media and the Postsecular City.' In Beaumont, J., Molendijk, A. and Jedan, C., eds., *Exploring the Postsecular: The Religious, The Political, the Urban*, Leiden: Brill, 281–308. Schrooten, M. 2012. 'Moving ethnography online: Researching Brazilian migrants' online togetherness.' *Ethnic and Racial Studies* 35(10): 1794–1809. McKay, D. 2011. 'On the Face of Facebook: Historical Images and Personhood in Filipino Social Networking.' *History and Anthropology* 21(4): 483–502. Nur Muhammad, R., Horst, H. A., Papoutsaki, E. and Dodson, G. 2015. 'Uyghur Transnational Identity on Facebook: On the Development of a Young Diaspora.' *Identities* (forthcoming): 1–15.

69 Postill, J. 2008. 'Localizing the Internet Beyond Communities and Networks.' *New Media & Society* 10(3): 413.

70 Coleman, G. 2012. *Coding Freedom: The Ethics and Aesthetics of Hacking*. Princeton, NJ: Princeton University Press.

71 Uimonen, P. 2012. *Digital Drama*. New York: Routledge.

72 An exception being Barendregt, B. 2012. 'Diverse Digital Worlds.' In Horst, H. and Miller, D., eds. *Digital Anthropology*. Oxford: Berg. 203–24.

73 Boellstorff, T. 2008. *Coming of Age in Second Life*. Princeton, NJ: Princeton University Press. See also Hine, C. 2000. *Virtual Ethnography*. London: Sage.

74 Information and Communication Technologies For Development.

75 e.g. Tacchi, J. 2012. 'Digital Engagement.' In Horst, H. and Miller, D., eds. *Digital Anthropology*. London: Berg. 225–41.

76 e.g. Van Dijk, J. 2013. 'Inequalities in the Network Society.' Orton-Johnson, K. and Prior, N., eds. *Digital Sociology*. London: Palgrave Macmillan.

77 e.g. Graham, M. 2014. 'Internet Geographies: Data Shadows and Digital Divisions of Labour.' Graham, M. and Dutton, W., eds. *The Internet and Society*. Oxford: Oxford University Press., 99–116.

78 Dalsgaard, S. 2008. 'Facework on Facebook: The presentation of Self in Virtual Life and its Role in the US Elections.' *Anthropology Today* 24(6): 8–12. Kuntsman, A. and Stein, R. 2015. *Digital Militarism: Israel's Occupation in the Social Media Age*. Stanford, CA: Stanford University Press.

79 Broadbent, S. 2011. *L'Intimite au Travail*. Paris: Fyp Editions. Gershon, I. 2010. *Breakup 2.0: Disconnecting Over New Media*. Cornell: Cornell University Press.

80 e.g. Rangaswamy, N. and Arora, P. 2015. 'The Mobile Internet in the Wild and Every Day: Digital Leisure in the Slums of Urban India.' *International Journal of Cultural Studies*.

Kumar, N. 2014. 'Facebook for Self-empowerment? A Study of Facebook Adoption in Urban India.' *New Media & Society* 16(7): 1122–37.

81 e.g. Gingrich, A. and Fox, R. G., eds. 2002. *Anthropology, By Comparison*. London: Routledge. In Holy, L., ed. 1987. *Comparative Anthropology*. Oxford and New York: Blackwell.

82 Cultural relativism is the practice of judging human behaviour in terms of the local cultural context.

Chapter 3

1 Costa, E. 2016. *Social Media in Southeast Turkey*. London: UCL Press.

2 Increasingly in commercial contexts.

3 Miller lived near rather than in his field site, but was present on most days.

4 Miller, D. 1998. *A Theory of Shopping*. Cambridge: Polity Press.

5 Along with Ciara Green. A strange man knocking on doors alone would be a very ineffective research technique in England.

6 The exception is Miller, D. and Sinanan, J. Forthcoming. *Visualising Facebook*. London: UCL Press. The book relies considerably upon this direct counting of actual postings.

7 For example Kala Shreen of the Center for Creativity, Heritage and Development, Chennai, for our films from India.

8 www.ucl.ac.uk/why-we-post

9 Boellstorff, T., Nardi, B., Pearce, C. and Taylor, T. 2012. *Ethnography and Virtual Worlds: A Handbook of Method*. Princeton, NJ: Princeton University Press.

10 An indirect is a post that appears to be directed towards an individual without specifying who he or she is.

Chapter 4

1 However, we are cognizant that this is a small sample. As is made clear in the conclusion to this chapter, we think these figures are more important as a defence against the kind of generalisations made by literature claiming 'all people do this or that on social media', and less important as the base for generalisations in their own right.

2 Where a particular field site is left out of the chart or a table, this is specifically because of a very low response rate to that particular question. There are instances where the percentages within a field site might add up to 99 per cent or 101 per cent instead of 100 per cent. This is due to rounding of the decimal points to the nearest integer.

3 McDonald, T. Forthcoming. *Social Media in Rural China*. London: UCL Press.

4 Data from an independent survey conducted by Wang among 238 rural migrants in industrial China.

5 Spyer's blog on this is http://blogs.ucl.ac.uk/global-social-media/2014/08/31/the-qualitative-insights-we-get-from-applying-questionnaires/

6 Miller, D. 2011. *Tales from Facebook*. Cambridge: Polity Press.

7 Independent survey conducted by Xinyuan Wang among 200 smartphone users in the industrial China field site.

8 More details of people's engagement with commerce are described in Chapter 6, which is devoted to this topic.

9 McDonald, T. Forthcoming. *Social Media in Rural China*. London: UCL Press. Wang, X. Forthcoming. *Social Media in Industrial China*. London: UCL Press.

10 Miller, D. 2011. *Tales from Facebook*. Cambridge: Polity Press.

11 Bernard, H. R. 2011. *Research methods in anthropology: Qualitative and quantitative approaches*. Lanham, MD: Altamira Press.

12 For ethical reasons the responses to all our surveys were completely anonymised.

13 The books in the Why We Post series, as listed at the end of this volume.

14 Although it will be evident by now how often we still failed in this quest.

Chapter 5

1   Buckingham, D. 2003. *Media Education: Literacy, Learning and Contemporary Culture.* Cambridge: Polity Press.

2   Ito, M., Horst, H., Bittanti, M., boyd, d., Herr-Stephenson, B., Lange, P. G., Pascoe, C. J. and Robinson, L. 2008. *Living and Learning with New Media: Summary of Findings from the Digital Youth Project.* Cambridge, MA: The MIT Press; Ito, M. et al. 2010. *Hanging Out, Messing Around, and Geeking Out.* Cambridge, MA: The MIT Press.

3   Anthropologists have frequently challenged this distinction between formal and informal learning. For example see Borofsky, R. 1987. *Making History: Pukapukan and Anthropological Constructions of Knowledge.* Cambridge: Cambridge University Press. Akinnaso, F. N. 1992. 'Schooling, Language and Knowledge in Literate and Nonliterate societies.' *Comparative Studies in Society and History* 34: 68–109.

4   Lange, P. 2014. *Kids on YouTube.* Walnut Creek, CA: Left Coast Press.

5   Wesch. M. (lecturer and dir.). 2008. 'An Anthropological Introduction to YouTube.' YouTube, 26 July 2008. http://www.youtube.com/watch?v=TPAO- lZ4_hU, accessed 14 September 2014.

6   Scobie, W. 2011. 'An Anthropological Introduction to YouTube by Michael Wesch.' *American Anthropologist* 113(4): 661–2.

7   Key contributions to the anthropology of learning came from the work of Jean Lave. See Lave, J.1993. *Situated Learning: Legitimate Peripheral Participation.* Cambridge: Cambridge University Press. Particularly influential in relation to informal learning online is Wenger, E. 1998. *Communities of Practice: Learning, Meaning, and Identity.* Cambridge: Cambridge University Press. For instance see Kimble, C., Hildreth, P. M. and Bourdon, I., eds. 2008. *Communities of Practice: Creating Learning Environments for Educators.* Charlotte, NC: Information Age.

8   Ito, M., Horst, H., Bittanti, M., boyd, d., Herr-Stephenson, B., Lange, P. G., Pascoe, C. J. and Robinson, L. 2008. *Living and Learning with New Media: Summary of Findings from the Digital Youth Project.* Cambridge, MA: The MIT Press.

9   boyd, d. 2014. *It's Complicated: The Social Lives of Networked Teens.* New Haven, CT; London: Yale University Press.

10 Clark, L. S. 2013. *The Parent App.* Oxford: Oxford University Press.

11 Livingstone, S. and Sefton-Green, J. Forthcoming. *The Class: Connections and Disconnections in the Digital Age.* New York: New York University Press.

12 For examples see Cross, M. 2011. *Bloggerati, Twitterati: How Blogs and Twitter are Transforming Popular Culture.* Santa Barbara, CA: Praeger. Wallis, C. 2013. *Technomobility in China: Young Migrant Women and Mobile Phones.* New York; London: New York University Press.

13 Livingstone, S., Mascheroni, G., Ólafsson, K. and Haddon, L., with EU Kids Online and Net Children Go Mobile. 2014. *Children's Online Risks and Opportunities: Comparative Findings from EU Kids Online and Net Children Go Mobile.* November 2014. http://eprints.lse.ac.uk/60513/. Hasebrink, U., Livingstone, S. and Haddon, L. 2008. *Comparing Children's Online Opportunities and Risks across Europe: Cross-National Comparisons for EU Kids Online.* 2nd edition. http://eprints.lse.ac.uk/24368/

14 It is important to emphasise that this 'rule of thumb' comparison of economic development is between our field sites, rather than between the countries of our research.

15 For examples see Fong, V. L. 2004. *Only Hope: Coming of Age under China's One-child Policy.* Stanford, CA: Stanford University Press. Kipnis, A. B. 2011. *Governing Educational Desire: Culture, Politics, and Schooling in China.* Chicago, IL: University of Chicago Press.

16 By default Snapchat users are not able to forward such images. However, most users are aware that they can easily capture and then forward received Snapchat images via the phone's built-in screen capture function.

17 Smith, P. K. and Brain, P. 2000. 'Bullying in Schools: Lessons from Two Decades of Research.' *Aggressive Behavior* 26(1): 1–9.

18 Hull, G. and Schultz, K. 2002. *School's Out: Bridging Out-of-school Literacies with Classroom Practice.* New York, NY: Teachers College Press.

19 Street, B. 2003. 'What's "New" in New Literacy Studies? Critical Approaches to Literacy in Theory and Practice.' *Current Issues in Comparative Education* 5(2): 77–91.

20 Potter, J. 2011. 'New Literacies, New Practices and Learner Research: Across the Semi-Permeable Membrane between Home and School.' *Lifelong Learning in Europe* (3): 174–80.

21 A film showing this example is one of many such illustrative films that can be found at www. ucl.ac.uk/wh-we-post

22 These are groups formed by the school to encourage and organise parental participation in the running of the school.

Chapter 6

1 Adorno, T. W. 1991. 'Free time.' *The Culture Industry: Selected Essays on Mass Culture.* Bernstein, J. M., ed. London: Routledge. 162–70. Broadbent, S. 2011. *L'Intimite au Travail.* Paris: Fyp Editions. Grint, K. 2005. *The Sociology of Work: Introduction.* Cambridge: Polity Press.

2 Broadbent, S. 2012. 'Approaches to Personal Communication.' In Horst, H. and Miller, D., eds. *Digital Anthropology.* 127–45. London, Oxford: Berg.

3 Baba, M. L. 1998. 'The Anthropology of Work in the Fortune 1000: A Critical Retrospective.' *Anthropology of Work Review* 18(4): 17–28. Jordan, A. 2003. *Business Anthropology.* Long Grove: Waveland Press. Ortiz, S. 1994. 'Work, the Division of Labour and Co-operation.' In Ingold, T., ed. *Companion Encyclopedia of Anthropology.* London: Taylor & Francis. Wallman, S., ed. 1979. *Social Anthropology of Work.* Vol. 19. London: Academic Press.

4 Holmström, M. 1976. *South Indian Factory Workers: Their Life and Their World.* Cambridge: Cambridge University Press. Vidyarthi, L. P., ed. 1984. *Applied Anthropology in India: Principles, Problems, and Case Studies.* New Delhi: Kitab Mahal.

5 De Neve, G. 2005. *The everyday Politics of Labour: Working Lives in India's Informal Economy.* Oxford: Berghahn Books. Holmström, M. 1976. *South Indian Factory Workers: Their Life and Their World.* Cambridge: Cambridge University Press.

6 See Fig. 4.21.

7 https://press.linkedin.com/about-linkedin (28 August 2015)

8 The Italian term for artisanal businesses, '*imprese artigiane*', encompasses much more than handicrafts, including any kind of activity performed with your hands, from agriculture to plumbing, pottery to hairdressing.

9 boyd, d. 2014. *It's Complicated: The Social Lives of Networked Teens.* New Haven, CT; London: Yale University Press.

10 Fuller, C. J. and Narasimhan, H. 2007. 'Information Technology Professionals and the New-rich Middle Class in Chennai (Madras).' *Modern Asian Studies* 41(1): 121–50. Nisbett, N. 2009. *Growing Up in the Knowledge Society: Living the IT Dream in Bangalore.* New Delhi: Routledge.

11 http://blogs.ucl.ac.uk/global-social-media/2013/11/24/what-will-we-learn-from-the-fall-of-facebook/

12 It is only supposition, but possibly the reason for this limited concern is an awareness that if a company seriously offended them there are increasingly alternatives available.

13 An expansion of the barcode that proliferated into many sectors (even some gravestones) for a while – http://www.theatlantic.com/technology/archive/2014/05/qr-codes-for-the-dead/370901/

14 Lee, K., Kim, J. H. and Woo, W. T., eds. 2009. *Power and Sustainability of the Chinese State.* New York: Routledge.

15 http://www.nytimes.com/2008/07/26/business/worldbusiness/26internet.html?_r=0

16 Which is also why our survey shows them 'liking' advertisements, even if they don't then purchase the products. For more details see the discussion of Fig. 4.19 above.

17 Goldfarb, A. and Tucker, C. 2011. 'Online Display Advertising: Targeting and Obtrusiveness.' *Marketing Science* 30(3): 389–404.

18 This is not so evident from Fig. 4.19, but the question asked there was slightly different. In any case we view ethnographic evidence gathered over 15 months as far more authoritative than a survey question response.

19 This is the subject of one of our films on ucl.ac.uk/why-we-post

20 The subject of another film on ucl.ac.uk/why-we-post

21 We are looking at this from the perspective of everyday users. We recognise that for a company for whom social media advertising is low-cost, even a tiny proportional uptake may be worthwhile.

22 See also Chu, J. Y. 2010. *Cosmologies of Credit: Transnational Mobility and the Politics of Destination in China.* Durham, NC: Duke University Press.

23 Stafford, C. 1995. *The Roads of Chinese Childhood: Learning and Identification in Angang.* Cambridge; New York: Cambridge University Press.

24 http://www.wantchinatimes.com/news-subclass-cnt.aspx?id=20140205000127 &cid=1102

25 Zelizer, V. 2011. *Economic Lives.* Princeton, NJ: Princeton University Press.

26 McKay, D. 2007. 'Sending Dollars Shows Feeling: Emotions and Economies in Filipino Migration.' *Mobilities* 2(2): 175–94.

27 These should not therefore be confused with other new digital commercial practices such as Airbnb or Uber, which are all about using the same digital facilities for making money.

28 Sahlins, M. 1972. *Stone Age Economics.* Chicago: Aldine-Atherton.

Chapter 7

1 See Prensky, M. 2001. 'Digital Natives, Digital Immigrants.' *On the Horizon* 9(5): 1–6.

2 See Miller, D. and Slater, D. 2000. *The Internet: An Ethnographic Approach.* Oxford: Berg.

3 See detailed discussion about human society's anxiety about 'new' technology in Marvin, C. 1988. *When Old Technologies were New.* New York: Oxford University Press.

4 Plato. 2008 (360 BC). *Phaedrus.* Charleston, SC: Forgotten Books.

5 See Turkle, S. 2011. *Alone Together: Why We Expect More from Technology and Less from Each Other.* New York: Basic Books.

6 See Carr, N. 2011. *The Shallows: What the Internet Is Doing to Our Brains.* New York: W. W. Norton & Company.

7 Horst, H. and Miller, D., eds. 2012. *Digital Anthropology.* London: Berg. 11–15. See also Butler, J. 1990. *Gender Trouble.* New York: Routledge. Baker, L. D. 1998. *From Savage to Negro: Anthropology and the Construction of Race.* Los Angeles, CA: University of California Press.

8 Miller, D. & Sinanan, J. 2014. *Webcam.* Cambridge: Polity Press.

9 See the discussion of key concepts used to analyse different ways of personal connection in Baym, N. 2010. *Personal Connections in the Digital Age.* Cambridge: Polity Press. 6–12.

10 See Goffman, E. 1975. *Frame Analysis.* Harmondsworth: Penguin.

11 See Aarsand, P. A. 2008. 'Frame Switches and Identity Performances: Alternating Between Online and Offline.' *Text & Talk.* 28(2): 147–65.

12 Lomborg, S. 2014. *Social Media, Social Genres: Making Sense of the Ordinary.* London: Routledge.

13 This is possible on Facebook, but the facility is not used much by our informants.

14 See Yan, Y. 1996. *The Flow of Gifts: Reciprocity and Social Networks in a Chinese Village.* Stanford, CA: Stanford University Press.

15 In China one can also use the QQ group ('*QQ qun*') function, which is similar to WhatsApp groups in using offline contacts to form online conversation groups. As with WhatsApp, this allows one to have a variety of such groups – more in keeping with the way we relate to friendship offline.

16 See the discussion of 'scalable sociality' in Chapter 1 of this volume.

17 See Jankowiak, W. 2002. "Proper Men and Proper Women: Parental Affection in the Chinese Family.' Brownell, S. and Wasserstrom, J., eds. *Chinese Femininities/Chinese Masculinities: A Reader.* Berkeley, CA: University of California Press. 361–81.

18 Miller, D. 2015. 'The Tragic Dénouement of English Sociality.' *Cultural Anthropology* 30(2): 336–57. This is also a main theme in Miller, D. 2016. *Social Media in an English Village.* London: UCL Press.

19 See Broadbent, S. 2012. 'Approaches to Digital Communication.' Horst, H. and Miller, D., eds. *Digital Anthropology.* London: Berg. 127–45.

20 Broadbent, S. 2012. 'Approaches to Digital Communication.' Horst, H. and Miller, D., eds. *Digital Anthropology.* London: Berg. 127–45.

21 See Fig. 4.2.

22 As with many of these generalisations, they vary by genre of platform use. People are not worried about followers on Twitter or Instagram, where these may not be regarded as social

connections, but they are concerned when it comes to platforms where there is a connotation of personal relationships.

23 This is a key theme in McDonald, T. Forthcoming. *Social Media in Rural China*. London: UCL Press.

24 How social media have facilitated the transformation of people's social networks and the creation of individual-based forms of sociality is a key topic in Costa, E. 2016. *Social Media in Southeast Turkey*. London: UCL Press.

25 See Sennett, R. 1977. *The Fall of Public Man*. New York: Knopf.

26 See Giddens, A. 1991. *Modernity and Self-identity: Self and Society in the Late Modern Age*. Cambridge: Polity Press.

27 Goffman, E. 1975. *Frame Analysis*. Harmondsworth: Penguin. Also see Brubaker, R. and Cooper, F., 2000. 'Beyond "Identity"'. *Theory and Society* 29: 1–47.

28 See Chapter 11.

29 See Miller, D. 2011. *Tales from Facebook*. Cambridge: Polity Press.

30 See the detailed analysis in Wang, X. Forthcoming. *Social Media in Industrial China*. London: UCL Press.

31 See Bargh, J.A. et al. 2002. 'Can You See the Real Me? Activation and Expression of the "True Self" on the Internet.' *Journal of Social Issues* 58(1): 33–48.

32 For a general critique of this idea that digital technologies reduce our humanity see Miller, D. and Sinanan, J. 2014. *Webcam*. Cambridge: Polity Press. Chapter 1.

33 Turkle, S. 1997. *Life on the Screen: Identity in the Age of the Internet*. New York: Simon and Schuster.

34 See Baym, N. 1999. *Tune In, Log On: Soaps, Fandom, and Online Community*. New York: Sage.

35 See Hampton, K. and Wellman, B. 2003. 'Neighboring in Netville: How the Internet Supports Community and Social Capital in a Wired Suburb.' *City and Community* 2(4): 277–311.

36 See Livingstone, S. 2008. 'Taking Risky Opportunities in Youthful Content Creation: Teenagers' Use of Social Networking Sites for Intimacy, Privacy and Self-expression.' *New Media & Society* 10: 393–411.

Chapter 8

1 Rheingold, H. 1993. Virtual Community: Homesteading in the Electronic Frontier. New York: Adddison-Wesley. Turkle, S. 1997. *Life on the Screen: Identity in the Age of the Internet*. New York: Simon and Schuster.

2 Plant, S. 1997. *Zeros and Ones: Digital Women and the New Technoculture*. London: Fourth Estate.

3 Among others see Haraway, D. 1991. 'A Cyborg Manifesto: Science, Technology and Social Feminism in the Late Twentieth Century.' *Simians, Cyborgs and Women: The reinvention of Nature*. New York: Routledge.

4 Ortner, S. B. 1972. 'Is Female to Male as Nature Is to Culture?' *Feminist Studies* 1(2): 5–31.

5 Castells, M. 1997. *The Power of Identity. The Information Age: Economy, Society and Culture Vol II*. Cambridge, MA; Oxford: Blackwell. Shade, L. R. 2002. *Gender and Community in the Social Construction of the Internet*. New York: Peter Lang.

6 Wajcman, J. 2004. *TechnoFeminism*. Cambridge: Polity Press.

7 Livingstone, S. 2008. 'Taking Risky Opportunities in Youthful Content Creation: Teenagers' Use of Social Networking Sites for Intimacy, Privacy and Self-expression.' *New Media & Society* 10: 393–411. Van Doorn, N., Van Zoonen, L. and Wyatt, S. 2007. 'Writing from Experience: Presentations of Gender Identity on Weblogs.' *European Journal of Women's Studies* 14(2): 143–59. Paechter, C. 2013. 'Young Women Online: Collaboratively Constructing Identities.' *Pedagogy, Culture and Society* 21(1): 111–27. Gray, M. L. 2009. *Out in the Country: Youth, Media, and Queer Visibility in Rural America*. New York: New York University Press.

8 boyd, d. 2014. *It's Complicated: The Social Lives of Networked Teens*. New Haven, CT; London: Yale University Press.

9 With the expression 'public-facing' social media we refer to those online spaces that are visible to a large network of people, ranging from hundreds up to an unlimited number.

10 Butler, J. 1990. *Gender Trouble*. New York: Routledge.
11 See Fig. 4.7.
12 Van Dijck, J. 2013c. '"You Have One Identity"': Performing the Self on Facebook and LinkedIn.' *Media, Culture & Society* 35(2): 199–215.
13 Miller, D. and Sinanan, J. Forthcoming. *Visualising Facebook*. London: UCL Press.
14 Lesbian Gay Bisexual Transgender. For wider issues around visibility see, for example, Gray, M. L. 2009. *Out in the Country: Youth, Media, and Queer Visibility in Rural America*. New York: New York University Press.

Chapter 9

1 With respect to the impact of the mobile phones, see for example Jeffrey, R. and Doron, A. 2013. *The Great Indian Phone Book*. London: Hurst. Wallis, C. 2013. *Technomobility in China: Young Migrant Women and Mobile Phones*. New York; London: New York University Press. Miller, D. and Horst, H. 2006. *The Cell Phone*. Oxford: Berg.
2 Samsung as a brand has had a global lead in market share from 2012 to current years for low-cost smartphones. See http://www.idc.com/prodserv/smartphone-market-share.jsp (accessed: 26 August 2015).
3 A key figure in such discussion has been Amartya Sen, for example Sen, A. 1992. *Inequality Re-examined*. Cambridge, MA: Harvard University Press. A major recent discussion about the causes of contemporary inequality is Piketty, T. 2014. *Capital in the Twenty-First Century*. Cambridge, MA: Belknap Press.
4 Bourdieu, Pierre. 1984. *Distinction: A Social Critique of the Judgment of Taste*. Cambridge, MA: Harvard University Press.
5 Skeggs, B. 1997. *Formations of Class and Gender: Becoming Respectable*. London: Sage.
6 Tacchi, J. 2012. 'Digital Engagement.' Horst, H. and Miller, D., eds. *Digital Anthropology*. London: Berg. 225–41.
7 Graham, M. 2014. 'Internet Geographies: Data Shadows and Digital Divisions of Labour.' Graham, M. and Dutton, W., eds. *Society and the Internet*. Oxford: Oxford University Press. 99–116.
8 There are many potentially relevant literatures here. One which we admit to having largely neglected, as couched in policy rather than ethnographic concerns, is that on ICTs and development. See, for example, Slater, D. 2014. *New Media, Development and Globalization: Making Connections in the Global South*. Cambridge: Polity Press. For an approach influenced by Sen see Kleine, D. 2013. *Technologies of Choice: ICT's Development and the Capabilities Approach*. Cambridge, MA: The MIT Press.
9 Chen, W. and Wellman, B. 2004. 'The Global Digital Divide Within and Between Countries.' *IT & Society* 1(7): 39–45; Zickuhr, K. 2013. *Who's Not Online and Why*. Rep. Washington DC: Pew Research Center's Internet & American Life Project.
10 Warschauer, M. 2004. *Technology and Social Inclusion: Rethinking the Digital Divide*. Cambridge, MA: The MIT Press.
11 Rainie, L. and Wellman, B. 2012. *Networked*. Cambridge, MA: The MIT Press. 257–9.
12 Rheingold, H. 2012. *Net Smart: How to Thrive On Line*. Cambridge, MA: The MIT Press.
13 Graham, M. 2014. 'Internet Geographies: Data Shadows and Digital Divisions of Labour.' Graham, M. and Dutton, W., eds. *Society and the Internet*. Oxford: Oxford University Press. 99–116.
14 The techno-utopian view is mirrored by the dystopian arguments that technology is bad for society because it makes us more dependent on it, more isolated and more exposed to institutional control and alienated. See for example Carr, N. 2011. *The Shallows: What the Internet Is Doing to Our Brains*. New York: W. W. Norton & Company. Turkle, S. 2011. *Alone Together: Why We Expect More from Technology and Less from Each Other*. New York: Basic Books. Morozov, E. 2012. *The Net Delusion: The Dark Side of Internet Freedom*. New York, NY: Public Affairs.
15 Among the best WE know are: Kelly, K. 1994. *Out of Control: The Rise of Neo-biological Civilization*. Reading, MA: Addison-Wesley. Johnson, S. 2001. *Emergence: The Connected Lives of Ants, Brains, Cities, and Software*. New York: Scribner. Shirky, C. 2008. *Here Comes Everybody: The Power of Organizing without Organizations*. New York: Penguin.

16 Rheingold, H. 1993. *Virtual Community: Homesteading in the Electronic Frontier*. New York: Addison-Wesley. Turkle, S. 1997. *Life on the Screen: Identity in the Age of the Internet*. New York: Simon and Schuster.

17 Barlow, J. 'A Declaration of the Independence of Cyberspace.' Electronic Frontier Foundation, 8 February 1996. Web. Accessed 7 July 2015.

18 boyd, d. 2014. *It's Complicated: The Social Lives of Networked Teens*. New Haven, CT; London: Yale University Press. 16.

19 boyd, d. 2014. *It's Complicated: The Social Lives of Networked Teens*. New Haven, CT; London: Yale University Press. 23.

20 boyd, d. 2013. 'White Flight in Networked Publics? How Race and Class Shaped American Teen Engagement with Myspace and Facebook.' Nakamura, L. and Chow-White, P., eds. *Race after the Internet*. New York: Routledge. 203–22.

21 Clark, L. S. 2013. *The Parent App*. Oxford: Oxford University Press.

22 An important example is Qiu, J. L. 2009. *Working-Class Network Society: Communication Technology and the Information Have-Less in Urban China*. Cambridge. Cambridge, MA: The MIT Press. Wallis, C. 2013. *Technomobility in China: Young Migrant Women and Mobile Phones*. New York; London: New York University Press.

23 This act does not signal the parents' lack of care for the children; traditionally there is an expectation that this is a temporary experience and not an informal adoption. Sandra and all her brothers and sisters were reclaimed by their parents and they are still attached by family bonds.

24 Bahia was the centre of the Portuguese colonial effort in the new world, based on mostly slave labour running plantations of products such as sugar cane. According to recent census data, Salvador, the regional capital, has more than 700,000 people of African descent; it is the largest black population outside of Africa, and also the most vulnerable locally in socio-economic terms.

25 There are cases in which this opportunity improved the life of the child, giving him or her the opportunity to study and be treated with respect. However, the majority of these exchanges leave deep scars as the child is treated as a servant, often taken to look after other children of nearly the same age, but without receiving the emotional attention given to the actual sons and daughters.

26 Weber, M. 2002 (1905). *The Protestant Ethic and the Spirit of Capitalism*. London: Penguin Books.

27 The reproduction of inequality, by those experiencing it, is often referred to as 'symbolic violence', outlined by Bourdieu, P. and Wacquant, L. 1992. *Symbolic Violence. An Invitation to Reflective Sociology*. Chicago, IL: University of Chicago Press. 167–73.

28 Bourdieu, Pierre. 1984. *Distinction: A Social Critique of the Judgment of Taste*. Cambridge, MA: Harvard University Press.

29 See examples of these practices in Miller, D. and Sinanan, J. Forthcoming. *Visualising Facebook*. London: UCL Press.

30 The word 'vlogger' is a contraction of 'video bloggers'. It describes the group of people who create online content through recording and sharing videos, particularly through YouTube.

31 In anthropological research levelling mechanisms were described as part of peasant societies, and they work by inhibiting an individual's efforts to evolve economically. This levelling relates to a shared understanding that common goods are limited; one only increases one's wealth to the detriment of all the others. This model has evolved from the study of peasant societies, but applies to a wider variety of cases. See Rubel, A. J. 1977. '"Limited Good" and "Social Comparison": Two Theories, One Problem.' *Ethos* 5(2): 224–38.

Chapter 10

1 Among other sources see http://www.al-monitor.com/pulse/originals/2013/09/turkeys-akp-twitter-election.html; http://www.wsj.com/articles/SB10001424127887323527004579079151479634742; http://www.hurriyetdailynews.com/ruling-akp-hires-thousands-for-new-social-media-campaign.aspx?pageID=238&nID=54479&NewsCatID=338

2 See Castells, M. 1996. *The Rise of the Network Society. The Information Age: Economy, Society and Culture Vol. I*. Oxford: Blackwell and Castells, M. 1997. *The Power of Identity. The*

Information Age: Economy, Society and Culture Vol II. Cambridge, MA; Oxford: Blackwell, for some of the most influential theories of the internet and networked organisation. See also Oates, S., Owen, D. and Gibson, R. K., eds. 2006. *The Internet and Politics. Citizens, Voters and Activists.* New York: Routledge. Klotz, R. J. 2004. *The Politics of Internet Communication.* Lanham, MD: Rowman & Littlefield.

3 See Fountain, J. E. 2001. *Building the Virtual State: Information Technology and Institutional Change.* Washington, DC: Brookings Institution Press; Narayan, G. 2007. 'Addressing the Digital Divide: E-governance and M-governance in a Hub and Spoke model.' *The Electronic Journal on Information Systems in Developing Countries* 31(1): 1–14 and Norris, P. 2001. *Digital Divide: Civic Engagement, Information Poverty, and the Internet Worldwide.* Cambridge: Cambridge University Press.

4 Papacharissi, Z. 2010b. 'The virtual sphere 2.0: The Internet, the Public Sphere, and Beyond.' Chadwick, A. and Howard, P. N., eds. *Routledge Handbook of Internet Politics.* Oxford: Taylor & Francis. 230–45. Papacharissi, Z. 2004. 'Democracy Online: Civility, Politeness, and the Democratic Potential of Online Political Discussion Groups.' *New Media & Society* 6(2): 259–83.

5 Gerbaudo, P. 2012. *Tweets and the Streets: Social media and contemporary activism.* London: Pluto Press. Clay. S. 2011 'The Political Power of Social Media.' *Foreign Affairs* 90: 128–41. Seib, P. 2012. *Real-time Diplomacy: Politics and Power in the Social Media Era.* Basingstoke: Palgrave Macmillan.

6 Chadwick, A., and Howard, P. N., eds. 2010. *Routledge Handbook of Internet Politics.* Oxford: Taylor & Francis. Postill, J. 2012. 'Digital Politics and Political Engagement.' In Horst, H. and Miller, D., eds. *Digital Anthropology.* London: Berg.

7 Heeks, R. 2001. 'Building E-governance for Development: A Framework for National and Donor Action.' http://www.man.ac.uk/idpm/idpm_dp.htm#ig. Chadwick, A. 2003. 'Bringing E-Democracy Back In: Why it Matters for Future Research on E-Governance.' *Social Science Computer Review* 21(4): 443–55. Dawes, S. S. 2008. 'The Evolution and Continuing Challenges of E-governance.' *Public Administration Review* 68(1): 86–102.

8 Dahlberg, L. 2001. 'The Internet and Democratic Discourse: Exploring the Prospects of Online Deliberative Forums Extending the Public Sphere.' *Information, Communication & Society* 4(4): 615–33. Fenton, N. and Barassi, V. 2011. 'Alternative Media and Social Networking Sites: The Politics of Individuation and Political Participation.' *The Communication Review* 14(3): 179–96. Habermas, J. 1969. *The Structural Transformation of the Public Sphere: An Inquiry into a Category of Bourgeois Society.* Cambridge, MA: The MIT Press.

9 Gerbaudo, P. 2012. *Tweets and the Streets: Social Media and Contemporary Activism.* London: Pluto Press. Hussain, M. M. and Howard, P. N. 2012. *Opening Closed Regimes: Civil Society, Information Infrastructure, and Political Islam.* IN Anduiza, E., Jensen, M. and Jorba, L., eds. *Comparing Digital Politics: Civic Engagement and Political Participation.* Cambridge: Cambridge University Press. Hussain, M. M. and Howard, P. N. 2013. 'What Best Explains Successful Protest Cascades? Icts and the Fuzzy Causes of the Arab Spring.' International Studies Review 15.1: 48–66. Lim, M. 2012. 'Clicks, Cabs, and Coffee Houses: Social Media and Oppositional Movements in Egypt, 2004–2011.' *Journal of Communication* 62(2): 231–48. Salvatore, A., ed. 2011. 'Between Everyday Life and Political Revolution: The Social Web in the Middle East.' *Oriente Moderno*, n.s. XCI/1, 2011. Tufekci, Z. 2014. 'The Medium and the Movement: Digital Tools, Social Movement Politics, and the End of the Free Rider Problem.' *Policy & Internet* 6 (2): 202–8: Tufekci, Z. and Wilson, C. 2012. 'Social Media and the Decision to Participate in Political Protest: Observation from Tahrir Square.' *Journal of Communication* 62 (2): 363–79.

10 Fuchs, C. 2012. 'Social Media, Riots, and Revolutions.' *Capital & Class* 36(3): 383–91. Morozov, E. 2012. *The Net Delusion: The Dark Side of Internet Freedom.* New York, NY: Public Affairs.

11 Coleman, G. 2012. 'Phreaks, Hackers, and Trolls: The politics of Transgression and Spectacle.' Maniberg, M., ed. *The Social Media Reader.* New York: New York University Press. 99–119. Coleman, G. 2014. *Hacker, Hoaxer, Whistleblower, Spy: The Many Faces of Anonymous.* London; Brooklyn, NY: Verso.

12 Although several analyses of internet politics and social media's role in political engagement contribute to debates on democracy, civil society and governance, they also start

from a similar position by engaging with what political engagement means locally. See, for example, Tufekci, Z. 2014. 'The Medium and the Movement: Digital Tools, Social Movement Politics, and the End of the Free Rider Problem.' *Policy & Internet* 6(2): 202–8. Tufekci, Z. and Wilson, C. 2012. 'Social Media and the Decision to Participate in Political Protest: Observation from Tahrir Square.' *Journal of Communication* 62(2): 363–79. Lim, M. 2012. 'Clicks, Cabs, and Coffee Houses: Social Media and Oppositional Movements in Egypt, 2004–2011.' *Journal of Communication* 62(2): 231–48. Lim, M. 2013. 'Many Clicks but Little Sticks: Social Media Activism in Indonesia.' *Journal of Contemporary Asia* 43(4): 636–57; Morozov, E. 2009. 'Iran: Downside to the "Twitter Revolution".' *Dissent* 56(4): 10–14.

13 The Hong Kong Umbrella Movement/Occupy Central is the most recent example. See Fu, K. W. and Chan, C. H. 2015. 'Networked Collective Action in the 2014 Hong Kong Occupy Movement: Analysing a Facebook Sharing Network.' *International Conference on Public Policy*, ICPP 2015. Tsui, L. 2015. 'The Coming Colonization of Hong Kong Cyberspace: Government Responses to the Use of New Technologies by the Umbrella Movement.' *Chinese Journal of Communication*. Forthcoming: 1–9.

14 For more comprehensive discussions of how social media is used in relation to politics, see the individual volumes in this series.

15 See for internet censorship in China MacKinnon, R. 2008. 'Flatter World and Thicker Walls? Blogs, Censorship and Civic Discourse in China.' *Public Choice* 134(1–2): 31–46. See also for internet censorship in Turkey Akdeniz, Y. and Altiparmak, K. 2008. *Internet: Restricted Access: A critical Assessment of Internet Content Regulation and Censorship in Turkey.* Akdenizli, B., ed. 2015. *Digital Transformations in Turkey: Current Perspectives in Communication Studies.* Lanham, MD: Lexington Books.

16 Noelle-Neumann, E. 1974. 'The Spiral of Silence: A Theory of Public Opinion.' *Journal of Communication* 24(2): 43–51. The Pew Research Center investigated how the 'spiral of silence' played out among social media users in the US, in which individuals avoided posting views on political topics where they believed their friends would disagree with them. Hampton, K. N., Rainie, L., Lu, W., Dwyer, M., Shin, I. and Purcell, K. 2014. 'Social Media and the "Spiral of Silence".' Pew Research Center, Washington, DC. Available at: http://www.pewinternet.org/2014/08/26/social-media-and-the-spiral-of-silence/

17 Brants, K. 2005. Guest editor's introduction: 'The Internet and the Public Sphere.' *Political Communication* 22(2): 143--6; Papacharissi, Z. 2002. 'The Virtual Sphere: The Internet as a Public Sphere.' *New Media & Society* 4(1): 9–27; Poster, M. 1997. 'Cyberdemocracy: Internet and the Public Sphere.' *Internet Culture* 201: 218.

18 King, G., Pan, J. and Roberts, M. E. 2013. 'How Censorship in China Allows Government Criticism But Silences Collective Expression.' *American Political Science Review* 107(2): 326–43.

19 PKK is the Kurdish militant organisation that has been involved in an armed struggle with the Turkish state from 1984 until 2013, when the ceasefire was declared. However, the state of this is unclear at the time of writing (summer 2015).

20 Ho, C. 2000. 'Popular Culture and the Aestheticization of Politics: Hegemonic Struggle and Postcolonial Nationalism in Trinidad Carnival.' *Transforming Anthropology* 9(1): 3–18.

Chapter 11

1 See Hjorth, L. and Hendry, N. 2015. 'A Snapshot of Social Media: Camera Phone Practices.' *Social Media+ Society*, 1(1), 2056305115580478. Gibbs, M., Meese, J., Arnold, M., Nansen, B. and Carter, M. 2015. '#Funeral and Instagram: Death, Social Media, and Platform Vernacular.' *Information, Communication & Society* 18(3): 255–68 and Cruz, E. G. and Meyer, E. 2012. 'Creation and Control in the Photographic Process: iPhones and the Emerging Fifth Moment of Photography.' *Photographies* 5(2) for more discussion on visual practices and social media platforms.

2 Ginsburg, F. 1995. 'Mediating Culture: Indigenous Media, Ethnographic Film, and the Production of Identity.' *Fields of vision: Essays in Film Studies, Visual Anthropology, and Photography.* Berkeley, CA: University of California Press, 258, MacDougall, D. 2005. *The Corporeal Image: Film, Ethnography, and the Senses.* Princeton, NJ: Princeton

University Press. Sprague, S. 1978. 'How I See the Yoruba See Themselves.' *Studies in the Anthropology of Visual Communications*. 5(1): 9–29; Edwards, E. 1992. *Anthropology and Photography 1860–1929*. Royal Anthropological Institute. Pinney, C. 2011. *Photography and Anthropology*. London: Reaktion.

3   "By looking at the range of posts, and photos in particular, we can do an ethnography of the range of culturally inflected relationships enmeshed and encoded in the visual.' Pink, S. 2001. 'Visual Ethnography.' *Images, Media and Representation in Research*. London; Thousand Oaks; New Delhi: Sage. See also Banks, M. and Morphy, H., eds. 1997. *Rethinking Visual Anthropology*. New Haven, CT: Yale University Press.

4   Ginsburg, F. 1995. 'Mediating Culture: Indigenous Media, Ethnographic Film, and the Production of Identity.' *Fields of Vision: Essays in Film Studies, Visual Anthropology, and Photography*. Berkeley, CA: University of California Press. MacDougall, D. 2005. *The Corporeal Image: Film, Ethnography, and the Senses*. Princeton, NJ: Princeton University Press. 3. See also Bateson, G. and Mead, M. 1942. 'Balinese character. A photographic analysis.' *Special Publications of the New York Academy of Science*: 17–92. Marshall, J. *A Kalahari Family*. Film, 2002. Gardner, R. *The Nuer*, Film, 1971.

5   Miller, D. and Sinanan, J. Forthcoming. *Visualising Facebook*. London: UCL Press.

6   Turkle, S. 1997. *Life on the Screen: Identity in the Age of the Internet*. New York: Simon and Schuster.

7   See http://www.theguardian.com/media-network/media-network-blog/2014/mar/13/selfies-social-media-love-digital-narcassism, http://www.theguardian.com/technology/2013/dec/06/selfies-status-updates-digital-bragging-web

8   By contrast, see http://www.theguardian.com/commentisfree/2014/sep/11/when-taking-selfies-in-trinidad-its-whats-on-the-outside-that-matters

9   For more on social uses of photography, see Van House, N. A. and Davis, M. 2005. 'The Social Life of Camera Phone Images.' *Proceedings of the Pervasive Image Capture and Sharing: New Social Practices and Implications for Technology Workshop (PICS 2005) at the Seventh International Conference on Ubiquitous Computing (UbiComp 2005)*. Voida, A. and Mynatt, E. D. 2005. 'Six Themes of the Communicative Appropriation of Photographic Images.' *Proceedings of the SIGCHI Conference on Human Factors in Computing Systems*. 171–80. ACM. David, G. 2010. 'Camera Phone Images, Videos and Live Streaming: A Contemporary Visual Trend.' *Visual Studies* 25(1): 89–98. Okabe, D. and Ito, M. 2006. 'Everyday Contexts of Camera Phone Use: Steps Toward Technosocial Ethnographic Frameworks.' Höflich, J. R, and Hartmann, M., eds. *Mobile Communication in Everyday Life: Ethnographic Views, Observations and Reflections*. Berlin: Frank & Timme. 79–102.

10   See Hjorth, L. 2007. 'Snapshot of Almost Contact: the Rise of Camera Phone Practices and a Case Study in Seoul, Korea.' *Continuum: Journal of Media & Cultural Studies* 21(2): 227–38 and Pink, S. 2011. 'Amateur Photographic Practice, Collective Representation and the Constitution of Place.' *Visual Studies* 26(2): 92–101.

11   See Dijck, J. van. 2008. 'Digital Photography: Communication, Identity, Memory.' *Visual Communication* 7: 57–76.

12   See Costa, E. 2016. *Social Media in Southeast Turkey*. London: UCL Press and Venkatraman, S. Forthcoming. *Social Media in South India*. London: UCL Press. Chapter 3.

13   '*Aburrido*' is Spanish for 'bored' and '*fome*' is Chilean slang for 'boring'.

14   Bourdieu, P. and Whiteside, S. 1996. *Photography: A Middle-brow Art*. Stanford, CA: Stanford University Press.

15   Bourdieu, P. and Bourdieu, M. C. 2004. 'The peasant and photography.' *Ethnography* 5(4): 601–16. (603).

16   For more on the relationship between comic books and increasing literacy see Bitz, M. 2004. 'The Comic Book Project: The Lives of Urban Youth.' *Art Education* 57(2): 33–46. See also Bitz, M. 2010. *When Commas Meet Kryptonite: Classroom Lessons from the Comic Book Project. Language and Literacy Series*. New York: Teachers College Press.

17   See Spyer, J. Forthcoming. *Social Media in Emergent Brazil*. London: UCL Press.

18   Ritchie, D. 2005. 'Frame-Shifting in Humor and Irony.' *Metaphor and Symbol* 20(4): 288.

19   Kermit the Frog provides a good example of how social media both facilitates the global spread of visual images yet simultaneously allows their rapid local re-contextualisation.

20   Ito, M. 2005. 'Mobile phones, Japanese Youth, and the Re-placement of Social Contact.' *Mobile Communication* 131–48. Ito, M. and Okabe, D. 2005. 'Intimate Visual Co-presence.' *Position paper for the Seventh International Conference on Ubiquitous Computing, Tokyo*.

Okabe, D. 2006. 'Everyday Contexts of Camera Phone Use: Steps Toward Techno-social Ethnographic Frameworks.' *Mobile Communications in Everyday Life: Ethnographic Views, Observations, and Reflections.*

21 For an extended discussion on camera phones and public and private spaces, see Lasén, A. and Gómez-Cruz, E. 2009. 'Digital Photography and Picture Sharing: Redefining the Public/private Divide.' *Knowledge, Technology & Policy* 22(3): 205–15.

22 Lindtner, S. et al. 2011. 'Towards a Framework of Publics: Re-encountering Media Sharing and its User.' *ACM Transactions on Computer-Human Interaction (TOCHI)* 18(2): 5. Ito, M. and Okabe, D. 2005. 'Intimate Visual Co-presence.' *Position paper for the Seventh International Conference on Ubiquitous Computing, Tokyo.* Boellstorff, T. 2008. *Coming of Age in Second Life.* Princeton, NJ: Princeton University Press.

23 Lindtner, S. et al. 2011. 'Towards a Framework of Publics: Re-encountering Media Sharing and its User.' *ACM Transactions on Computer-Human Interaction (TOCHI)* 18(2): 5. Warner, M. 2002. 'Publics and Counterpublics.' *Public Culture* 14(1): 49–90.

24 Marwick, A. 2011. 'I Tweet Honestly, I Tweet Passionately: Twitter Users, Context Collapse, and the Imagined Audience.' *New Media & Society* 13(1): 114–33.

25 Bubel, C. M. 2008. 'Film Audiences as Overhearers.' *Journal of Pragmatics* 40: 55–71.

26 Several of the films made about Trinidad for this project relate to this theme. See also Miller, D. 2011. *Tales from Facebook.* Cambridge: Polity.

27 See Barthes, R.1977. 'Rhetoric of the Image.' *Image-Music-Text.* New York: Noonday. 32–7.

28 See Hjorth, L. 2007. 'Snapshot of Almost Contact: The Rise of Camera Phone Practices and a Case Study in Seoul, Korea.' *Continuum: Journal of Media & Cultural Studies* 21(2): 227–38 and Koskinen, I. 2006. 'Managing Banality in Mobile Multimedia.' *The Social Construction and Usage of Communication Technologies: European and Asian Experiences.* Pertierra, R. ed. 48–60. Singapore: Singapore University Press.

29 This echoes Gunning's 'truth claim' in photography which relies on indexicality and visual accuracy of photographs. See Gunning, T. 2004. 'What's the Point of an Index? Or, Faking Photographs.' *NORDICOM Review* 5 (1/2 September): 41.

30 For an elaboration of this argument see Miller, D. 2016. 'Photography in the Age of Snapchat.' Anthropology and Photography. 1.

Chapter 12

1 We found it impossible to avoid some overlap in some of the insights and points being made between this chapter and the earlier chapter comparing online and offline lives. Where this occurs, however, we have mainly used different examples and related the text to different issues here.

2 Dumont, L. 1980. *Homo Hierarchicus: The Caste System and its Implications.* Chicago: University of Chicago Press. 45. For a more comprehensive theoretical overview see Morris, B. 1991. *Western Conceptions of the Individual.* Oxford: Berg.

3 See for example Giddens, A. 1991a. Modernity and Self-identity: Self and Society in the Late Modern Age. Cambridge: Polity Press. 1991b. *The Consequences of Modernity.* Cambridge: Polity Press. Putnam, R. 2000. *Bowling Alone: The Collapse and Revival of American Community.* New York: London: Simon & Schuster.

4 De Tocqueville, A. 1994 (1840). *Democracy in America.* London: David Campbell.

5 See especially Chapters 2 and 3 of Giddens, A. 1991a. *Modernity and Self-identity: Self and Society in the Late Modern Age.* Cambridge: Polity Press. In Giddens' approach this narrative is essential for the self in order to select from the multiple meanings and individual choices offered by late modernity.

6 This has been a constant theme in the Western media, probably the dominant stance to social media within the press. Typical examples with respect to Facebook would include:-http://www.dailymail.co.uk/news/article-2419419/All-lonely-Facebook-friends-Study-shows-social-media-makes-MORE-lonely-unhappy-LESS-sociable.html; http://www.newyorker.com/tech/elements/how-facebook-makes-us-unhappy;http://www.theguardian.com/media-network/media-network-blog/2014/mar/13/selfie-social-media-love-digital-narcassism

7   For a complete theory of the rise of network society see Castells, M. 2000. *The Information Age: Economy, Society and Culture*, updated edition, 3 vols. Oxford: Blackwell. See also Van Dijk, J. 1999. *The Network Society: Social Aspects of New Media*. London: Sage.
8   Rainie, L. and Wellman, B. 2012. *Networked*. Cambridge, MA: The MIT Press.
9   See the discussion of this term also in Papacharissi, Z. 2010a. *A Private Sphere: Democracy in a Digital Age*. 138– 44. Cambridge: Polity Press. For a similar conception of networked self seePapacharissi, Z. ed. 2011. *A Networked Self: Identity, Community and Culture on Social Network Sites*. London: Routledge and Cohen, J. E. 2012. *Configuring the Networked Self: Law, Code, and the Play of Everyday Practice*. New Haven, CT and London: Yale University Press.
10 Rainie, L. and Wellman, B. 2012. *Networked*. Cambridge, MA: The MIT Press. 13.
11 Rainie, L. and Wellman, B. 2012. *Networked*. Cambridge, MA: The MIT Press. 38–9.
12 Rainie, L. and Wellman, B. 2012. *Networked*. Cambridge, MA: The MIT Press. 124–5. In particular Rainie and Wellman argue that 'Facebook is both the epitome of networked individualism – each person is an individual participant – *and* of the networked operating system as a whole.' Rainie, L. and Wellman, B. 2012. *Networked*. Cambridge, MA: The MIT Press. 144.
13 See also Baym, N. 2010. *Personal Connections in the Digital Age*. Cambridge: Polity Press. 6–12. The work argues for the continued power of people to shape technologies without this involving a certain decrease in sociality.
14 Fox, R. 1967. *Kinship and Marriage*. Harmondsworth: Penguin.
15 Mendleson, A. and Papacharissi, Z. 2001. 'Look at Us: collective narcissism in college student Facebook photo galleries.' Papcharissi, Z., ed. *A Networked Self*. 251– 73. Hogan, B. and Wellman, B. 'The relational self-portrait: selfies meet social networks.' Graham, M. and Dutton, W., eds. *Society and the Internet*. Oxford: Oxford University Press. Despite these titles the actual content of both papers places an emphasis upon social relations commensurate with the arguments made in this chapter.
16 In a non-peer-reviewed big data study conducted by *Time* magazine, Makati City and Pasig, Philippines emerged as the city with the highest rate of selfies per capita. The study is available online at http://time.com/selfies-cities-world-rankings accessed on 20 July 2015.
17 Nicolescu, R. Forthcoming. *Social Media in Southeast Italy*. London: UCL Press. Chapter 5.
18 From the hundreds of articles on this themes see for example Andrejevic, M. 2002. 'The Work of Being Watched.' *Critical Studies in Media Communication* 19(2): 230–48. boyd, d. 2008. 'Facebook's Privacy Trainwreck: Exposure, Invasion, and Social Convergence.' *Convergence* 14(1): 13–20. Etzioni, A. 1999. *The Limits of Privacy*. New York: Basic Books. Fuchs, C. 2012b. 'The Political Economy of Privacy on Facebook.' *Television & New Media* 13(2): 139–59, Madden, M. 2012. *Privacy Management on Social Media Sites: Most Users Choose Restricted Privacy Settings while Profile 'Pruning' and Unfriending People is on the Rise*. Pew Research Center's Internet & American Life Project. Trepte, S. and Reinecke, L., eds. 2011. *Privacy Online: Perspectives on Privacy and Self-Disclosure in the Social Web*. New York: Springer. Utz, S. and Kramer, N. 2009. 'The Privacy Paradox on Social Network Sites Revisited: The Role of Individual Characteristics and Group Norms.' *Cyberpsychology: Journal of Psychosocial Research on Cyberspace* 3(2).
19 See boyd, d. 2008. 'Facebook's Privacy Trainwreck: Exposure, Invasion, and Social Convergence.' *Convergence* 14(1) 13–20.
20 See detailed discussion about Chinese concepts of the 'public' and the 'private' at Chan, Y. K. 2000. 'Privacy in the Family: Its Hierarchical and Asymmetric Nature.' *Journal of Comparative Family Studies* 31(1): 1–17. Nicolescu, R. Forthcoming. *Social Media in Southeast Italy*. London: UCL Press.
21 For many factory workers those social media contacts who thereby come to know about their dreams, worries, complaints or other secrets do not know their real name and other offline social identities, and so cannot harm their offline reputation.
22 Turkle, S. 2011. *Alone Together: Why We Expect More from Technology and Less from Each Other*. New York: Basic Books.
23 Hampton, K. and Wellman, B. 2003. 'Neighboring in Netville: How the Internet Supports Community and Social Capital in a Wired Suburb.' *City and Community* 2(4): 277–311.
24 For detailed examples see Miller, D. and Sinanan, J. 2014. *Webcam*. Cambridge: Polity Press. Chapter 1.
25 For a discussion of what Miller calls the 'Goldilocks Strategy' see Miller, D. 2016. *Social Media in an English Village*. London: UCL Press. Chapter 4.

26 See further discussion of temporal aspects of communication media, such as synchronous/ asynchronous in Baym, N. 2010. *Personal Connections in the Digital Age*. Cambridge: Polity Press. pp.7–8.
27 See also Chapter 7.
28 Hebdige, D. 1979. *Subculture: The Meaning of Style*. London: Methuen.

Chapter 13

1   Layard, R. 2011. *Happiness: Lessons for a New Science*. London: Penguin.
2   Rousseau, Jean-Jacques. 2010 (1754). *Discourse on the Origin and Foundations of Inequality Among Men*, Rosenblatt, H., trans and ed. Boston, MA: Bedford/St. Martin's.
3   Durkheim, E. 1997 (1893). *The Division of Labor in Society*, Halls, W. D., trans. New York: The Free Press. Durkheim, E. 1979 (1897). *Suicide: A Study in Sociology*, Spaulding, J. A. and Simpson, G., trans. New York: The Free Press.
4   James, W. 2012 (1902). *The Varieties of Religious Experience*. Boston, MA: Bedford/St. Martin's.
5   Weber, M. 2002 (1905). *The Protestant Ethic and the Spirit of Capitalism*. London: Penguin Books.
6   Locke, J. 1979 (1689). *An Essay Concerning Human Understanding*, Nidditch, P. H., ed. Oxford: Oxford University Press.
7   Comte, A. 1875. *System of Positive Polity*. London: Longmans, Green and Co.
8   Thin, N. 2005. 'Happiness and the Sad Topics of Anthropology.' *WeD Working Paper 10*. ESRC Research Group on Wellbeing in Developing Countries.
9   While many anthropologists approach topics such as desires, satisfaction and belonging, which may play a part in individuals' happiness, the concept of happiness is rarely explicitly theorised.
10 Sen, A. 1999. *Development As Freedom*. Oxford: Oxford University Press.
11 GDP has been long known to have little correlation with 'happiness', as evidenced by Gallup surveys measuring wellbeing using the Cantril Self-Anchoring Scale. See Cantril, H. 1965. *The Pattern of Human Concerns*. New Brunswick, NJ: Rutgers University Press.
12 "Gross National Happiness." 2008. Centre for Bhutan Studies and GNH Research, http://www.grossnationalhappiness.com/gnhIndex/intruductionGNH.aspx.
13 Helliwell, J., Layard, R. and Sachs, J., eds. 2015. *World Happiness Report 2015*. New York: Sustainable Development Solutions Network.
14 "Human Development Index." 2014. United Nations Development Programme, http://hdr.undp.org/en/statistics/hdi/.
15 Maslow, A. H. 1943. 'A Theory of Human Motivation.' *Psychological Review* 50(4): 370–96.
16 Helliwell, J., Layard, R. and Sachs, J., eds. 2015. *World Happiness Report 2015*. New York: Sustainable Development Solutions Network. 13.
17 Thin, N. 2005. 'Happiness and the Sad Topics of Anthropology.' *WeD Working Paper 10*. ESRC Research Group on Wellbeing in Developing Countries.
18 Wali, A. 2012. 'A Different Measure of Well-Being.' Vital Topics Forum. Johnston, B. R., ed. *American Anthropologist* 114(1): 12.
19 Tandoc, E. C. Jr., Ferruci, P. and Duffy, M. 2015. 'Facebook Use, Envy, and Depression Among College Students: Is Facebooking Depressing?' *Computers in Human Behavior* 43. 139–46.
20 Kross, E., Verduyn, P., Demiralp, E., Park, J., Lee, D. S., Lin, N., Shablack, H., Jonides, J. and Ybarra, O. 2013. 'Facebook Use Predicts Declines in Subjective Well-Being in Young Adults.' *PLoS ONE* 8(8): e69841.
21 Muise, A., Christofides, E. and Desmarais, S. 2009. 'More Information Than You Ever Wanted: Does Facebook Bring Out the Green-eyed Monster of Jealousy?' *Cyberpsychological Behavior* 12(4): 441–4.
22 Tiggeman, M. and Slater, A., 2013. 'NetGirls: The Internet, Facebook and Body Image Concern in Adolescent Girls.' *International Journal of Eating Disorders* 46(6): 630–3.
23 O'Keeffe, G. S. and Clarke-Pearson, K. 2011. 'Clinical Report—The Impact of Social Media on Children, Adolescents, and Families.' American Academy of Pediatrics, http://pediatrics.

aappublications.org/content/early/2011/03/28/peds.2011-0054.full.pdf+html?ijkey = 76f29031adb1f95a04cca23436b5ccdebfd5cd9f.

24 O'Keeffe, G. S. and Clarke-Pearson, K. 2011. 'Clinical Report—The Impact of Social Media on Children, Adolescents, and Families.' American Academy of Pediatrics, http://pediatrics. aappublications.org/content/early/2011/03/28/peds.2011-0054.full.pdf+html?ijkey = 76f29031adb1f95a04cca23436b5ccdebfd5cd9f.

25 Tandoc, E. C. Jr., Ferruci, P. and Duffy, M. 2015. 'Facebook Use, Envy, and Depression Among College Students: Is Facebooking Depressing?' *Computers in Human Behavior* 43: 139–46.

26 Sagioglou, C. and Greitemeyer, T. 2014. 'Facebook's Emotional Consequences: Why Facebook Causes a Decrease in Mood and Why People Still Use It.' *Computers in Human Behavior* 35: 359–63.

27 Lauren, A., Jelenchick, J., Eickhoff, C. and Moreno, M. A. 2013. 'Facebook Depression? Social Networking Site Use and Depression in Older Adolescents.' *Journal of Adolescent Health* 52(1): 128–30.

28 Hiscott, R. 2014. 'Why You Feel Terrible After Spending Too Much Time On Facebook.' *The Huffington Post*, http://www.huffingtonpost.com/2014/07/17/facebook-study_n_5595890.html, 18 July 2014.

29 Valenzuela, S., Park, N. and Kee, K. F. 2009. 'Is There Social Capital in a Social Network Site?: Facebook Use and College Students' Life Satisfaction, Trust and Participation.' *Journal of Computer-Mediated Communication* 14(4): 875–901.

30 Kramer, A. D., Guillory, J. E. and Hancock, J. T. 2014. 'Experimental Evidence of Massive-Scale Emotional Contagion through Social Networks.' *Proceedings of the National Academy of Sciences* 111(24): 8788–90.

31 Miller and Slater suggest that the internet itself (and social media by extension) does not exist prior to its usage, but is created through the individual acts of users – much as linguists follow J. L. Austin's notion of performative utterance, which suggests that illocutionary acts not only describe a given reality, but also change the social reality they are describing. As such social media platforms are simply the environment in which content may shift what that particular medium is and what it means to the user. See Miller, D. and Slater, D. 2000. *The Internet: An Ethnographic Approach.* Oxford: Berg. Austin, J. L. 1962. *How to Do Things With Words.* Oxford: Oxford University Press.

32 See Fig. 4.26 for the results and an explanation of the survey.

33 For the sites in Trinidad and England the word 'happier' was used, as it was in India where 'happy' is part of commonly used Tanglish (Tamil and English). It was translated as '*más feliz*' in Chile, '*mais feliz*' in Brazil, and '*piu felice*' in Italy. In Turkey the word '*mutlu*' was used, which is the most common of various words that could be translated as 'happy'. In China the concept of '*kuaile*' (meaning happy, joyful, cheerful) was used, as opposed to '*xingfu*' which highlights a more 'profound' form of happiness, reflecting the fact that social media is primarily a source of entertainment.

34 Appadurai, A. 2004. 'The Capacity to Aspire: Culture and the Terms of Recognition.' Rao, V. and Walton, M., eds. *Culture and Public Action.* Stanford, CA: Stanford University Press. 59–84.

35 Wang, X. Forthcoming. *Social Media in Industrial China.* London: UCL Press.

36 Haynes, N. Forthcoming. *Social Media in Northern Chile.* London: UCL Press.

37 Frazier, L. 2007. *Salt in the Sand: Memory, Violence, and the Nation-State in Chile, 1890 to the Present.* Durham, NC: Duke University Press.

38 Spyer, J. Forthcoming. *Social Media in Emergent Brazil.* London: UCL Press.

39 McDonald, T. Forthcoming. *Social Media in Rural China.* London: UCL Press.

40 Wang, R. R. 2002. 'Globalizing the Heart of the Dragon: The Impact of Technology on Confucian Ethical Values.' *Journal of Chinese Philosophy* 29(4): 553–69.

41 Rainey, L. D. 2010. *Confucius & Confucianism: The Essentials.* Malden, MA: Wiley-Blackwell. 16.

42 Miller, D. 2011. *Tales from Facebook.* Cambridge: Polity Press.

43 Sinanan, J. Forthcoming. *Social Media in Trinidad.* London: UCL Press.

44 YY is a major Chinese video-based social network with over 300 million users.

45 Unlike migrant factory workers, who seldom use their real name and real photographs on QQ, tending instead to create a fantasy world online using images collected from the

internet, middle-class Chinese increasingly prefer WeChat to QQ. On WeChat the percentage of real names is much higher than on QQ.

46 Nicolescu, R. Forthcoming. *Social Media in Southeast Italy*. London: UCL Press.
47 Costa, E. 2016. *Social Media in Southeast Turkey*. London: UCL Press.
48 Venkatraman, S. Forthcoming. *Social Media in South India*. London: UCL Press.
49 Hogan, B. 2010. 'The Presentation of Self in the Age of Social Media: Distinguishing Performances and Exhibitions Online.' *Bulletin of Science, Technology, and Society* 30(6): 377–86.
50 See Fig. 4.26.

Chapter 14

1   Miller, D. 2014. 'Hospices: The Potential for New Media.' http://www.ucl.ac.uk/anthropology/people/academic_staff/d_miller/mil-28
2   Miller, D. and Sinanan, J. 2014. *Webcam*. Cambridge: Polity Press. Chapter 1.
3   Miller, D. and Sinanan, J. 2014. *Webcam*. Cambridge: Polity Press. Chapter 1.
4   Van Dijck, J. 2007. *Mediated Memories in the Digital Age*. Stanford, CA: Stanford University Press.
5   Thompson, C. 2013. *Smarter Than You Think*. London: Penguin.
6   Miller, D. 2015. 'Photography in the Age of Snapchat.' Anthropology and Photography.
7   Miller, D. and Sinanan, J. 2014. *Webcam*. Cambridge: Polity Press. Chapter 1.
8   See for example Fig. 4.9.
9   Jeffrey, R. and Doron, A. 2013. *The Great Indian Phone Book*. London: Hurst.
10 Wallis, C. 2011. 'New Media Practices in China: Youth Patterns, Processes, and Politics.' *International Journal of Communication* 5:406–36.
11 According to a national report, 83.4 per cent of all internet users in China use mobile phones to access the internet. China Internet Network Information Center. 2014. 34th Statistical Report on Internet Development in China. Retrieved 28 March 2015 from http://www1.cnnic.cn/IDR/ReportDownloads/201411/P020141102574314897888.pdf
12 For the prediction of a 20-fold growth over the next five years see http://www.theguardian.com/world/2014/jun/05/internet-use-mobile-phones-africa-predicted-increase-20-fold
13 *The Economist*. 28 February 2015.
14 Graham, M. 2014. 'Internet Geographies: Data Shadows and Digital Divisions of Labour.' Graham, M. and Dutton, W., eds. *Society and the Internet*. Oxford: Oxford University Press. 99–116.
15 *The Economist*. 13 September 2014.
16 In this connection, it is worth noting the growing popularity among urban Chinese internet users of online shopping websites offering brand name goods at fixed prices, for example JD.com and Tmall, who similarly regard the need for interactions in order to make purchases as a considerable hassle.
17 For example Simmel, G. 1968. *The Conflict in Modern Culture and other Essays*. New York: Teachers College Press.
18 See Miller, D. and Horst, H. 2012. 'Introduction.' In Horst, H. and Miller, D., eds. *Digital Anthropology*. London: Berg: 4–11.
19 Malaby, T. 2009. *Making Virtual Worlds*. Ithaca, NY: Cornell University Press.
20 Coleman, G. 2010. 'Ethnographic Approaches to Digital Media.' *Annual Review of Anthropology* 39. 487–505.
21 Kelty, C. 2008. *Two Bits: The Cultural Significance of Free Software*. Durham, NC: Duke University Press.
22 Horst, H. and Miller, D., eds. 2012. *Digital Anthropology*. London: Berg: 28–30.
23 http://blogs.ucl.ac.uk/global-social-media/2013/02/14/my-whatsapp-field-trip/
24 See discussion of the 'newness' of social media at Gershon, I. and Bell, J. A. 2013. 'Introduction: The Newness of New Media.' *Culture, Theory and Critique* 54(3): 259–64.
25 See Wang, X. Forthcoming. *Social Media in Industrial China*. London: UCL Press. Chapter 2.
26 Sinanan, J. Forthcoming. *Social Media in Trinidad*. London: UCL Press.
27 Wang, X. Forthcoming. *Social Media in Industrial China*. London: UCL Press.

Appendix

1   http://www.ucl.ac.uk/why-we-post
2   http://www.youtube.com/whywepost
3   You can register for the English version of this course on the FutureLearn platform https://www.futurelearn.com/
4   The translations of the university course may be found through UCL eXtend.

References

Aarsand, P. A. 2008. 'Frame switches and identity performances: alternating between online and offline.' *Text & Talk* 28(2): 147–65.

Adorno, T. W. and Horkheimer, M. 2002. *Dialectic of Enlightenment.* Stanford, CA: Stanford University Press.

Adorno, T. W. 1991. 'Free time.' Bernstein, J. M., ed. *The Culture Industry: Selected essays on mass culture.* 162–70.

Akdeniz, Y. and Altiparmak, K. 2008. *Internet: restricted access: a critical assessment of Internet content regulation and censorship in Turkey.* http://privacy.cyber-rights.org.tr/?page_id=256

Akdenizli, B., ed. 2015. *Digital transformation in Turkey: current perspectives in communication studies.* Maryland: Lexington Books.

Akinnaso, F. N. 1992. 'Schooling, language and knowledge in literate and nonliterate societies.' *Comparative Studies in Society and History* 34: 68–109.

Alev Degim, I., Johnson, J. and Fu, T., eds. 2015. *Interpersonal Interactions Across Borders.* Amsterdam: Institute of Network Cultures.

Andrejevic, M. 2002. 'The work of being watched.' *Critical Studies in Media Communication* 19(2): 230–48.

Appadurai, A. 2002. 'The Capacity to Aspire: Culture and the Terms of Recognition.' Rao, V. and Walton, M., eds. *Culture and Public Action.* Stanford, CA: Stanford University Press. 59–84.

Askew, K. and Wilk, R. 2002. *Anthropology of Media: A Reader.* Oxford: Blackwell Publishing.

Austin, J. L. 1962. *How to Do Things with Words.* Oxford: Oxford University Press.

Baba, M. L. 1998. 'The anthropology of work in the Fortune 1000: a critical retrospective.' *Anthropology of Work Review* 18(4):17–28.

Baker, L. D. 1998. *From Savage to Negro: Anthropology and the Construction of Race.* Los Angeles, CA: University of California Press.

Banks, M. and Morphy, H., eds. 1997. *Rethinking Visual Anthropology.* New Haven, CT: Yale University Press.

Barendregt, B. 2012. 'Diverse Digital Worlds.' Horst, H. and Miller, D., eds. *Digital Anthropology.* London: Berg. 203–24.

Bargh, J.A., et. al. 2002. 'Can You See the Real Me? Activation and Expression of the "True Self" on the Internet.' *Journal of Social Issues* 58(1): 33–48.

Barlow, J. 1996. 'A Declaration of the Independence of Cyberspace.' *Electronic Frontier Foundation*, 8 February 1996 (accessed on web. 7 July 2015).

Barthes, R. 1977. 'The Rhetoric of the Image.' *Image-Music-Text.* New York: Noonday.

Barthes, R. 1977. 'Rhetoric of the Image.' *Image-Music-Text.* New York: Noonday.

Bateson, G. and Mead, M. 1942. 'Balinese character. A photographic analysis.' *Special Publications of the New York Academic of Science.* New York. 17–92.

Baym, N. 2010. *Personal Connections in the Digital Age.* Cambridge: Polity Press.

Baym, N. 1999. *Tune In, Log On: Soaps, Fandom, and Online Community.* New York: Sage.

Bernal, V. 2014. *Nation as Network.* Chicago, IL: University of Chicago Press.

Bernard, H. R. 2011. *Research methods in anthropology: Qualitative and quantitative approaches.* Lanham, MD: Altamira Press.

Bitz, M. 2010. *When Commas Meet Kryptonite: Classroom Lessons from the Comic Book Project. Language and Literacy Series.* New York: Teachers College Press.

Bitz, M. 2004. 'The comic book project: The lives of urban youth.' *Art Education* 57(2): 33–46.

Boase, J. and Wellman, B. 2006. 'Personal Relationships: On and Off the Internet.' Perlman, D. and Vangelisti, A., eds. *Handbook of Personal Relations.* Cambridge: Cambridge University Press.

Boellstorff, T., Nardi, B., Pearce, C. and Taylor, T. 2012. *Ethnography and Virtual Worlds: A handbook of method.* Princeton, NJ: Princeton University Press.

Boellstorff, T. 2008. *Coming of Age in Second Life.* Princeton, NJ: Princeton University Press.

Borofsky, R. 1987. *Making history: Pukapukan and anthropological constructions of knowledge.* Cambridge: Cambridge University Press.

Bourdieu, P. and Whiteside, S. 1996. *Photography: A middle-brow art.* Stanford, CA: Stanford University Press.

Bourdieu, P. 1984. *Distinction: A social critique of the judgment of taste.* Cambridge, MA: Harvard University Press.

Bourdieu, P. 1972. *Outline to a Theory of Practice.* Cambridge: Cambridge University Press.

Bourdieu, P. and Wacquant, L. 1992. 'Symbolic Violence.' In *An Invitation to Reflective Sociology.* Chicago: University of Chicago Press. 167–73.

Bourdieu, P. and Bourdieu, M. C. 2004. 'The peasant and photography.' *Ethnography* 5(4): 601–16.

boyd, d. 2014. *It's complicated: The social lives of networked teens.* New Haven, CT; London: Yale University Press.

boyd, d. 2013. 'White Flight in Networked Publics? How Race and Class Shaped American Teen Engagement with MySpace and Facebook.' Nakamura, L. and Chow-White. P., eds. *Race After the Internet.* New York: Routledge. 203–22.

boyd, d. 2008. 'Facebook's Privacy Trainwreck: Exposure, Invasion, and Social Convergence.' *Convergence* 14(1): 13–20.

boyd, d. and Ellison, N. B. 2007. 'Social Network Sites: Definition, History and Scholarship.' *Journal of Computer-Mediated Communication* 13(1): 210–30.

Brants, K. 2005. Guest editor's introduction: 'The Internet and the public sphere.' *Political Communication* 22(2): 143–6.

Broadbent, S. 2011. *L'Intimite au Travail.* Paris: Fyp Editions.

Broadbent, S. 2012. 'Approaches to Personal Communication.' Horst, H. and Miller, D., eds. *Digital Anthropology.* London, Oxford: Berg. 127–45.

Brubaker, R. and Cooper, F. 2000. 'Beyond "Identity".' *Theory and Society* 29: 1–47.

Bubel, C. M. 2008. 'Film Audiences as Overhearers.' *Journal of Pragmatics* 40: 55–71.

Buckingham, D. 2003. *Media education: literacy, learning and contemporary culture.* Cambridge: Polity Press.

Butler, J. 1990. *Gender Trouble.* New York: Routledge.

Cantril, H. 1965. *The Pattern of Human Concerns.* New Brunswick, NJ: Rutgers University Press.

Carr, N. 2011. *The Shallows: What the Internet Is Doing to Our Brains.* New York: W. W. Norton & Company.

Castells, M. 2000. *The Information Age: Economy, Society and Culture,* Updated edition, 3 volumes. Oxford: Blackwell.

Castells, M. 1997. *The Power of Identity. The Information Age: Economy, Society and Culture Vol II of 3.* Oxford, UK: Blackwell.

Castells, M. 1996. *The Rise of the Network Society. The Information Age: Economy, Society and Culture Vol. I of 3.* Oxford: Blackwell.

Chadwick, A. and Howard, P. N. 2010. *Routledge handbook of Internet politics.* Oxford: Taylor & Francis.

Chadwick, A. 2003. 'Bringing E-Democracy Back In: Why it Matters for Future Research on E-Governance.' *Social Science Computer Review* 21(4): 443–55.

Chambers, D. 2013. *Social Media and Personal Relationships: Online Intimacies and Networked Friendship.* Basingstoke: Palgrave Macmillan.

Chan, Y. K. 2000. 'Privacy in the Family: Its Hierarchical and Asymmetric Nature.' *Journal of Comparative Family Studies* 31(1): 1–17.

Chen, W. and Wellman, B. 2004. 'The global digital divide within and between countries.' *IT & Society* 1(7): 39–45.

Chu, J. Y. 2010. *Cosmologies of credit: transnational mobility and the politics of destination in China.* Durham, NC: Duke University Press.

Clark, L. S. 2013. *The Parent App.* Oxford: Oxford University Press.

Clay, S. 2011 'The political power of social media.' *Foreign Affairs* 90: 128–41.

Cohen, J. E. 2012. *Configuring the Networked Self: Law, Code, and the Play of Everyday Practice.* New Haven, CT: Yale University Press.

Coleman, G. 2014. *Hacker, hoaxer, whistleblower, spy: The many faces of Anonymous.* London; Brooklyn, NY: Verso.

Coleman, G. 2012a. *Coding Freedom: The Ethics and Aesthetics of Hacking.* Princeton, NJ: Princeton University Press.

Coleman, G. 2012b. 'Phreaks, hackers, and trolls: The politics of transgression and spectacle.' Maniberg, M., ed. *The social media reader. New York: New York University Press.* 99–119.

Coleman, G. 2010. 'Ethnographic Approaches to Digital Media.' *Annual Review of Anthropology* 39: 487–505.

Comte, A. 1875. *System of Positive Polity.* London: Longmans, Green and Co.

Costa, E. 2016. *Social Media in Southeast Turkey.* London: UCL Press.

Couldry, N. 2015. 'Social Media: Human Life.' *Social Media + Society* 1(2).

Cross, M. 2011. *Bloggerati, Twitterati: How Blogs and Twitter are transforming popular culture.* Santa Barbara, CA: Praeger.

Cruz, E. G. and Meyer, E. 2012. 'Creation and Control in the Photographic Process: iPhones and the Emerging Fifth Moment of Photography.' *Photographies* 5(2).

Culnan, M. J., McHugh, P. J. and Zubillaga, J. I. 2010. 'How large US companies can use Twitter and other social media to gain business value.' *MIS Quarterly Executive* 9(4): 243–59.

Dahlberg, L. 2001. 'The Internet and democratic discourse: Exploring the prospects of online deliberative forums extending the public sphere.' *Information, Communication & Society* 4(4): 615–33.

Dalsgaard, S. 2008. 'Facework on Facebook: The presentation of self in virtual life and its role in the US elections.' *Anthropology Today* 24(6): 8–12.

David, G. 2010. 'Camera phone images, videos and live streaming: a contemporary visual trend.' *Visual Studies* 25(1): 89–98.

Dawes, S. S. 2008. 'The evolution and continuing challenges of e-governance.' *Public Administration Review* 68(1): 86–102.

De Neve, G. 2005. *The everyday politics of labour: Working lives in India's informal economy.* Oxford: Berghahn Books.

De Tocqueville, A. 1994 (1835). *Democracy in America.* London: David Campbell.

Dumont, L. 1980. *Homo Hierarchicus: The Caste System and its Implications.* Chicago: University of Chicago Press.

Durkheim, E. 1979 (1897). *Suicide: A Study in Sociology.* Spaulding, J. A. and Simpson, G., trans. New York: The Free Press.

Durkheim, E. 1997 (1893). *The Division of Labor in Society.* Halls, W. D., trans. New York: The Free Press.

Edwards, E. 1992. *Anthropology and Photography 1860–1929.* Royal Anthropological Institute.

Ellison, N. B., Steinfield, C. and Lampe, C. 2007. 'The benefits of Facebook "friends": Exploring the relationship between college students' use of online social networks and social capital.' *Journal of Computer-Mediated Communication* 12(3).

Etzioni, A. 1999. *The limits of privacy.* New York: Basic Books.

Fenton, N. and Barassi, V. 2011. 'Alternative media and social networking sites: The politics of individuation and political participation.' *The Communication Review* 14(3): 179–96.

Fong, V. L. 2004. *Only hope: coming of age under China's one-child policy.* Stanford, CA: Stanford University Press.

Fountain, J. E. 2001. *Building the Virtual State: Information Technology and Institutional Change.* Washington, DC: Brookings Institution Press.

Fox, R. 1967. *Kinship and Marriage.* Harmondsworth: Penguin.

Frazier, L. 2007. *Salt in the Sand: Memory, Violence, and the Nation-State in Chile, 1890 to the Present.* Durham, NC: Duke University Press.

Fu, K. W. and Chan, C. H. 2015. 'Networked collective action in the 2014 Hong Kong Occupy Movement: analysing a Facebook sharing network.' *International Conference on Public Policy, ICPP 2015.*

Fuchs, C. 2013. *Social Media: A Critical Introduction.* London: Sage.

Fuchs, C. 2012a. 'Social media, riots, and revolutions.' *Capital & Class* 36(3): 383–91.

Fuchs, C. 2012b. 'The Political Economy of Privacy on Facebook.' *Television & New Media* 13(2): 139–59.

Fuller, C. J. and Narasimhan, H. 2007. 'Information technology professionals and the new-rich middle class in Chennai (Madras).' *Modern Asian Studies* 41(1): 121–50.

Gardner, R. 1971. *The Nuer* (Director of the film).

Gerbaudo, P. 2012. *Tweets and the streets: Social media and contemporary activism.* London: Pluto Press.

Gershon, I. 2010. *Breakup 2.0: Disconnecting Over New Media*. Ithaca, NY: Cornell University Press.

Gershon, I. and Bell, J. A. 2013. Introduction: 'The Newness of New Media.' *Culture, Theory and Critique* 54(3): 259–64.

Gershon, I. 2011. 'Un-Friend My Heart: Facebook, Promiscuity and Heartbreak in a Neoliberal Age.' *Anthropological Quarterly* 84(4): 865–94.

Gibbs, M., Meese, J., Arnold, M., Nansen, B. and Carter, M. 2015. '#Funeral and Instagram: death, social media, and platform vernacular.' *Information, Communication & Society* 18(3): 255–68.

Giddens, A. 1991a. *Modernity and Self-identity: Self and Society in the Late Modern Age.* Cambridge: Polity Press.

Giddens, A. 1991b. *The Consequences of Modernity.* Cambridge: Polity Press.

Gingrich, A. and Fox, R. G., eds. 2002. *Anthropology, by Comparison.* London: Routledge.

Ginsburg, F., Abu-Lughod, L. and Larkin, B., eds. 2002. *Media Worlds.* Berkeley, CA: University of California Press.

Ginsburg, F. 1995. 'Mediating culture: indigenous media, ethnographic film, and the production of identity.' *Fields of vision: Essays in film studies, visual anthropology, and photography.* Berkeley, CA: University of California Press.

Godelier, M. 2012. *The Metamorphosis of Kinship.* London: Verso.

Goffman, E. 1975. *Frame Analysis.* Harmondsworth: Penguin.

Goffman, E. 1959. *The Presentation of the Self in Everyday Life.* Garden City, NY: Anchor Books.

Goldfarb, A. and Tucker, C. 2011. 'Online Display Advertising: Targeting and Obtrusiveness.' *Marketing Science* 30(3): 389–404.

Graham, M. and Dutton, W., eds. 2014. *Society and the Internet.* Oxford: Oxford University Press.

Graham, M. 2014. 'Internet Geographies: data shadows and digital divisions of labour.' Graham, M. and Dutton, W., eds. *Society and the Internet.* Oxford: Oxford University Press. 99–116.

Gray, M. L. 2009. *Out in the Country: Youth, Media, and Queer Visibility in Rural America.* New York: New York University Press.

Greschke, H. 2012. *Is there a home in cyberspace? The Internet in migrants' everyday life and the emergence of global communities.* New York: Routledge.

Grint, K. 2005. *The sociology of work: introduction.* Cambridge: Polity Press.

Gross National Happiness. Centre for Bhutan Studies and GNH Research, http://www.grossnationalhappiness.com/gnhIndex/intruductionGNH.aspx, 2008.

Gunning, T. 2004. 'What's the Point of an Index? Or, Faking Photographs.' *NORDICOM Review* 5 (1/2 September): 41.

Habermas, J. 1969. *The Structural Transformation of the Public Sphere: An Inquiry into a Category of Bourgeois Society.* Cambridge, MA: The MIT Press.

Hampton, K. N., Rainie, L., Lu, W., Dwyer M., Shin, I. and Purcell, K. 2014. 'Social Media and the "Spiral of Silence".' Pew Research Center, Washington, DC. Available at: http://www.pewinternet.org/2014/08/26/social-media-and-the-spiral-of-silence/

Hampton, K. and Wellman, B. 2003. 'Neighboring in Netville: How the Internet Supports Community and Social Capital in a Wired Suburb.' *City and Community* 2(4): 277–311.

Hanna, R., Rohm, A. and Crittenden, V. L. 2010. 'We're all connected: The power of the social media ecosystem.' *Business Horizons* 54(3): 265–73.

Haraway, D. 1991. 'A Cyborg Manifesto: Science, Technology and Social Feminism in the Late Twentieth Century.' *Simians, Cyborgs and Women: The reinvention of Nature.* New York: Routledge.

Hasebrink, U., Livingstone, S. and Haddon, L. 2008. *Comparing children's online opportunities and risks across Europe: cross-national comparisons for EU Kids Online.* 2nd edition. http://eprints.lse.ac.uk/24368/

Haynes, N. Forthcoming. *Social Media in Northern Chile.* London: UCL Press.

Hebdige, D. 1979. *Subculture: the meaning of Style.* London: Methuen.

Heeks, R. 2001. *Building e-governance for development: A framework for national and donor action.* Institute for Development Policy and Management, University of Manchester.

Helliwell, J., Layard, R. and Sachs, J., eds. 2015. *World Happiness Report 2015*. New York: Sustainable Development Solutions Network.

Hine, C. 2000. *Virtual ethnography*. London: Sage.

Hiscott, R. 2014. 'Why You Feel Terrible After Spending Too Much Time On Facebook.' *The Huffington Post* (18 July 2014) http://www.huffingtonpost.com/2014/07/17/facebook-study_n_5595890.html

Hjorth, L. 2009. 'Gifts of Presence: A Case Study of a South Korean Virtual Community, Cyworld's Mini-Hompy.' Goggin, G. and McLelland, M., eds. *Internationalising the Internet*. London: Routledge. 237–51.

Hjorth, L. and Hendry, N. 2015. 'A Snapshot of Social Media: Camera Phone Practices.' *Social Media + Society* 1(1).

Hjorth, L. 2010. 'The Game of Being Social: Web 2.0, Social Media, and Online Games.' *Iowa Journal of Communication* 42(1): 73–92.

Hjorth, L. 2007. 'Snapshot of Almost Contact: The Rise of Camera Phone Practices and a Case Study in Seoul, Korea.' *Continuum: Journal of Media & Cultural Studies* 21(2): 227–38.

Ho, C. 2000. 'Popular Culture and the Aestheticization of Politics: Hegemonic Struggle and Postcolonial Nationalism in Trinidad Carnival.' *Transforming Anthropology* 9(1): 3–18.

Hogan, B. and Wellman, B. 2014. 'The relational self-portrait: selfies meet social networks.' Graham, M. and Dutton, W., eds. *Society and The Internet*. Oxford: Oxford University Press.

Hogan, B., 2010. 'The Presentation of Self in the Age of Social Media: Distinguishing Performances and Exhibitions Online.' *Bulletin of Science, Technology, and Society* 30(6): 377–86.

Holmström, M. 1976. *South Indian factory workers: Their life and their world*. Cambridge: Cambridge University Press.

Holy, L., ed. 1987. *Comparative Anthropology*. Oxford and New York: Blackwell.

Horst, H. and Miller, D., eds. 2012 *Digital Anthropology*. London: Berg.

http://blogs.ucl.ac.uk/global-social-media/2013/11/24/what-will-we-learn-from-the-fall-of-facebook/

http://blogs.ucl.ac.uk/global-social-media/2014/08/31/the-qualitative-insights-we-get-from-applying-questionnaires/

http://time.com/selfies-cities-world-rankings (accessed on 20 July 2015).

http://www.al-monitor.com/pulse/originals/2013/09/turkeys-akp-twitter-election.html

http://www.dailymail.co.uk/news/article-2419419/All-lonely-Facebook-friends-Study-shows-social-media-makes-MORE-lonely-unhappy-LESS-sociable.html

http://www.danah.org/researchBibs/sns.php

http://www.hurriyetdailynews.com/ruling-akp-hires-thousands-for-new-social-media-campaign.aspx?pageID=238&nID=54479&NewsCatID=338

http://www.idc.com/prodserv/smartphone-market-share.jsp (accessed on 26 August 2015)

http://www.media-anthropology.net/

http://www.newyorker.com/tech/elements/how-facebook-makes-us-unhappy

http://www.nytimes.com/2008/07/26/business/worldbusiness/26internet.html?_r=0

http://www.theatlantic.com/technology/archive/2014/05/qr-codes-for-the-dead/370901/

http://www.theguardian.com/commentisfree/2014/sep/11/when-taking-selfies-in-trinidad-its-whats-on-the-outside-that-matters

http://www.theguardian.com/media-network/media-network-blog/2014/mar/13/selfie-social-media-love-digital-narcassism, http://www.theguardian.com/technology/2013/dec/06/selfies-status-updates-digital-bragging-web

http://www.theguardian.com/media-network/media-network-blog/2014/mar/13/selfie-social-media-love-digital-narcassism

http://www.theguardian.com/world/2014/jun/05/internet-use-mobile-phones-africa-predicted-increase-20-fold

http://www.wantchinatimes.com/news-subclass-cnt.aspx?id=20140205000127&cid=1102

http://www.whywepost.com

http://www.wsj.com/articles/SB10001424127887323527004579079151479634742

http://www.youtube.com/whywepost

https://press.linkedin.com/about-linkedin (accessed on 28 August 2015)

Hull, G. and Schultz, K. 2002. *School's Out: Bridging out-of-school literacies with classroom practice*. New York: Teachers College Press.

Human Development Index. United Nations Development Programme, http://hdr.undp.org/en/statistics/hdi/, 2014.

Hunsiger, J. and Senft, T., eds. 2014. *The Social Media Handbook*. New York: Routledge.

Hussain, M. M. and Howard, P. N. 2012. 'Opening Closed Regimes: Civil Society, Information Infrastructure, and Political Islam.' Anduiza, E., Jensen, M. and Jorba, L., eds. *Comparing Digital Politics: Civic Engagement and Political Participation*. Cambridge: Cambridge University Press.

Hussain, M. M. and Howard. P. 2013 'What best explains successful protest cascades? ICTs and the fuzzy causes of the Arab Spring.' *International Studies Review* 15.1: 48–66.

Ito, M. et al. 2010. *Hanging Out, Messing Around, and Geeking Out*. Cambridge, MA: The MIT Press.

Ito, M., Horst, H., Bittanti, M., boyd, d., Herr-Stephenson, B., Lange, P. G., Pascoe, C. J. and Robinson, L. 2008. *Living and Learning with New Media: Summary of Findings from the Digital Youth Project*. Cambridge, MA: The MIT Press.

Ito, M. 2005. 'Mobile phones, Japanese youth, and the re-placement of social contact.' *Mobile Communication*. 131–48.

Ito, M. and Okabe, D. 2005. 'Intimate visual co-presence.' *Position paper for the Seventh International Conference on Ubiquitous Computing, Tokyo*.

James, W. 2012 (1902). *The Varieties of Religious Experience*. Boston, MA: Bedford/St. Martin's.

Jankowiak, W. 2002. 'Proper men and proper women: parental affection in the Chinese family.' Browned, S. and Wasserstrom, J., eds. *Chinese Femininities/Chinese Masculinities: A Reader*. Berkeley, CA: University of California Press. 361–81.

Jeffrey, R. and Doron, A. 2013. *The Great Indian Phone Book*. London: Hurst.

Johnson, S. 2001. *Emergence: The Connected Lives of Ants, Brains, Cities, and Software*. New York: Scribner.

Jones, G. Schieflin, B. and Smith, R. 2011. 'When Friends Who Talk Together Stalk Together: Online Gossip as Meta communication.' Thurlow, C. and K. Mroczek, K., eds. *Digital Discourse: Language in the New Media*. Oxford: Oxford University Press. 26–47.

Jordan, A. 2003. *Business Anthropology*. Long Grove: Waveland Press.

Jussila, J., Kärkkäinen, H. and Leino, M. 2011. 'Benefits of Social Media in Business-to-Business Customer Interface in Innovation.' *Proceedings of the 15th International Academic MindTrek Conference: Envisioning Future Media Environments*. 167–74.

Kelly, K. 1994. *Out of Control: The Rise of Neo-biological Civilization*. Reading, MA: Addison-Wesley.

Kelty, C. 2008. *Two Bits: The Cultural Significance of Free Software*. Durham, NC: Duke University Press.

Kimble, C., Hildreth, P. M. and Bourdon, I. eds. 2008. *Communities of practice: creating learning environments for educators*. Charlotte, NC: Information Age.

King, G., Pan, J. and Roberts, M. E. 2013. 'How censorship in China allows government criticism but silences collective expression.' *American Political Science Review* 107(2): 326–43.

Kipnis, A. B. 2011. 'Governing educational desire: culture, politics, and schooling in China.' Chicago: University of Chicago Press.

Kleine, D. 2013. *Technologies of Choice: ICT's Development and the Capabilities Approach*. Cambridge, MA: The MIT Press.

Klotz, R. J. 2004. *The politics of Internet communication*. Lanham: Rowman & Littlefield.

Koskinen, I. 2006. 'Managing banality in mobile multimedia.' Pertierra, R. ed. *The Social Construction and Usage of Communication Technologies: European and Asian Experiences*. Singapore: Singapore University Press. 48–60.

Kramer, A. D., Guillory, J. E. and Hancock, J. T. 2014. 'Experimental evidence of massive-scale emotional contagion through social networks.' *Proceedings of the National Academy of Sciences* 111(24): 8788–90.

Krasnova, H., Wenniger,H., Widjaja,T. and Buxmann, P. 2013. 'Envy on Facebook: A Hidden Threat to Users' Life Satisfaction?' *Wirtschaftsinformatik Proceedings*: Paper 92.

Kross, E., Verduyn, P., Demiralp, E., Park, J., Lee, D. S., Lin, N., Shablack, H., Jonides, J., Ybarra, O. 2013. 'Facebook Use Predicts Declines in Subjective Well-Being in Young Adults.' *PLoS ONE* 8(8): e69841.

Kumar, N. 2014. 'Facebook for self-empowerment? A study of Facebook adoption in urban India.' *New Media & Society* 16(7): 1122–37.

Kuntsman, A. and Stein, R. 2015. *Digital Militarism: Israel's Occupation in the Social Media Age*. Stanford, CA: Stanford University Press.

Landzelius, K., ed. 2006. *Native on the Net*. London: Routledge.

Lange, P. 2014. *Kids on YouTube*. Walnut Creek, CA: Left Coast Press.

Lasén, A. and Gómez-Cruz, E. 2009. 'Digital photography and picture sharing: redefining the public/private divide.' *Knowledge, Technology & Policy* 22(3): 205–15.

Lauren, A., Jelenchick, J., Eickhoff, C. and Moreno, M. A. 2013. 'Facebook Depression? Social Networking Site Use and Depression in Older Adolescents.' *Journal of Adolescent Health* 52(1): 128–30.

Lave, J. 1993. *Situated learning: legitimate peripheral participation*. Cambridge: Cambridge University Press.

Layard, R. 2011. *Happiness: Lessons for a New Science*. London: Penguin.

Lee, K., Kim, J. H. and Woo, W. T., eds. 2009. *Power and Sustainability of the Chinese State*. New York: Routledge.

Lenhart, A. 2015. *Teens, Social Media & Technology Overview*. http://www.pewinternet.org/2015/04/09/teens-social-media-technology-2015/(accessed 9 May 2015).

Levine, G. ed. 1971. *Georg Simmel on Individuality and Social Forms*. Chicago, IL: Chicago University Press.

Lim, M. 2013. 'Many clicks but little sticks: Social media activism in Indonesia.' *Journal of Contemporary Asia* 43(4): 636–57.

Lim, M. 2012. 'Clicks, cabs, and coffee houses: Social media and oppositional movements in Egypt, 2004–2011.' *Journal of Communication* 62(2): 231–48.

Lindtner, S. et al. 2011. 'Towards a framework of publics: Re-encountering media sharing and its user.' *ACM Transactions on Computer-Human Interaction (TOCHI)* 18(2): 5.

Livingstone, S. and Sefton-Green, J. Forthcoming. 2015. *The Class: Connections and disconnections in the digital age*. New York: New York University Press.

Livingstone, S. 2009. *Children and the Internet*. Cambridge: Polity Press.

Livingstone, S. 2008. 'Taking risky opportunities in youthful content creation: Teenagers' use of social networking sites for intimacy, privacy and self-expression.' *New Media & Society* 10: 393–411.

Livingstone, S., Mascheroni, G., Ólafsson, K. and Haddon, L. with EU Kids Online and Net Children Go Mobile. 2014. *Children's online risks and opportunities: Comparative findings from EU Kids Online and Net Children Go Mobile,* November 2014.

Locke, J. 1979 (1689). *An Essay Concerning Human Understanding*. Nidditch, P. H, ed. Oxford: Oxford University Press.

Lomborg, S. 2014. *Social Media, Social Genres: Making Sense of the Ordinary*. London: Routledge.

MacDougall, D. 2005. *The corporeal image: Film, ethnography, and the senses*. Princeton, NJ: Princeton University Press.

MacKinnon, R. 2008. 'Flatter world and thicker walls? Blogs, censorship and civic discourse in China.' *Public Choice* 134(1–2): 31–46.

Madden, M. 2012. *Privacy Management on Social Media Sites: Most Users Choose Restricted Privacy Settings while Profile 'Pruning' and Unfriending People is on the Rise*. Pew Research Center's Internet & American Life Project.

Madianou, M. and Miller, D. 2012. *Migration and New Media*. London: Routledge.

Malaby, T. 2009. *Making Virtual Worlds*. Ithaca, NY: Cornell University Press.

Mangold, W. G. and Faulds, D. J. 2009. 'Social media: The new hybrid element of the promotion mix.' *Business Horizons* 52 (4): 357–65.

Marshall, J. 2002. *A Kalahari Family* (director of the film)

Marvin, C. 1988. *When Old Technologies Were New*. New York: Oxford University Press.

Marwick. A. and boyd, d. 2014. 'Networked privacy: How teenagers negotiate context in social media.' *New Media & Society* 16(7): 1051–67.

Marwick, A. 2011. '"I tweet honestly, I tweet passionately": Twitter users, context collapse, and the imagined audience.' *New Media & Society* 13(1): 114–33.

Maslow, A. H. 1943. 'A Theory of Human Motivation.' *Psychological Review* 50(4): 370–96.

Mauss, M. 1966. *The Gift*. London: Cohen and West.

McDonald, T. Forthcoming. *Social Media in Rural China*. London: UCL Press.

McKay, D. 2011. 'On the face of Facebook: historical images and personhood in Filipino social networking.' *History and Anthropology* 21(4): 483–502.

McKay, D. 2007. 'Sending Dollars Shows Feeling: Emotions and Economies in Filipino Migration.' *Mobilities* 2(2): 175–94.

McLaughlin, C. and Vitak, J. 2012. 'Norm evolution and violation on Facebook.' *New Media & Society* 14(2): 299–315.

Mehdizadeh, S. 2010. 'Self-Presentation 2.0: Narcissism and Self-Esteem on Facebook.' *Cyberpsychology, Behaviour and Social Networking* 13(4): 357–64.

Mendleson, A. and Papacharissi, Z. 2010. 'Look at Us: collective narcissism in college student Facebook photo galleries.' Papcharissi, Z., ed. *A networked self: Identity, community, and culture on social network sites*. New York: Routledge. 351–273.

Miller, D. and Sinanan, J. Forthcoming. *Visualising Facebook*. London: UCL Press.

Miller, D. 2016. *Social Media in an English Village*. London: UCL Press.

Miller, D. and Sinanan, J. 2014. *Webcam*. Cambridge: Polity Press.

Miller, D. and Horst, H. 2012 'Introduction.' Horst, H. and Miller, D., eds. *Digital Anthropology*. London: Berg.

Miller, D. 2011. *Tales from Facebook*. Cambridge: Polity Press.

Miller, D. and Horst, H. 2006. *The Cell Phone*. Oxford: Berg.

Miller, D. and Slater, D. 2000. *The Internet: An Ethnographic Approach*. Oxford: Berg.

Miller, D. 1998. *A Theory of Shopping*. Cambridge: Polity Press.

Miller, D. 2015. 'Photography in the Age of Snapchat.' *Anthropology and Photography* 1.

Miller, D. 2015. 'The Tragic Dénouement of English Sociality.' *Cultural Anthropology* 30(2): 336–57.

Miller, D. 2014. 'Hospices: The Potential for New Media.' http://www.ucl.ac.uk/anthropology/people/academic_staff/d_miller/mil-28

Morozov, E. 2012. *The Net Delusion: The Dark Side of Internet Freedom*. New York, NY: Public Affairs.

Morozov, E. 2009. 'Iran: Downside to the "Twitter Revolution".' *Dissent* 56(4): 10–14.

Morris, B. 1991. *Western Conceptions of the Individual*. Oxford: Berg.

Muise, A., Christofides, E. and Desmarais, S. 2009. 'More information than you ever wanted: does Facebook bring out the green-eyed monster of jealousy?' *Cyberpsychological Behavior* 12(4): 441–4.

Narayan, G. 2007. 'Addressing the digital divide: E-governance and m-governance in a hub and spoke model.' *The Electronic Journal on Information Systems in Developing Countries* 31(1):1–14.

Naughton, J. 2012. *From Guttenberg to Zuckerberg*. London: Quercus.

Nicolescu, R. Forthcoming. *Social Media in Southeast Italy*. London: UCL Press.

Nisbett, N. 2009. *Growing Up in the Knowledge Society: Living the IT Dream in Bangalore*. New Delhi: Routledge.

Noelle-Neumann, E. 1974. 'The spiral of silence: a theory of public opinion.' *Journal of Communication* 24(2): 43–51.

Noor Al-Deen, H. and Hendricks, J., eds. 2012. *Social Media: Usage and Impact*. Lanham, MD: Lexington Books.

Norris, P. 2001. *Digital divide: Civic engagement, information poverty, and the Internet worldwide*. Cambridge: Cambridge University Press.

Nur Muhammad, R., Horst, H. A., Papoutsaki, E. and Dodson, G. 2015. 'Uyghur transnational identity on Facebook: on the development of a young diaspora.' *Identities*. Forthcoming. 1–15.

O'Keeffe, G.S. and Clarke-Pearson, K. 2011. *Clinical Report–The Impact of Social Media on Children, Adolescents, and Families*. American Academy of Pediatrics, http://pediatrics.aappublications.org/content/early/2011/03/28/peds.2011-0054.full.pdf+html?ijkey=76f29031adb1f95a04cca23436b5ccdebfd5cd9f.

Oates, S., Owen, D. and Gibson, R. K., eds. 2006. *The Internet and Politics. Citizens, Voters and Activists*. New York: Routledge.

Okabe, D. and Ito, M. 2006. 'Everyday contexts of camera phone use: Steps toward technosocial ethnographic frmeworks'. Höflich, J. R. and Hartmann, M., eds. *Mobile Communication in Everyday Life: Ethnographic Views, Observations and Reflections*. Berlin: Frank & Timme. 79–102.

Oosterbaan, M. 2010a. 'Virtual Migration. Brazilian Diasporic Media and the Reconfigurations of Place and Space.' *Revue Européenne des Migrations Internationales* 26(1): 81–102.

Oosterbaan, M. 2010b. 'Virtual Re-evangelization: Brazilian Churches, Media and the Postsecular City.' Beaumont, J. Molendijk, A. and Jedan, C, eds. *Exploring the Postsecular: the religious, the political, the urban*. Leiden: Brill. 281–308.

Ortiz, S. 1994. 'Work, the Division of Labour and Co-operation.' Ingold, T., ed. *Companion encyclopedia of anthropology*. London: Taylor & Francis.

Ortner, S. B. 1972. 'Is Female to Male as Nature Is to Culture?' *Feminist Studies* 1(2): 5–31.

Paechter, C. 2013. 'Young Women online: collaboratively constructing identities.' *Pedagogy, Culture and Society,* 21(1): 111–27.

Papacharissi, Z., ed. 2011. *A networked self: Identity, community, and culture on social network sites.* London: Routledge.

Papacharissi, Z. 2010a. *A Private Sphere: Democracy in a Digital Age.* Cambridge: Polity Press. 138–44.

Papacharissi, Z. 2010b. 'The virtual sphere 2.0: The Internet, the public sphere, and beyond.' *Chadwick, A. and Howard, P. N., eds. Routledge handbook of Internet politics.* London: Routledge. 230–45.

Papacharissi, Z. 2004. 'Democracy online: Civility, politeness, and the democratic potential of online political discussion groups.' *New Media & Society* 6(2): 259–83.

Papacharissi, Z. 2002. 'The virtual sphere: The internet as a public sphere.' *New Media & Society* 4(1): 9–27.

Parks, M. 2011. 'Social network sites as virtual communities.' Papacharissi, Z., ed. *A networked self: Identity, community, and culture on social network sites.* London: Routledge. 105–23.

Piketty, T. 2014. *Capital in the Twenty-First Century.* Cambridge: Belknap Press.

Pink, S. 2001. *'Doing Visual Ethnography:' Images, Media and Representation in Research.* London: Sage.

Pink, S. 2011. 'Amateur photographic practice, collective representation and the constitution of place.' *Visual Studies* 26(2): 92–101.

Pinney, C. 2011. *Photography and Anthropology.* London: Reaktion.

Plant, S. 1997. *Zeros and Ones: Digital Women and the New Technoculture.* London: Fourth Estate.

Plato. 2008 (360 BC). *Phaedrus.* Charleston, SC: Forgotten Books.

Poster, M. 1997. 'Cyberdemocracy: Internet and the public sphere.' *Internet culture* 201: 218.

Postill, J. 2012. 'Digital Politics and Political Engagement.' Horst, H and Miller, D., eds. *Digital Anthropology.* London: Berg.

Postill, J. 2008. 'Localising the internet beyond community and networks.' *New Media & Society* 10(3) 413–31.

Potter, J. 2011. 'New literacies, new practices and learner research: Across the semi-permeable membrane between home and school.' *Lifelong Learning in Europe* 3:174–80.

Prensky, Marc. 2001. 'Digital Natives, Digital Immigrants'. *On the Horizon* 9(5): 1–6.

Putnam, R. 2000. *Bowling Alone: The Collapse and Revival of American Community.* New York: London: Simon & Schuster.

Qiu, J. L. 2009. *Working-Class Network Society: Communication Technology and the Information Have-Less in Urban China.* Cambridge, MA: The MIT Press.

Qiu, L., Lin, H. and Leung, A. K-y. 2013. 'Cultural Differences and Switching of In-Group Sharing Behavior Between an American (Facebook) and a Chinese (Renren) Social Networking Site.' *Journal of Cross-Cultural Psychology* 44(1): 106–21.

Rainey,L.D.2010.*Confucius&Confucianism:TheEssentials.*Malden,MA:Oxford:Wiley-Blackwell.

Rainie, L. and Wellman, B. 2012. *Networked.* Cambridge, MA: The MIT Press.

Rangaswamy, N. and Arora, P. 2015. 'The mobile internet in the wild and every day: Digital leisure in the slums of urban India.' *International Journal of Cultural Studies.*

Rantanen, T. 2005. *The Media and Globalization.* New York: Sage.

Rheingold, H. 2012. *Net Smart: How to Thrive Online.* Cambridge, MA: The MIT Press.

Rheingold, H. 1993. *Virtual Community: Homesteading on the Electronic Frontier.* New York: Addison-Wesley.

Ritchie, D. 2005. 'Frame-Shifting in Humor and Irony.' *Metaphor and Symbol* 20(4): 288.

Rousseau, Jean-Jacques. 2010 (1754). *Discourse on the Origin and Foundations of Inequality Among Men.* Rosenblatt, H., trans and ed. Boston, MA: Bedford/St. Martin's.

Rubel, A. J. 1977. '"Limited Good" and "Social Comparison": Two Theories, One Problem.' *Ethos* 5(2): 224–38.

Sagioglou, C. and Greitemeyer, T. 2014. 'Facebook's Emotional Consequences: Why Facebook Causes a Decrease in Mood and Why People Still Use It.' *Computers in Human Behavior* 35: 359–63.

Sahlins, M. 1972. *Stone Age Economics.* Chicago, IL: Aldine-Atherton.

Salvatore, A., ed. 2011. 'Between Everyday Life and Political Revolution: the Social Web in the Middle East.' *Oriente Moderno,* n.s. XCI/1, 2011.

Schrooten, M. 2012. 'Moving ethnography online: Researching Brazilian migrants' online togetherness.' *Ethnic and Racial Studies* 35(10): 1794–1809.

Scobie, W. 2011. 'An Anthropological Introduction to YouTube by Michael Wesch.' *American Anthropologist* 113(4): 661–2.

See Yan, Y. 1996. *The Flow of Gifts: Reciprocity and Social Networks in a Chinese Village*. Stanford, CA: Stanford University Press.

Seib, P. 2012. *Real-time diplomacy: Politics and power in the social media era*. Basingstoke: Palgrave Macmillan.

Sen, A. 1999. *Development as Freedom*. Oxford: Oxford University Press.

Sen, A. 1992. *Inequality Re-examined*. Cambridge, MA: Harvard University Press.

Sennett, R. 1977. *The Fall of Public Man*. New York: Knopf.

Shade, L. R. 2002. *Gender and Community in the Social Construction of the Internet*. New York: Peter Lang.

Shirky, C. 2008. *Here Comes Everybody: The Power of Organizing without Organizations*. New York: Penguin.

Simmel, G. 1968. *The Conflict in Modern Culture and other Essays*. New York: Teachers College Press.

Simmel, G. and Wolff, Kurt H. 1950. *The Sociology of Georg Simmel*. Glencoe, IL: Free Press.

Sinanan, J. Forthcoming. *Social Media in Trinidad*. London: UCL Press.

Skeggs, B. 1997. *Formations of Class and Gender: Becoming Respectable*. London: Sage.

Slater, D. 2014. *New Media, Development and Globalization: Making Connections in the Global South*. Cambridge: Polity Press.

Smith, P. K. and Brain, P. 2000. 'Bullying in schools: Lessons from two decades of research.' *Aggressive Behavior* 26(1): 1–9.

Sprague, S. 1978. 'How I see the Yoruba see themselves.' *Studies in the Anthropology of Visual Communications* 5(1): 9–29.

Spyer, J. Forthcoming. *Social Media in Emergent Brazil*. London: UCL Press.

Stafford, C. 1995. *The Roads of Chinese Childhood: Learning and Identification in Angang*. Cambridge: Cambridge University Press.

Street, B. 2003. 'What's "new" in New Literacy Studies? Critical approaches to literacy in theory and practice.' *Current Issues in Comparative Education* 5(2): 77–91.

Tacchi, J. 2012. 'Digital Engagement.' Horst, H. and Miller, D., eds. *Digital Anthropology*. London: Berg. 225–41.

Tandoc, E. C. Jr., Ferruci, P. and Duffy, M. 2015. 'Facebook Use, Envy, and Depression Among College Students: Is Facebooking Depressing?' *Computers in Human Behavior* 43: 139–46.

The 34th Statistical Report on Internet Development in China. Retrieved 28 March 2015. http://www1.cnnic.cn/IDR/ReportDownloads/201411/P020141102574314897888.pdf

The Economist, 28 February 2015.

The Economist, 13 September 2014.

Thin, N. 2005. 'Happiness and the Sad Topics of Anthropology.' *WeD Working Paper 10*. ESRC Research Group on Wellbeing in Developing Countries.

Thompson, C. 2013. *Smarter than you think*. London: Penguin.

Tiggeman, M. and Slater, A., 2013. 'NetGirls: The Internet, Facebook, and Body Image Concern in Adolescent Girls.' *International Journal of Eating Disorders* 46(6): 630–3.

Trepte, S. and Reinecke, L., eds. 2011. *Privacy Online: Perspectives on Privacy and Self-Disclosure in the Social Web*. New York: Springer.

Tsui, L. 2015. 'The coming colonization of Hong Kong cyberspace: government responses to the use of new technologies by the umbrella movement.' *Chinese Journal of Communication*. 2015. 1–9.

Tufekci, Z. 2014. 'The Medium and the Movement: Digital Tools, Social Movement Politics, and the End of the Free Rider Problem.' *Policy & Internet* 6(2): 202–8.

Tufekci, Z. and Wilson, C. 2012. 'Social media and the decision to participate in political protest: Observation from Tahrir Square.' *Journal of Communication* 62(2): 363–79.

Turkle, S. 2011. *Alone Together: Why We Expect More from Technology and Less from Each Other*. New York: Basic Books.

Turkle, S. 1997. *Life on the screen: Identity in the Age of the Internet*. New York: Simon and Schuster.

Uimonen, P. 2012. *Digital Drama*. New York: Routledge.

Utz, S. and Kramer, N. 2009. 'The privacy paradox on social network sites revisited: The role of individual characteristics and group norms.' *Cyberpsychology: Journal of Psychosocial Research on Cyberspace* 3(2).

Valenzuela, S., Park, N. and Kee, K. F. 2009. 'Is There Social Capital in a Social Network Site? Facebook Use and College Students' Life Satisfaction, Trust, and Participation.' *Journal of Computer-Mediated Communication* 14(4): 875–901.

Van Dijck, J. 2013a. *The Culture of Connectivity*. Oxford: Oxford University Press.

Van Dijk, J. 2013. 'Inequalities in the Network Society.' Orton-Johnson, K. and Prior, N., eds. *Digital Sociology*. London: Palgrave Macmillan.

Van Dijck, J. 2007. *Mediated Memories in the Digital Age*. Stanford, CA: Stanford University Press.

Van Dijk, J. 1999. *The Network Society: Social Aspects of New Media*. London: Sage.

Van Dijck, J. 2013b. '"You have one identity": performing the self on Facebook and LinkedIn.' *Media, Culture & Society* 35(2): 199–215.

Van Dijck, J. 2008. 'Digital photography: Communication, identity, memory.' *Visual Communication* 7:57–76.

Van Doorn, N., Van Zoonen, L. and Wyatt, S. 2007. 'Writing from experience: Presentations of Gender Identity on Weblogs.' *European Journal of Women's Studies* 14(2): 143–59.

Van House, N. A. and Davis, M. 2005. 'The social life of cameraphone images.' *Proceedings of the Pervasive Image Capture and Sharing: New Social Practices and Implications for Technology Workshop (PICS 2005) at the Seventh International Conference on Ubiquitous Computing (UbiComp 2005)*.

Venkatraman, S. Forthcoming. *Social Media in South India*. London: UCL Press.

Vidyarthi, L. P., ed. 1984. *Applied anthropology in India: principles, problems, and case studies*. New Delhi: Kitab Mahal.

Voida, A. and Mynatt, E. D. 2005. 'Six themes of the communicative appropriation of photographic images.' *Proceedings of the SIGCHI 2005 conference on Human Factors in computing systems*. 171–80.

Wajcman, J. 2004. *TechnoFeminism*. Cambridge: Polity Press.

Wali, A. 2012. 'A Different Measure of Well-Being.' *Vital Topics Forum*. Johnston, B. R. ed. *American Anthropologist* 114(1): 12.

Wallis, C. 2013. *Technomobility in China: young migrant women and mobile phones*. New York, London: New York University Press.

Wallis, C. 2011. 'New Media Practices in China: Youth Patterns, Processes, and Politics.' *International Journal of Communication* 5:406–36.

Wallman, S., ed. 1979. *Social Anthropology of Work*. London: Academic Press.

Wang, R. R. 2002. 'Globalizing the Heart of the Dragon: The Impact of Technology on Confucian Ethical Values.' *Journal of Chinese Philosophy* 29(4): 553–69.

Wang, X. Forthcoming. *Social Media in Industrial China*. London: UCL Press.

Warner, M. 2002. 'Publics and counterpublics.' *Public culture* 14(1): 49–90.

Warschauer, M. 2004. *Technology and Social Inclusion: Rethinking the Digital Divide*. Cambridge, MA: The MIT Press.

Weber, M. 2002 (1905). *The Protestant Ethic and the Spirit of Capitalism*. London: Penguin Books.

Weller, K. et al., eds. 2013. *Twitter and Society*. New York: Peter Lang.

Wenger, E. 1998. *Communities of practice: learning, meaning, and identity*. Cambridge: Cambridge University Press.

Wesch. M. (lecturer and dir.). 2008. *An Anthropological Introduction to YouTube*. YouTube, 26 July 2008. http://www.youtube.com/watch?v=TPAO-1Z4_hU, (accessed 14 September 2014).

Wilson, R., Gosling, S. and Graham, L. 2012. 'A Review of Facebook Research in the Social Sciences.' *Perspectives on Psychological Science* 7(3): 203–20.

Xiong, C. and Lv, Y. 2013. 'Social network service and social development in China.' *Studies in Communication Sciences* 13(2): 133–8.

Zelizer, V. 2011. *Economic Lives*. Princeton, NJ: Princeton University Press.

Zickuhr, K. 2013. *Who's Not Online and Why*. Washington DC: Pew Research Center's Internet & American Life Project.

Index

abuse, physical, emotional, sexual
Brazilian girl 134
access to social media in workplace/
educational institution during working
hours **62**
accounts, setting up
older people allow younger 46
advertising 57
from companies targeted to people 92
on social media 91–2
susceptibility to, on or offline 59
African divination systems 23
Afro-Trinidadian men, 'gangsta' image 120
afternoon and evening greetings circulated on
Facebook in Tamil Nadu **167**
age distribution of survey respondents across
field sites **69**
amount spent on social media/online
games **60**
anonymity of Chinese social media
lack of privacy 11
material online 40
QZone profiles 117
anthropology 23
definition 183
ethnography, 'participant observation' 28
field sites, politics or migration 30
involvement, genuine friendships 28
living among different people 29
photography, photographers involved 157
positive benefits 40
study of kinship 22
anti-Japanese sentiment 148–9
appropriate and inappropriate behaviour 22
adaptation to people 31
Arab Spring, political action 144
arts students and visual identity, Tanzania 23
attitudes towards social media 62
'authentic' emotional states 204
'authenticity', big concern 101
autonomy, respect for young people's 72
avatars for befriending of strangers, 'mask' 56
average number of friends on primary
social media
QQ in China, Facebook in all other sites **43**

baby-toddler groups, class system
in England 83
Balduíno (fictional name), Brazil
growing criminality 220

high level of social inequality 219–20
Pentecostal Christianity 220
behaviour genres, socialising on
social media 211
'BFF' (Best Friend Forever), school pupils 5
Brazil, expansion of Protestant churches
affluence and power 188
contribution to gender equality 123
cordial relations offline, genial relations on
social media 103
distracting or positive in workplace 63–4
growth of tourism industry 123
low paid manual workers
education for social mobility 132
social media visibility of LGBT people 124
women, increased job opportunities, more
public visibility 123
Brazilian field site
adult activity on social media 170
Afro-descended girl, domestic servant at
five years old 134
fear of negative consequences in politics 146
footballers, Nike brand 61
parents, social media as positive 73
practice, 'dar os filhos' ('giving their
children') 134
social media as young person's space 105
social project in setting up account 46
teachers, social media as 'bad internet' 73
visibility to new wealth 160
wedding, display on Facebook account
134–5
broadcasting, public 207
businesses 'liked' followed on social media **61**
buying behaviour **59**

Calvin, John, Protestant
drive for upward social mobility 135
capacities, increased
learning skills, public voice 196–7
car access for men, ability to travel
in China, Turkey 122
Castells, M. The Rise of the Network Society 20
class consciousness in China, platform usage
210
cheating husbands, increase, Turkey, southeast
202–3
child-centred policy project 71
children's use of social media, appropriate
age 62

253

humour and irony on social media
  from lower class Trinidadians 137–8
humour, connecting through, on social media
  138
hunger strike of activist group leader,
  Kublalsingh 151–2

ICT *see* Information and Communication
  Technologies
identity ascription in ancient times
  particular class, occupation, social role,
    place of origin 110
illiteracy in Brazil 101, 170
illiterate populations in India, 'conversations'
  visual 207
image leaking 176
image posting of school work success for
  parents 81–2
images, appropriateness of 176
images of babies taken at professional studios
  and posted by parents on QQ **161**
images of fantasies of consumption
  China, QQ **159–60**
images of food taken at family gatherings in
  southeast Turkey **168**, **169**
images showing how facial expressions can
  emulate those of '*emojis*' in Snapchat
  178–9
India, south
  appearance on Facebook 163
  children of poor families, positive attitudes
    to social media 73–4
  communication between family members,
    WhatsApp 108
  discouragement of teacher-parent
    communications 82
  'emergent class' 89
  encouragement to sons to use social media
    74
  entrepreneurial activities from home 95
  everyday greetings on photographs 165
  Facebook as platform of choice 96
  Facebook criticism from parents to teachers
    82
  fear of negative consequences in politics 146
  friends 45
  gender in traditional family role 118
  happiness as social value 204
  humour about politics 150
  kinship, age, gender, class, caste groups 185
  leaked photographs of women, from their
    mobile phones 176
  lower class parents 74
  no serious political content by social media
    users 146
  official ban on social media use in schools 79
  Parent-Teacher Association (PTA) 82
  prohibition for unmarried women to own
    mobiles 74
  realization of prominence through social
    media, abuse of women 65
  restrictions on behaviour of women 50
  school encouragement as an educational
    tool 63
  social media as 'fictive kin' 105
  social media for friends, not family 47

social media marketing 61
  claims to cosmopolitanism 140
social media to flirt 122–3
spending on social media 60
storytelling business, educational 96
traditional social divisions, retention of
  137
use of social media by wealthy 73
weaving as home and family work 86
wealthy families, children 73
Indian field site comments
  Christian conversion of Hindus, Islamic
    terrorism, criticism of Pakistan 150
Indian IT sector
  focus on educational credentials 89
indigenous ancestry in Chile, no primary
  focus 27
indigenous populations study, Chile, Santiago
  27
'individual against government' 131
individual-based network, rise 21
individualisation rise 28, 181–92
  selfie, self-expression or narcissism 186
individuals in Italy
  burden to create positive image 203
industrial Chinese site
  floating population of migrant workers 7
inequalities of access 131
inequality 128–41
  wealth distribution and poverty 129
Information and Communication Technologies
  (ICTs)
  banning of 70
  transformation relationship between formal
    and informal education 76
'information capitalism' 182
Instagram and Snapchat, for young people 15
Instagram, Facebook, WhatsApp 90
Instagram photographs, Chilean field site 197
Instagram, strangers welcome 5
Interdisciplinary Center for Intercultural and
  indigenous Studies, Chile, Santiago 27
internet, communication, information
  geographies, inequalities of 23
internet 'morality' 180
internet representation
  egalitarianism, freedom of speech.
    democracy 131
Internet Revolution 182
internet services, MSM and AOL 2
Internet Studies 10
intimacy and intimidation 76, 77
intimacy to anonymity, scalable sociality
  105–9
Islamic State (IS) 143
isolation on social media 181, 202
Italian celebrities as role model 59
Italian field site
  barriers to student–teacher friending 80
  high unemployment 133
  limited school–parent communication via
    social media 83
  reservations on schools 75
  to underprivileged, social media an
    obligation 133
Italian sociability offline 44

Lightning Source UK Ltd.
Milton Keynes UK
UKOW06f1357100917
308875UK00002B/7/P